CLIO & ME

An Intellectual Autobiography

CASTALIA HOUSE

Non-Fiction

Equality: The Impossible Quest by Martin van Creveld
A History of Strategy: From Sun Tzu to William S. Lind
     by Martin van Creveld
4th Generation Warfare Handbook
     by William S. Lind and Gregory A. Thiele
Do We Need God To Be Good? by C.R. Hallpike
The Nine Laws by Ivan Throne
MAGA Mindset: Making YOU and America Great Again by Mike Cernovich
Compost Everything: Extreme Composting by David the Good
Grow or Die: Survival Gardening by David the Good
Push the Zone: Growing Tropical Plants Beyond the Tropics
     by David the Good

Fiction

An Equation of Almost Infinite Complexity by J. Mulrooney
Brings the Lightning by Peter Grant
Loki's Child by Fenris Wulf
Six Expressions of Death by Mojo Mori
The Missionaries by Owen Stanley

Military Science Fiction

The Eden Plague by David VanDyke
Reaper's Run by David VanDyke
Skull's Shadows by David VanDyke
There Will Be War Volumes I and II ed. Jerry Pournelle
Riding the Red Horse Volume 1 ed. Tom Kratman and Vox Day

Science Fiction

Victoria: A Novel of Fourth Generation War by Thomas Hobbes
The End of the World as We Knew It by Nick Cole
CTRL-ALT REVOLT! by Nick Cole
Somewhither by John C. Wright
City Beyond Time by John C. Wright
Awake in the Night Land by John C. Wright
Back From the Dead by Rolf Nelson
Mutiny in Space by Rod Walker
Alien Game by Rod Walker

CLIO & ME

An Intellectual Autobiography

MARTIN VAN CREVELD

CASTALIA HOUSE

Clio & Me

Martin van Creveld

Published by Castalia House
Tampere, Finland
www.castaliahouse.com

ISBN: 978-952-7065-53-2

Contents

Note to the Reader   i

Introduction   iii

1   Apprenticeship   1

2   Young Historian   47

3   Defense Consultant   87

4   Breaking Free   141

5   As I Please   185

6   Looking Forward   225

Some Works Consulted   235

List of Publications   237

Notes   239

Note to the Reader

As the introduction says, originally, this book was written as long ago as 2003. At the time my primary intention was to help my stepson Jonathan, who was just entering the study of history, with no intention of publication. Over the years, however, I have mentioned it to a few of friends and acquaintances and showed it to those of them who were interested. Almost all said they liked it very much. So, when one of them, Damien O'Connell, of the Marine Corps University, Quantico, VA, suggested that I publish it, I was induced to say, why not?

Even so, it took a long time. What really set me going was a short book about Hegel I picked up a few months ago for completely different reasons. It reminded me that, modest as my contribution to the study of the philosophy of history has been, I, too, had something to say about the subject.

However, I am no longer the same person I was thirteen years ago. I have stopped working at Hebrew University. This happened after the university, following some unpleasantness with a female student who, it seems, had been planted in my class specifically to snitch on me, decided that my views on women and feminism were unacceptable. Rather than apologize and agree to have what I value most in life, i.e. freedom of speech, taken away, I decided to retire. I also have fewer hairs on my head and in many ways no longer feel as confident as I did a decade ago. Both the loss of hair and the decline in confidence are typical symptoms of old age. Perhaps it was this loss of confidence which made me modify some parts of the book instead of simply leaving it as it was. As to freedom of speech, it was George Bernard Shaw who said, "Beware of old men; they have nothing to lose."

I hope that some eager young students in Israel and abroad, the kind who value scholarship and the rewards it can bring, both to themselves and to society at large, will find what I have to say interesting. It is to them that this book is dedicated.

Mevasseret Zion, 2016

Introduction

Relatives, friends, students, colleagues, and journalists have often asked me what I see in the study of history, particularly military history, and how I ever got into that esoteric field. I always answered as best I could but never thought I would try to put my answer down in writing. In my family people only write their memoirs when they are very old and ready to go, which I am not. My stepson and best friend, Jonathan Lewy, has been bitten by the scholarship bug. As an undergraduate student of history at Hebrew University, he read Marc Bloch's *The Historian's Craft*, which, as he was not slow to point out, was written when Bloch was exactly as old as I was in 2003. Jonathan has often asked me why I did not try to produce a similar work, and I have often evaded the question even in my own mind.

Jonathan, who in the meantime earned his PhD and did a post-doc at Harvard, is nothing if not persistent. But I did not want to produce yet another volume on the philosophy of history and the technique of teaching it. Instead, I decided I would try to answer the above questions, and others like them, by writing an intellectual autobiography. Why and how did I come to be a historian? What does the study of history really mean to me? Why, in my view, does it merit being studied, what for, and how? How did I master my craft? What problems did I meet, and how did I try to solve them? Where do I get my ideas? What does "scientific" history mean, and how does it differ from other kinds? What does it take to write a book, and what is doing so like? Can history be used for looking into the future, and, if so, how does one go about it? How should history, in fact the humanities and social sciences in general, be taught at the university level? What are the differences between civilian universities and military ones? How does one prepare a talk, and how does one deal with the media? What are the advantages of the scholarly life, and what are the disadvantages? Should one take it up?

As I got to work, I soon found myself in a dilemma. On the one hand, I did not want to appear as some sort of disembodied spirit. Like anybody else, I do have a life outside the purely intellectual one. Moreover, the two are interrelated. I have often wondered about the impact health may have on creativity and *vice versa*. So, incidentally, did Friedrich Nietzsche, to mention but one. On the other hand, I did not think my personal life is of great interest either to Jonathan, who already knows it all, or to other people. In the end I compromised. I tried to put in only as much of my non-professional life as I considered absolutely essential to explain where I come from and to make the narrative coherent. Unlike a few writers whom I consulted and to some extent used as my model, I do not think it matters who attended to my bodily needs when I was a child. Like them, I shall be very happy to strike out the name of anybody who feels offended by what I have to say. With the aid of word processing and e-books, which most of them did not have, doing so is easy enough.

I very much hope that this book will have something to offer the type of young, earnest students with whom it has been my great fortune to work throughout my academic career. Nevertheless, in the end it was Jonathan whom it was written for. Therefore, whatever the reaction of others, I pray that he at any rate will not be disappointed.

Chapter 1

Apprenticeship

I like to keep calendars in which I jot down my appointments. But I have never kept a diary of my activities and thoughts. Worse still, to prevent my study from filling up, I have, or at any rate had, a habit of going over my correspondence and throwing away the parts of it I think I no longer need. When Rachel, my first wife, and I separated in 1984, most of the photographs I had of my previous life stayed with her in my former home. So did all my correspondence—there were no computers yet—and quite a few newspaper articles I had published or that had been published about me. The end result is that the documentation behind the following pages is exceptionally poor. In essence, all I have to go on is my memory, and we all know what tricks that can play. At one point I read Betty Friedan's autobiography *and* a biography written about her by somebody else. They made me wonder which one presented a more faithful portrait of her.

As to using other sources to check on what one thinks one remembers, doing so is not always possible. Even when it is possible, it may only make things worse. Looking at the few photographs I still have, I wonder whether I can really remember what I see. There I am, three years old and looking quite happy, having a bath in an old-fashioned tin tub. Can I honestly say I remember

the episode and the fun I had? Or was the picture that made me feel as if I could remember sitting there? Suppose somebody had taken the trouble to fake a picture of me at that age. Provided only it did not display obvious errors of commission and omission, which as a historian it would be my job to detect, I would almost certainly have ended by remembering that episode, too.

This being an intellectual autobiography, I have in front of me some of the books I read, those I wrote, and some of the reviews of the latter. However, I rarely reread my own books. When I do look at them, I tend to find them irritating. Nor, after the first few years, did I do more than take a passing glance at what others wrote about me. In this respect I like to look forward to the next task, not backward to the last one.

Yet I did read some books in preparation for this work. As it happened, the last thing I wrote before I started working on it in 2003 was a short biography of Moshe Dayan. His autobiography, *Story of My Life*, taught me not to badmouth anybody, at least not on paper. Others included Johan Huizinga's essay *My Path to History*, A. J. P. Taylor's *A Personal Story*, Friedrich Nietzsche's *Ecce Homo: How One Becomes What One Is*, and H. Stuart Hughes' *History as Art and as Science*. Some provided me with guides as to what to do and not to do. Others triggered my own thoughts. Preparing the final draft, I had the good fortune of coming across E. O. Wilson's *Letters to a Young Scientist* (2014). It confirmed what I had suspected for a long time past: namely that, however small my achievements in comparison with those of many great scholars and scientists, my way of finding problems and trying to solve them is, in many ways, not too different from theirs.

Paradoxically, among the works I found the least useful was Bloch's *The Historian's Craft*. Not because it is no good, but because it is too good. As a result, over the years much of it has come to seem self-evident. That includes the relevance of remote periods; the importance of psychological factors; the need for in-depth comparisons as the best tool for gaining understanding; and the impossibility of separating history from the other humanities and social sciences. For some of us, the greatest triumph consists precisely of being taken for granted and, perhaps, forgotten. But don't worry: they have their exits and their entrances.

Whenever I came across an interesting passage, I marked it, using small plastic paperclips that do not damage the paper as much as aluminum ones do. Having finished with it, I removed the clips for reuse, trying not to lose even one. This is one of the games I like to play with myself. As the reader will see, it is by no means the only or most important one. Needless to say, any errors in this volume are the fault of the authors I consulted. Needless to say, any merit it may have is mine alone.

People have said—referring to Clausewitz, I myself have done so—that great historians often trace the beginning of their interest to some radical change in their environment that affected their lives and forced them to think about the past. I am probably not a great historian, which may explain why this is not the case with me. Instead, I think my first conscious encounter with history came around 1956 when I was ten years old. Having come to Israel in 1950, my family and I were living in Ramat Gan, a town near Tel Aviv, in an apartment located on the third floor. On the ground floor there was a large room, or so it seemed to me, that served all the residents of the building for storing their discarded belongings. And what belongings they were! I distinctly remember odd pieces of old-fashioned furniture, broken-down electric lamps, framed pictures, various utensils, curtains, porcelain, cutlery, heaps of old newspapers, and God knows what else. To get at many of them, one had to climb over some items and crawl into the nooks and crannies that separated them. Which, of course, added to the attraction.

Unlike some others whose autobiographies I read, I did not leap straight out of Zeus's brow. I was a child, and along with my two younger brothers and our downstairs neighbor, I loved to poke around in the room, in which our bicycles were also stored. One day I came across a brown cloth sack. Tied with a string, it was standing near the door; since it was too heavy for me to move, I opened it. Inside, I discovered a few dozen Dutch books. To this day I do not know to whom the books belonged. Still, it stands to reason that they had been dumped by my parents, Leon and Greet (*née* Wijler) van Creveld, who had brought them along when they immigrated to Israel six years earlier, even though they themselves always told me they could no longer remember doing so.

Having been born in 1946, at the time we moved to Israel I was just over four years old. At home we continued to speak Dutch, though gradually it became so riddled with Hebrew as to resemble pidgin. I remember some strange expressions that would have made purists in both languages wince. Such as, for example, *ten li et haju* (give me the meat sauce) and *la'asot schoenepoetsen* (literally, to do polish your shoes). It was only much later that I learned to appreciate the humor in this. To this day, I speak all languages in Dutch; but then, after sixty something years, my Dutch accent is not perfect either.

At the age of seven I took lessons in reading and writing my native language from a friend of my parents, Ms. Dora Oppenheimer. Her principal tool was a *leesplankje*, or little reading-tablet. Measuring about fifteen inches by ten, it was a device the present generation cannot even imagine. There were three tiers of words, each surmounted by a picture of what it stood for: *aap* (ape), *noot* (nut), Wim (short for William), Mies (the name of the cat shown in the picture), and so forth. There were lots of little wooden letters, as in scrabble, and you were supposed to put the right letter on its counterpart under the picture. The highlight of each lesson came at the end when you were permitted to push the letters back into the metal box from which they had come. Sliding along, they formed a train; and of course you made appropriate noises to accompany them on their way.

aap	roos	zeef	muur	voet	neus
lam	gijs	riem	muis	ei	juk
jet	wip	does	hok	bok	kous

A leesplankje, the device on which I learnt to read Dutch

Thanks to Ms. Oppenheimer, I had no trouble reading the books I found. Most were meant for adults, and I did not find them interesting. I can only recall two titles. One was a historical novel about the first South African War (1881), written for juveniles from the point of view of the brave Boers who had defeated the wicked British at the Battle of Majuba Hill. The other and, to me, much more important one, was called *Wereldgeschiedenis in een Nootedop* (World History in a Nutshell). It was a book of general—meaning, at that time, almost exclusively European—history designed for children my age.

The book opened with King Menes of Egypt, who reigned so long ago that it was almost unimaginable. Yet, as the author explained, if you took fifty hundred-year old people and linked them hand to hand, they would reach back as far as him. The text mentioned World War I, which in good Dutch fashion was presented as a tragedy for European civilization, but not Hitler and National Socialism. Hence it must have been published between 1924 and 1933, which was when my parents, who were born in 1918 and 1920, respectively, went to school. Most attractive of all, each chapter ended with a black silhouette that illustrated one of the themes just discussed. Among them, if I am not mistaken, was the legend of the monk Berthold Schwarz inventing gunpowder and being blown up for his pains.

I remember, or think I can remember, the chapter on Henry VIII, who had no fewer than six wives. Also the one on Louis XIV, who was so conceited he had an entire claque to laugh at his jokes. I also remember, or think I can remember, the last chapter. Its subject was twentieth-century technical progress. The acme of that progress was represented by a picture of a streamlined electric train of the kind that, in the nineteen twenties, was starting to replace the old steam-driven ones.

The story that impressed me most, though, was the one about the wars fought by the Greeks against the Persians in 490–480 B.C. Here were a people, small but brave. Their freedom was threatened by this great foreign king who, however, was so foolish that he had the Hellespont whipped for destroying a bridge he had built over it. They fought against much stronger enemies, made the supreme sacrifice at Thermopylae—I remember reading the famous verse about Leonidas and his 300 Spartans—and ended up victorious. They fired my imagination with their heroism; next, they went on to build all those magnificent temples with the beautiful capitals. In the evenings, helping my parents do the dishes, I used to lecture them about what I had read. Almost then and there I decided I would become a historian. As to what historians actually did, it took me years to find out. In a way, I am still finding out more with every passing day.

Years later my parents, considering *Wereldgeschiedenis in a Nootedop* too childish for me, asked and got my permission to lend it to some acquaintances of theirs who lived in Dimona, far from Ramat Gan. The book was lost, a fact I have regretted ever since. Much later still a Dutch student of mine explained to me that it was not a one-time creation but part of an ongoing educational series that was reissued in updated form every few years. She gave me a more recent edition, published in the late nineteen sixties or early nineteen seventies, but I was grievously disappointed by its contents. They seemed juvenile, ill-organized, and not nearly as entertaining as I remembered. Though there were some illustrations, the silhouettes, which to me had been the best part of the book, were missing. Perhaps because I was afraid of further disappointments, I did not try to locate the original volume. There are situations when trying to refresh one's memories will only destroy those that already exist.

I cannot remember what other history, if any, I read at that time. I had a reader's card at one of those bookstores that also lent out books. Once, my curiosity having been aroused by I do not remember what, I asked the librarian to give me *The Communist Manifesto*. However, she said she did not have it. I did not lose any sleep over it and was quite happy to borrow a book by Karl May instead. Perhaps Winnetou, Old Shatterhand, and their friends saved me from becoming a Communist.

Another source of knowledge was the Dutch version of *Readers' Digest*. Having been born with a cleft palate, I had to visit my dentist every two or three weeks. It was in her waiting room that I found *Het Beste (The Best)*. What caught my attention was the immense variety of topics covered. They ranged from a story about a Canadian dog that had climbed a tree but could not come down and had to be rescued to one about the wonders of the U.S. Tactical Air Force, which was ready to go anywhere, at any time (and, presumably, drop bombs on anybody). Since then, my curiosity has been omnivorous. When bored, I will even read a telephone book. Indeed, it is surprising how much a volume of the yellow pages can teach you about a city.

My interest in history was an open secret. For my Bar Mitzvah, which was celebrated in 1959, my parents presented me, in addition to a tennis racket, with a Hebrew edition of Caldwell and Merrill's *Popular History of the World*. It was a big green volume, and I received it on the evening before the actual ceremony of reading from the

Map from Caldwell and Merrill. What first brought me to military history.

Torah. By the next morning I had already finished half of it, with the result that, arriving at the synagogue, I could hardly keep my eyes open. This time the chapter that impressed me the most was the one on the early years of World War II. It was called "The Mighty Offensive of the Axis Power." Looking back, it probably formed the real beginning of my interest in military history.

My family was not orthodox by any means. But my mother had vague feelings of guilt that my brothers and I might not be learning as much about our Jewish heritage as we ought to. To correct this problem I, my brother, and our downstairs neighbor were sent to a rabbi, who gave us private lessons in Judaism. About the only thing I can remember was his telling us that, as part of the events commemorated in the festival of Purim, the wicked Persian Queen Vashti used to strip Jewish girls naked, whip them, and make them work on the Shabbat. Referring back to the book of *Esther*, I claimed that the story had no basis in historical fact, causing our studies with him to come to an abrupt end. As I learned much later, incidentally, our teacher was right. Such a tradition does indeed exist. Though where the rabbis took it from God knows; apparently, some of them are not as pure as they claim to be.

It was probably my mother's concern, too, which accounts for the fact that, along with Caldwell and Merrill, I was given an equally big volume on Jewish history. It had been authored by a well-known historian, Simon Dubnow (1860–1941). Its title, in Hebrew, was *A History of the Eternal People*. I took one look at it and put it aside. For one thing, it was older and was printed in an unattractive, out-of date font. More important, we young Israelis had our fill of the Eternal People, a phrase we had often heard and detested with all our hearts.

To the extent that we studied Jewish history at all, it seemed to consist of little but an endless list of rabbis. Until the emancipation— which we knew was supposed to be something great and wonderful, though only half-understood, thing—they lived in ghettoes. There, they spent their time writing incomprehensible books about incomprehensible topics and trying to escape frequent pogroms. What, for example, was one to make of a ninth- or tenth-century "genius" (in the Rabbinic tradition, almost anyone with a beard is a "genius") named Sa'adia who, living in Mesopotamia, had the bright idea of compiling a dictionary of rhyming words so as to help poets in their works?

Our teachers, drawing on what one can only call anti-Semitic stereotypes, imbued us with the idea that Diaspora Jews were despicable and cowardly types. Now they tried to please the gentiles; now they ran from them. Having failed to do either, when the Holocaust came, they went "like cattle to the slaughter," as the saying went. We actually had to memorize a song that compared them to "calves." No wonder we looked down on them and did not want anything to do with them. So bad was the teaching that, reading about the "Aryan"

part of Warsaw, I had no idea what Aryan meant. To me it had
something to do with lions, given that one of the Hebrew terms for
that animal is *ari*.

It might be objected that the Old Testament, which we did study,
contains plenty of Jewish history. That is true, but there was a
catch. Israel in the 1950s and 1960s was a secular society with strong
socialist leanings. The country's most important leader, David Ben
Gurion, detested religion as only a turn-of-the-twentieth century
socialist could. It was rumored that members of left-wing youth
movements used to hunt down young *haredim* (orthodox people) to
cut off their side-locks. However, I myself never saw this being done,
nor met anyone who participated in such activities.

All this put our teachers in a conundrum. Understood as history,
the Bible was the basis on which the Zionist claim to the Land of
Israel was based. It was also a Holy Book believed to be inspired
directly by God. We modern Israelis, though, did not believe in God,
least of all in a personal one who supervised things here on Earth.
Had we done so, we might have had to start practicing Judaism as
orthodox people did. But then everybody "knew" that the orthodox
were a backward minority who had not yet discovered the light of
modern civilization. Nor, if truth be said, did my encounter with
the rabbi with the naked girls on his brain give me any reason to
think otherwise.

Worse still for the Bible, it was full of miracles that just could not
be true. What, for example, was one to make of the story of the
ten plagues? I remember one of our teachers discussing the problem
when we were fourteen or so. She, of course, was an enlightened
woman. On one occasion, she presented herself in a man's shorts,
complete with fly. Miracles were the last thing in which she believed.
Not believing in miracles and perhaps having read of the theories of
Immanuel Velikovsky, which were popular at that time, she tried to
find a "natural" explanation for the blood and other plagues. However, doing so only led her into another dilemma. Supposing the

plagues were caused by natural phenomena, how could Moses have known each one was coming and make his predictions accordingly? She ended by shrugging the question off. I recall the episode as if it took place yesterday; not a bad indication of how we used to think.

Its historical significance apart, supposedly the reasons why we studied the Old Testament were its "poetic qualities" and "high moral values." However, those values and those qualities meant little to us youngsters. It was only years later that I understood, or thought I began to understand, the full grandeur of the Book of Books. What little Judaism we did study was taught so sanctimoniously as to make us youngsters reject it lock, stock, and barrel. One outcome was that, for each song we had to learn about the various feast days, we made up one that was a caricature of it. Some of the caricatures were obscene; others merely silly.

In the whole of Jewish history, the only episode to affect me deeply was that of Masada. I first visited it in the winter of 1962, climbing the mountain along with other Gadna—a paramilitary organization—youths so as to watch the sun rise over the Dead Sea. There was neither a cable car nor a proper path. This made the ascent much more dangerous than it has since become, particularly because it was a rainy day and the entire area was a vast sea of mud. We young Israelis were supposed to toughen ourselves in preparation for our military service, and we were very proud of our feat. But Masada had little to do with school or the kind of history we learned there. In fact, the best thing about Gadna was precisely that, to participate in its activities, one did not have to sit in front of a desk and do homework.

Not long ago I asked my father, 96 years old, why he had left the Netherlands for Israel. "So as not to feel Jewish," he shot back at me. If so, he succeeded. We young Israelis lived among ourselves and not as a minority in another people's land. Unlike our parents, we never had to worry whether this or that being said or not being said, done or not being done, to us was a result of our being Jewish

and the other guy being, or not being, anti-Semitic. We never had
to wonder whether the ringing of bells meant that a fire had broken
out or that a pogrom was in the making; never experienced what it
means to be branded as outsiders, discriminated against, persecuted,
and demonized. Nor did we know what living under a despotic
government where there is no such thing as human rights is like. My
parents and others have often told me that all this twists one's soul.
I can certainly believe it.

Another thing we were spared was the need to agonize over the
precise meaning of our Jewishness, what we had in common with
other people, and how we differed from them. Being Jewish was
something we accepted as self-evident. Weren't the main events in
our lives, such as births, weddings, deaths, rest days, and, above all,
school holidays, governed by the Jewish tradition? Other people had
their ways of life, we had ours, and may the devil take the rest. All
in all, a greater accolade to the success of Zionism can scarcely be
imagined. Even though, repelled by the sanctimonious way in which
that subject was taught, we, or at any rate I, did not realize the fact
until much later.

Other historians whose autobiographies I have read often express
their thanks to their former teachers. But I do not recall that school,
and high school in particular, did much to stimulate my interest in
history. The school I went to had the reputation of being among the
best in the country. It also had the reputation of being a place where
an iron discipline ruled; that was why we students called it "The
Barracks." One teacher in particular did what he could to terrorize
us. Reputed to be a former Etzel man, he was so thin that we used
to joke his pajamas had only one stripe.[1] In other words, he was
what we today we would call a terrorist. He used to enter classes
without warning so as to make sure the girls did not wear nail polish,
a terrible crime in those days. He also checked that we wore the
school uniform, that our shoes were polished, and that our desks
were arranged like soldiers on parade.

I personally did not mind the discipline. Perhaps I felt that way because the one I was used to at home was almost as strong. On the positive side, we had some excellent teachers, particularly of math, English, and French. The last-named subject was taught by a Ms. Laniado. She was a tall, thin woman with a high-pitched voice we loved to imitate. However, when she piped out, *"Monsieur x, au tableau s'il vous plait,"* which meant it was your turn to demonstrate your prowess, everybody trembled. She only taught me for two years, but thanks to her I can read this beautiful language fairly well.

I do remember the names of my history teachers, some of their peculiarities, and, if not the contents of what they taught, at any rate the broad themes we covered over the years. Some of them only held a B.A., though at a time when graduates were so few that their names were published in Israel's leading newspaper, a B.A. was not to be sneezed at. Others were highly educated men; there were, I think, no women among them. One or two held a PhD. At least one later became a university professor, specializing in Jewish history and the Holocaust.

My most vivid single memory is of a high school test. One day we fourteen- or fifteen-year-olds were handed a mimeographed page. On it were some tables with one half of their rubrics empty. We were supposed to "put the date opposite the event or the event opposite the date." The subject of the exam was ancient Middle Eastern history and the Babylonian King Hammurabi figured in it. Ever since I can remember, one of the things I have hated most is being made to memorize facts. To excuse the teacher, all I can say is he was young and inexperienced. Punning on his name, we called him "Creep."

I spent entire days reading history—among other things, I used some prize-money I got in order to buy William Shirer's *The Rise and Fall of the Third Reich.* Yet my future was by no means preordained, and I also had several other hobbies. One was physics, which at first I misunderstood for some kind of narrative history that dealt with subjects such as the nature of light, the atom, and so on. I spent the rest of the money I got buying a textbook on that subject; I remember how disappointed I was to find it full of equations that described such things as the relationship between the temperature of a gas and the pressure it exerted. Another hobby was tennis. In the dirt-poor Israel of those days tennis was considered an upper-middle class sport fit only for snobs. In fact my family was better off than most; yet I spent most of my childhood in an apartment measuring about 900 square feet with two brothers in a single room.

Finally, a third occupation that kept me busy for days on end was constructing models out of an erector set. Mine was probably the largest in the country, but even so I kept asking my grandmother in Rotterdam to send me additional parts for it. On one occasion I received an international award for an automatic gearbox I built. It was an elegant little mechanism that relied on centrifugal force to do its work. Much later I also built a Congreve clock, a sophisticated machine that has a rolling ball on an inclined plane instead of a pendulum, which actually kept time. I took photographs of it, but, unfortunately, they have been lost.

It may have been my interest in transmission systems that made my father think I might become an engineer. More likely it was his own frustrated ambitions. He himself had been trained as an economist. Before he went on pension, he made his living first as a banker and then as the vice president of Visa, Israel. However, he always remained an engineer at heart. He spent Friday afternoons lying under his car, a 1950 Citroen we had for so long that it ended up as the oldest one on the street. And which, my mother claimed, he used to put out of order on purpose so he could fix it later.

Partly because he may have hoped to make me do what he had missed, partly because he thought studying history might take me nowhere, economically speaking, he and my mother pushed me in the direction of the natural sciences. Given that the humanities were considered fit mainly for girls, I did not find it hard to agree. In fact I did study mathematics, including logarithms, trigonometry, analytical geometry, and some calculus, as well as physics and chemistry, at high school. I never became very good at them, and I remember practically nothing of what I was taught. On the positive side, I learned not to be afraid of figures. To this day, presented with an equation or graph, I do not hasten to turn the page as so many of my colleagues do.

I worked very hard at math, but retained my interest in history and the humanities in general. Homer, whom I first encountered in Hebrew translation when I was twelve years old, was a special favorite. The poems were full of the warriors' activities, triumphs, and defeats; alternating between extreme brutality, as when King Agamemnon lopped of the limbs of a dead enemy and rolled him in front of himself as if he were a log, to the tender scene where Hector takes leave of his wife and infant son. So much did I like them that I dropped my aversion to rote learning. On one occasion I even made a collection of toy-soldiers supposed to represent the heroes of the *Iliad*. I had Menelaus, Achilles, Patroclus, Aeneas, Odysseus, Ajax, and all the rest. They were mounted side by side on a sawn-off wooden ruler that could be pulled out of a cylindrical box originally containing tennis-balls. Much to my chagrin, I subsequently learned that I was the only one who cared about them, or even knew their names.

Then, as now, students specializing in the natural sciences looked down on the "humanists" as softheads, and I shared this attitude to some extent. On the other hand, my class contained many youngsters far more gifted in math than I was. I acquired the reputation of a rare bird. I was not a girl, nor did I study in the class called "literary." Still, instead of solving equations or performing chemical experiments, I quoted poetry. Indeed, I spent most literature classes secretly reading poems we were never supposed to study. To read a poem out of one's own free will was considered incredible; to show appreciation for the poetic qualities of the Jewish prayer book even more so. Occasionally, I talked about literary themes. One was the

tragedy of Hector the Trojan. Another was the courage of Sophocles'
Antigone; thanks to her having the highest quality of all, i.e. courage,
she became a favorite of mine and has remained so to the present day.
At the time I thought my literary interests were too elevated for most
of my friends to follow. Looking back, I am sure they were simply
confused by them.

High school ended in 1964 when my classmates and I matricu-
lated. The subjects I took were math, physics, and chemistry, along
with English, Hebrew grammar, and the Old Testament. At the last
moment there was an amusing incident, which at the time looked
anything but amusing. Instead of handing in my exam paper in math,
I mistakenly gave the supervisor the booklet containing my tables
of logarithms. This was not so bad in itself since we were allowed
to bring the tables into the examination room. However, between
the lines I had written all the various algebraic and trigonometric
formulae I needed. In other words, the booklet was the best possible
proof that I had cheated or, since I did not really use the formulae in
question, that I had intended to cheat. I went home quite happily
and took the rest of the day off.

The next morning, discovering the error, I panicked. I seized my
bicycle, raced to find my principal and deputy principal, and found
them in a Tel Aviv coffee house where they had gone to prepare the
next year's curriculum. They accepted my protestations that it had
all been a mistake, took my notebook with the exams in it, and sent
it to wherever it had to go. I ended by getting a B, which I regarded
as satisfactory. The time of inflated grades had not yet come, and for
entering the university it was good enough.

✳ ✳ ✳

By that time, the problem of what career path to take could
no longer be avoided. Hebrew University, unlike most American
universities, did not give you two years' grace to decide what field

really interested you. Instead, you had to join this or that department right away. Like so many other parents of aspiring historians, mine believed history was a bad choice, economically speaking. In their efforts to convince me to study math and the natural sciences, they enlisted the aid of Dr. Giulio Muggia, our downstairs neighbor. He was a psychiatrist and as good a friend as they come.

Like many old-fashioned psychiatrists, the kind who followed Freud and did not content themselves with prescribing drugs, Muggia was a highly cultured man with wide interests. Later, he was to help me study both Latin and ancient Greek. Among other things, he read Xenophon's *Anabasis* with me to help me prepare for an examination in that language; one which, in the end, I never took. His wife, Costanzia, taught me what little Italian grammar I know. Now, having carried out some elementary tests, he told my parents and me that my mind was decidedly "realistic," meaning, at that time, "inclined towards math," rather than the liberal arts. What he could not know was that I had happened to read about some of the questions he asked during his examination of me and was, accordingly, quite prepared to answer them. Whether, had it not been for this accident, I would have been declared fit for math is hard to say.

My parents, not yet content, also enlisted a teacher of mine and a young professor of mathematics at Tel Aviv University. The former, a Mr. Balaban, had given me private lessons in math and knew me very well. When I consulted him, he told me that a good historian was better than an average mathematician. He also said the mathematical outlook on the world was a very narrow one. I shall never forget how, doing so, he put his hands in front of his face to simulate blinkers; meanwhile, the six volumes of Winston Churchill's *History of the Second World War* were standing on the shelf right behind his back. The professor, a young man whose name I can no longer recall, countered my anxiety as to how I was to make a living by pointing out that jobs for bricklayers were not exactly available for the asking either. To this day, I am grateful to both of them.

In the end, since I refused to study engineering at the Technion in Haifa, it was decided I would go for physics and math. No sooner did I arrive at Hebrew University, though, than I switched to history, taking English as my second subject. Probably because I had been raised in Dutch, at school I had found English easy. I also came to like the language greatly. It seems to have a unique flexibility, which I admired and still admire. Not only is its vocabulary larger than that of any other, but the same word can often serve as a noun, verb, and adjective, too; I sometimes think one cannot know English well and be unintelligent at the same time. My parents resigned themselves to my decision. A degree in English would enable me to make my living by teaching that language, as another friend of theirs also did. The resulting life would be secure if somewhat humdrum. With some luck I might work my way up to giving private lessons to backward students until I owned a small apartment.

I, however, was disappointed with the English course which I found too literary and insufficiently "hardheaded" to my taste. Just what I meant by hardheaded I can no longer recall. Perhaps what troubled me was the fact that my teachers seemed to have absolutely no interest in the historical background of the various writers. The latter were presented as if they were pure spirit. A fault, I am told, that is quite common in university departments specializing in literature and the arts.

We studied English and American authors from William Chaucer to Saul Bellow, and I enjoyed most of them very much. However, I always thought I could invent the kind of "critical" rubbish that surrounded them just as well as my teachers could. Consequently, I seldom wrote down anything they said. During exams, inventing rubbish was just what I did. Instead of reading criticism, as I was supposed to, I made sure I knew the authors themselves inside out by reading through them not once but time after time after time; I understand that the American writer Erica Jong, whose books I read during the 1970s and 1980s and liked very much, did exactly the same. Early in my second year, I planned to abandon English and take up philosophy instead. That was too much for my parents, who put down their foot for the first and only time. As they saw it, one useless field was bad enough; but two?

At the time, there were no courses in military history at Hebrew University. Not once in five years did I see a map of a battlefield drawn up or hear a campaign being discussed in detail. That even applied to a course called "Roman Expansion in the Mediterranean." The closest we got was a thorough examination of the structure of the Roman legion. Even that was presented more as an administrative organization than as a tactical unit. We learned that each legion maintained a sort of bank into which soldiers put their savings, but not what kind of siege machinery it operated or the way it combined standards and bugles to exercise command in the field. In fact I believe that the first course specifically devoted to military history I ever attended had to wait until the sabbatical year I spent in London in 1975–76. The seminar leader was Brian Bond, and he was as good as they come.

Hebrew University did not have tutorials, and to this day I have no clear idea what that much-discussed method of teaching looks like or whether I would have benefited from it. My studies were divided between large, obligatory survey courses on the one hand and workshops and seminars on the other. The more one progressed, the fewer the survey courses and the more important the seminars. As to workshops, they were really seminars that focused on a very detailed examination of primary sources. Didactically speaking, they were the best courses of all; however, after the first year, they disappeared from the curriculum. The more advanced you were, the fewer the exams you had to take and the more numerous the pro-seminar papers and seminar papers, all crowned by a thesis at the M.A. level. Even for the few remaining examinations, you had to prepare on your own. You were given a reading list, but the subjects were planned in such a way as not to overlap with any course you had taken.

Many people found the outcome, namely a growing measure of independence, hard to cope with. I myself liked it very much if only because it caused my grades to improve year by year. I still believe it is the correct way to organize a curriculum. As to just what classes you take, it does not matter much so long as your teachers are first rate. It is also important that you get along with them. Not every teacher is suited for every student; the opposite, alas, is also true. Ultimately, the objective is to learn how to study, not to master this subject or that.

My most important, or should I say prominent, teacher was Professor Jacob L. Talmon. Like many scholars, he owed his fame primarily to his first book, *The Origins of Totalitarian Democracy*, written when he was studying with Lewis Namier during the late nineteen forties. His success encouraged him. He spent most of his professional life inquiring how the democratic ideals of liberty, justice and, above all, equality could have led to the monstrous regimes he had witnessed during his youth in the 1920s and 1930s; the day he finished proofreading his last book on that subject, his heart gave way and he died.

At the time I was his student, he was about fifty years old, newly married (for the first time), and at the height of his powers. A small, sharp-featured man, he was a great actor who accompanied thunderous prose with theatrical gestures. Some considered him the greatest Jewish historian since Josephus Flavius. Politically, he stood on the left, always warning against the consequences that would follow if Israel held on to the Territories it had occupied in June 1967. His strictures made him few friends among Israel's political elite. On one occasion Moshe Dayan, using a Biblical phrase out of context, called him "the worm of Jacob." On another he wrote an open letter to the newly-elected Prime Minister, Menahem Begin, imploring him to withdraw. Thereupon Begin declared that Talmon was the greatest expert on the history of any period before the twentieth century. Who, in his opinion, was the expert on *that* remains unclear.

He always announced that a professor was supposed to profess, something I did not understand then but later came to agree with. A professor who does not have a message of his own is the most superfluous creature on Earth; a clock that, primed with facts nobody else knows or cares about, goes tick-tock, tick-tock until death or an early pension relieves his students of his boring presence. Later still, though, I changed my mind. Professing is important, even vital. However, helping students read, study, and discuss various points of view so as to form their own opinions is no less so. Best of all is to combine the two approaches. But I never met anybody who could do so as, in my imagination, it should be done.

Talmon did command my admiration by his attitude to memorizing facts. He always claimed that, out of the four he knew, he had forgotten three but had forgotten which ones; perhaps that was going too far in the right direction. To make up for it, he once told me in private that, preparing to include a few paragraphs about Rosa Luxemburg in one of his books, he had studied her life as if he was going to write a five-hundred page biography of her.

In class he was as disorganized as he was provocative. He would announce a seminar on, say, "The Russian, Nazi, and Chinese Revolutions." In the end, out of the three he would only cover one and a half, leaving you in the lurch and making you wonder what on earth he had wanted to say. His favorite term, which he always accompanied by a theatrical wave of his right arm, was "paradoxical." The way he used it, "paradoxical" meant that two seemingly incompatible things nevertheless went together; the best example being, of course, democracy and totalitarianism, as first expounded by Rousseau in *Le Contract Social*. He also used it to mean "interesting," "fascinating," and "so sophisticated that only I am clever enough to grasp it and explain it to you."

No such paradoxes seemed to bedevil the Greek and Roman history courses I took. Here were professors who were decidedly well organized, down to earth, and hardheaded. They neither raised their voices nor used their arms to deal with the grand sweep of history as Talmon did. The most important among them was Alexander Fuks. Nothing delighted him more than finding "problems," meaning gaps and contradictions, in the ancient sources; trying to solve them, he and the rest insisted that every word one uttered or wrote should be substantiated and documented. Since then, I have often noticed how, the less material is available about any subject, the more massive the documentation that those who write about it use to hide their ignorance. As with Parkinson's Law, the number of footnotes grows to fill the available space.

Still it was these professors who taught me how to do historical detective work. A very good example was a paper I once did on the difference between "cause" (*aitia*) and "excuse" (*afourme*) as used by Thucydides in his *History of the Peloponnesian War*. Then as always, to think was to learn. Fuks helped. He insisted that I read everything ever written on the subject, including a hefty French *doctorat d'etat* as well as a German monograph originally published around 1830. He personally made sure I got the last-named volume by ordering it via the international lending service. Having done so, he did not allow me to defray the cost—a typical example of the generosity for which he was famous.

A question that preoccupied us very much, and which was typical of the "go ahead" atmosphere of the nineteen sixties, was how we budding historians were to arrive at "the truth" and explain it to others. The most important requirement was that history should be "objective." Like Moliere's bourgeois, who spoke prose without realizing it, we were all followers of the great nineteenth-century German historian Leopold von Ranke. At the opposite pole from "objective" stood "tendentious"—*sine ira et studio* was the ideal that was held up to us—and "romantic." Objectivity meant that, in theory at any rate, two trained historians looking at the same evidence should arrive at the same conclusions. Being unromantic caused the dry, matter-of-fact Hellenistic historian Polybius to be preferred over the "patriotic" Roman historian Livy. But even Livy was preferable to Plutarch, who, accused of being a "moralist," clearly represented the scum of the earth. At best, he might be utilized for checking on other authors. Regrettably, for some facts, he was the only available source. However, when it was a question of human motivation, he could not be trusted. Who would believe that this or that act had originated in high-mindedness and not in some form of self-interest?

Not only did history have to be "objective," but it was also supposed to be "scientific." Just as "objective" was contrasted with "tendentious" and "romantic," so "scientific" stood in opposition to "popular" on the one hand and "stagnant" on the other. Popular history was almost as bad as Plutarch. Its evident inferiority could be instantly recognized by the colorful language it used and also by the fact that it did not have footnotes. Worst of all, instead of seeking to identify "factors" and "processes," it focused on people, their peculiarities, and their peccadilloes. It was as if the fact that Cleopatra had this nose and no other could explain so serious and so weighty a phenomenon as the *history* we studied.

At the time, the most prominent representative of this offensive genre was Barbara Tuchman and, in particular, *The Guns of August*. Not only was it a best seller, but it was also said to have been read by that august personality, President Kennedy. Though they did not admit it, this fact made some of my teachers green with envy. I, too, envy her—for her books, not for having been president of the American Academy of Arts and Letters. But I do not think that her ability to write well is any reason to put her down. In my view, the wider the audience a historian reaches, the better he or she serves the society of which he or she is a member. Before the advent of electronic publishing threw everything into turmoil, a good scholarly book was one that was published in paperback. If, in addition, important decision-makers take the time to look at it, so much the better. Yet if truth be told, whether or not they do so has little to do with its quality.

There is, of course, another side to the gap between "scientific" and "popular" history. Many years later, it was brought to my attention in a peculiarly poignant way. When my stepdaughter Adi was thirteen years old, she came home with a problem. Her teacher had asked the class to write a two-page essay on "the secret" behind the victories of Napoleon Bonaparte. She wanted me to help, and I, having written a chapter in *Command in War* on precisely that subject, readily agreed. How do you compress such a topic into four hundred words and do it in such a way that a teenager, whose main interest in life at that time was horses, may understand? Having considered the matter, I decided that Napoleon's success was due to two cardinal factors. The first was the *corps d'armée* system which enabled him to vastly increase the range of his operations and, subsequently, invent strategy. The second was the unrivalled qualities of leadership that made men follow him through thick and thin and to which Heinrich Heine gave voice in his famous poem, *Die Grenadiere*. Adi wrote the paper and handed it in. A few days later it came back bearing the comment "beside the point." I never did anything like that again, nor did Adi ask me to.

As to the problem of stagnation, it rose out of the comparison with the natural sciences. As Bloch himself had written in the early 1940s, and as others have often repeated since, the humanities were developing an inferiority complex, one, incidentally, that was noted by Huizinga as far back as the 1890s. All around us science and technology were racing ahead, even to the point where they were reaching for outer space. Meanwhile, we, poor worms, were forever feeding on the same horse-pills, and, as often as not, perusing the same old sources that had already been studied a thousand times from a thousand different points of view. Were we making any "progress"? If so, precisely what did it consist of? Were we really better than our predecessors? If not, why bother?

Some people argued that, as a result of having at our disposal better tools such as aerial photography, radio-carbon dating, and, later, DNA analysis, we wrote better history, or at any rate were in a position to write better history, than those predecessors could. I personally doubted it and do so still; even when we do have better methods, that in itself does not guarantee better results. In any case, being in my early twenties, I did not take much interest in these and other historiographic problems. Compared to finding out what had actually happened, how and why, they seemed to me unnecessarily difficult and almost irrelevant. In this respect I agree with the famous English historian A. J. P. Taylor, who once wrote that the function of history is to answer the question, "What happened next?" Conversely, when Plato said that no one should start studying philosophy before reaching the age of thirty, he knew what he was talking about.

In the summer of 1966 some thirty of us students went to Italy, accompanied by two of our professors as well as my teacher of Latin and another female teacher who was later to teach me ancient Greek. For three weeks on end we visited Roman sites, crossing and recrossing the peninsula, passing no stone without noting its origins. Our interests ranged from the Forum Romanum and the Colosseum to the city of Reate (the present-day Rieti), which, we were told, had been the birthplace of Emperor Vespasian. In preparation for the trip, each of us students was assigned a subject to prepare and lecture on. Mine was the Etruscans, about whom I knew absolutely nothing. I plagiarized the article in the *Encyclopaedia Britannica* and was a little surprised when nobody caught me in the act. To the contrary, I earned high praise for starting with an explanation of the available sources. It was my first inkling that, when delivering a lecture, form is at least as important as contents. I also learned that my professors were not as omniscient as, until then, they had seemed to be. So tightly organized was the trip, and so numerous the sites we visited, that we were barely given time to feast our eyes on attractions which, though they were world-famous, happened to date to non-Roman times. The few we did see were the Uffizi Museum and Michaelangelo's *David*; even the Vatican we only visited because, luckily for it, apart from the Sistine Chapel, it also contained numerous Roman antiquities. I returned from the trip with a large collection of slides. Later, I used to show them to the few who cared.

Though my sympathy lay with the ancient historians, I gradually discovered that their methods had their limitations. By carefully examining every letter in some ancient Latin or Greek text, as well as reading literally everything that had been written about it by modern scholars, one might arrive at firm conclusions concerning the number of soldiers Sparta could field in the third century B.C. Equally interesting, one might find out whether it was as a tribune or a legate that Cato the Elder fought at the Battle of Cynoscephalae in 197 B.C. Depending on one's point of view, this was "critical" history at its worst or at its best. The crowning achievement, which might make a professor happy for an entire week, was to "prove" that Gaius Gracchus had been assassinated two days later, or two days earlier, than was generally supposed; the fact that "generally" only meant about five historians the world over was overlooked.

At first I was enthusiastic about the kind of mental exercise involved. It reminded me of the kind of plane geometry I had learned at school and which, for a time, had my classmates and me proving theorems for the sheer pleasure of doing so. We felt like the figures in Raphael's famous painting *The School of Athens*! Later, I realized that the method did not lead very far beyond such problems. One might, indeed, spend one's entire life filling gaps and resolving contradictions without ever producing something more worthwhile than a "definitive" statement concerning the language in which the same Cato addressed the Athenians when trying to enlist their support against King Antiochus III of Syria. When Talmon spoke contemptuously of "stamp collectors," he had a point.

What made the question important was the fact that, at the end of the second year, the curriculum began to diverge. History was divided into ancient, medieval, and modern (by now the latter has been divided into "early" and "late," but I have never been able to take that distinction seriously). It was up to you to decide which one you were going to specialize in. From high school I remembered the Middle Ages as a feudal mess. Sword-happy warlords interacted with superstitious prelates. They chased each other around over issues nobody could understand while socking a population consisting largely of illiterate clodhoppers. I did what I could to avoid the period in question; the fact that the department's best-known professor of medieval history, Joshua Prawer, was as bad at running seminars as he was good at delivering frontal lectures helped.

My decision to specialize in modern, rather than ancient, history grew directly out of the narrow approach taken by those who taught me the latter. Meeting one of them, an excellent teacher by the way, one day, I told him I would like to do my M.A. thesis on some "important," meaning the opposite of narrow, subject. He asked me what I had in mind, and I said I was thinking of a history of sport in the ancient world. At the time I was very much into long-distance running, the only form of exercise I was ever any good at. That made me think a book on sport might attract more readers than one on the date on which Gaius Gracchus was assassinated. "That is not an important subject," he answered. Then and there, I decided not to become an ancient historian.

As the fact that I can still reel off every Roman emperor from Caesar to Pertinax, complete with the years they reigned, proves, I owe a lot to those who taught me ancient history. What is more, what they had to say interested me so much that, after I had already become a member of the faculty, I took some extra courses with Professor Fuks. These were the mid-1970s, and he was in his early sixties. He was a man, who, as someone said of him, had the beauty of ancient Greece written all over his face.

His seminars took place not in a classroom but in his office. It was lined with slightly out-of-date books that had belonged to one of his deceased predecessors. All were in hard cover, creating a grave, respectable impression. Fuks smoked, and in the days before doing

so became a crime, his pipe, which was seldom unlit, helped create
a pleasant atmosphere conducive to learning. Since I myself have
never smoked, perhaps it was with Fuks that I picked up my liking
for the accoutrements of that activity as well as the smell of tobacco.
Absentminded as I am, I am afraid that I sometimes played with his
pipe cleaner, but it was characteristic of him that he never told me off.

We spent most of our time in class
taking turns translating Greek texts word
by word, letter by letter, and even accent
by accent. It was all in an attempt to
capture the author's meaning as closely
as possible. Since there were never more
than five or six students in a class, to
come unprepared could not pass unno-
ticed. Partly for this reason and partly
because Fuks was a magnificent teacher
who never lost patience, that hardly ever
happened. On the few occasions it did
happen, he never said a word. Nor did

*Prof. Alexander Fuks, my
revered teacher*

he have to, given that the question of what one was doing there rose
of itself and hovered in the air.

Whenever we encountered a difficulty that could not be overcome
on the spot, Fuks would stop. Next, he would ask the student who
had pointed it out to consult such and such sources and report back
in a week or two. If, having discovered that there was more to it
than met the eye and the student asked for another week, then that
was never a problem. I remember listening to a briefing on Tyche,
the Greek goddess of fortune, and preparing one on the meaning of
Oikoumene, "the inhabited world." A better form of mental exercise
could scarcely be imagined.

It was Fuks who taught me to appreciate the beauties of Greek literature, including Thucydides, Polybius, utopists such as Euhemerus
and Lucian, and, above all, Plato. Along with Lucretius, Nietzsche,

and Lao-Tzu, Plato is the only philosopher who was also a great poet. Not only is every character in the various dialogues sharply formed, but each one also speaks in the kind of language you would expect from him—as a doctor, say, or a politician. Though I have since moved to other fields, I can sympathize with the scholar who spends his entire career studying him.

Unlike Talmon, Fuks had no particular message to deliver, except, perhaps, that study and the quest for truth—meaning, at that time, objective, unshakeable, "scientific" truth—was the greatest and most wonderful enterprise anyone could embark on. That was why it had to be approached in a strictly conscientious way and the techniques for discovering it mastered—first by gathering all the facts and then by carefully putting them together as in a jigsaw puzzle.

He walked slowly with a limp. How he got it, I never found out. Normally, he was the most balanced of men, as placid as placid can be. But one day he burst out. We were studying the way the Romans had subjugated Greece, and specifically the Achaean League, leading up the destruction of Syracuse, one of the largest and most important Greek city-states, in 146 B.C. Suddenly, we heard him say, "Over two thousand years have passed, and I really do not care which side was in the right. But look, just look, at what the Romans did to those poor Greeks!"

His courses were superbly well organized, but they were never hurried. Time was left for the unexpected, allowing individual students to pursue their interests if they wanted to. I recall how, on one occasion, I spent a class comparing *The Republic* to George Orwell's *1984*. Later, I developed the talk into a paper called "Plato's Non-Republic." I read it to the members of Israeli Classical Association, who urged me to publish it. I, however, had come to the conclusion I had done an injustice both to Plato and, which was equally bad, to Fuks, who admired him so much. Feeling ashamed of myself, I decided not to. By that time, Fuks, who was suffering from skin cancer, was dying. At his funeral, people cried.

Education, the famous behaviorist Burton Skinner once wrote, is what is left after one forgets what one has learned. If so, then Fuks was far and away the best teacher I ever had. The uncompromising quest for truth apart, another thing he taught me was that, when it comes to studying the humanities and social sciences at the university level, curricula do not matter nearly as much as most people think. To be sure, one cannot do everything at once. Some things must come first and others last. Somebody must decide on the program and handle administrative trivia such as matching classes to classrooms, setting examination-dates, and the like. These and a thousand other details are essential for the smooth functioning of any department, and none of them will take care of themselves. I will even grant that, unless they are taken care of, the outcome will be a mess. Nevertheless, when everything is said and done, the only important thing is what happens in class.

Since I myself have turned to teaching, I have often tried to do as well as Fuks did. But I think I never quite succeeded. Perhaps I did not succeed because of my own limitations, particularly my impatience and tendency to rush ahead. Or because the texts I used in my attempt to imitate his methods were written not in Greek but in English, which meant that the students could, or thought they could, read and understand them without preparation. Or because they were simply not nearly as good as the ones he read with us. With all due respect, even Francis Bacon, whom I taught as part of a course on the Scientific Revolution, and Clausewitz are not Plato.

Having decided to pursue modern history, I did my finals in English in the summer of 1967. This was very soon after the Six-Day War had turned Israel from a small, unimportant country in the Middle East into a pocket empire with an army celebrated throughout the world. As usual, I made sure I knew the English and American authors we had studied inside out. However, I did not bother to read any criticism. Compared to reading *The Tempest*, for example, learning what professor so-and-so had said about it simply did not interest me.

Taking my history finals was another matter, and I prepared very seriously. The department had a student who was a few years older than I and whom I shall call G.A. He was the son of a captain of Israeli industry and was, by the standards of those days, filthy rich; he would go around saying such incredible things as, "When I was in Rome last week…" We became friendly, and he sometimes paid me to read books and to summarize them for him. He too intended to graduate. To prepare for the exam, he made me summarize everything there was to be had on seventeenth-century English history. I did my work, but this time he did not pay up. I chased him for weeks but failed to get a hold of him. In the end I decided that, since I had already read and summarized the books, I might as well take the examination myself. I did so and got an A+ As to G.A., with his booming voice, vivid imagination, and genial, convincing manner he was able to bamboozle others besides me, some professors included. Later, he disappeared into a mental asylum. At least that is what I heard.

I started my advance toward—or, given what excited my childish interest in Caldwell and Merrill's book, back to—military history sometime during the late nineteen sixties. My parents, their friends, and most of my teachers had gone through World War II, which was still considered the greatest event in history. Indeed, I would argue that it is only since the end of the Cold War that our perspective on these matters has changed. I could not learn enough about it. For example, at some point I was given Churchill's *History of the English Speaking People* but did not find it interesting. However, I *did* devour his *History of the Second World War*, particularly the first three volumes. Even more interesting were the Axis countries and their "mighty offensive." I collected paperbacks, many of which I still have, with titles such as *Rommel, the Desert Fox, Channel Dash*, and *I Flew for the Führer*. Perhaps I did this because I had not yet met

Plato and was, in any case, too young for him. Or because the society
in which I grew up considered war the greatest and most wonderful
thing on Earth; or because evil often looks fascinating until you meet
it face to face. I did my M.A. thesis on German strategy in the fateful years of
1940–41, teaching myself to read German as I went along. The thesis
was an expanded version of an M.A. seminar paper. The latter in turn
was an expanded version of a B.A. seminar paper that I did for Dr.
Bela Vago, an expert on Central European history who was the first
of my teachers that thought I was worth investing in. Even when
I did the original paper, I already knew that, to economize on time
and effort, I had to recycle my work. The most efficient way was to
submit different versions of the same paper to different professors.
On one occasion I lent a paper I had done to the wife of a friend of
mine so she could submit it in turn. I was delighted to learn she got
the same high grade for it I had. I myself, however, never made use
of other people's work. *Aliis licet, non tibi.*

When I submitted the original paper to Dr. Vago, I could not
know I would be stuck with the same subject for the next five years.
Since then I have learned that such is often the fate of graduate
students. For my M.A. thesis I got an A+ at the hands of a very
well-known professor who specialized in Nazi Germany and the
Holocaust but who almost certainly never read my 120-page paper.
In a way, it was my own fault. I had told him at the outset that I
was determined to get the highest possible grade and that I would
do whatever it took. He probably gave me the A+ to get rid of me,
knowing that, unless he did, I would pester him again and again with
fresh drafts. Later, he refused to support my request for a grant.

I submitted my M.A. thesis at the end of the first year of my post-
graduate studies. It was against the rules, but, luckily, my supervisor
was unaware of that fact. That meant I had the entire second year to
prepare for the final examination. No wonder I passed with flying
colors. Immediately thereafter, in the summer of 1969 I was married.

I was all of twenty-three years old. However, people married younger in those days, and I believed I was up to the burden.

* * *

At the wedding I gave my profession as "historian," making some of the assembled guests snigger. However, my mind was made up. I would read for a PhD, and I would become an academic historian. In Israel at that time there were very few universities, which meant that, practically, my only choice was to return to the place from whence I had come. I could have done my PhD in Israel, but I decided to go abroad. My reasoning was that, if it was my fate to work alongside my former teachers, I did not want to depend on them for my professional qualifications; it was a decision I have never regretted.

Originally, I hoped to go to Oxford and, specifically, to Oriel College. Oxford was where Talmon had done his PhD; he always talked about it in glowing terms as the greatest intellectual center in the world. Two other reasons were that I had never been much interested in French history and that, the efforts of Ms. Laniado notwithstanding, my French was not nearly as good as my English. As to the U.S., here is a story that will illustrate how I felt. At one point I had read a novel about a bunch of rich teenagers in New York. At the end of their adventures, which included flying around the skyscrapers in a private airplane, the hero was left with "only" twenty dollars in his pocket. That amounted to seventy Israeli pounds, a sum equal to my monthly rent. No wonder those distant shores were beyond our, or at any rate my, dreams.

In the event Oriel refused to accept me, a fact, I fondly hope, they still regret. To this day, I have never had an opportunity to speak at Oxford. Instead, I went to the London School of Economics (LSE). On the strength of an interview with Professor Leonard Schapiro, a great expert on modern Russian history and a kind man, I got a

Ford Foundation Grant. There was also some money from Hebrew University. Altogether, my wife and I had a little over 100 pounds a month, enough to get by if one economized on practically everything. This was 1969–71. Not only was there a song that used LSE to rhyme with LSD, but *Oh, Calcutta!* with its notorious nude scenes and bawdy songs was being performed at the Aldwych Theater right across the street. I was sorely tempted, but in the end I did not have what it took to go inside. I suppose I was afraid of being corrupted.

On the other hand, London was already beginning to change from the "swinging London" of the late 1960s into the "Britain down the drain" of the mid-1970s. Compared to the continent, it was a poor, shabby place. I well remember how disappointed some of my Dutch relatives were when they came to visit. For a couple of young Israelis, though, even Kilburn, a one-time solid Jewish neighborhood that was then well on the way to becoming first Irish and then West Indian, was almost too grand to be true. In the whole of Jerusalem there was just one supermarket that could compare with the one near the tube station. As to Harrods, the famous department store in Knightsbridge, so magnificent was it that we barely dared enter its doors.

I did my research at the libraries and archives where I first encountered those awe-inspiring creatures, *the microfilms* on which many captured German documents had been recorded. However, not having an office, I usually wrote at home. The more progress I made with my work, the more time I spent there instead of in town. Home consisted of two rooms rented from an elderly Jewish couple, Mr. and Ms. Levy. The bathroom was shared with a couple about our own age who lived across the corridor. They never washed, which had the advantage that we had the facility largely to ourselves. From their room came the sweet smell of what must have been marijuana.

I worked in our living room. It had a built-in kitchenette, and the table I used also served us when eating our meals. After my oldest son Eldad was born in 1970, he too sat on the table in his chair, and I would interrupt my labors to feed him a bottle or change his diapers. The window looked over a narrow garden some twenty meters long, with the underground running on the far side. Every few minutes a train passed by, causing the entire house to shake. Since I can write with a jackhammer at work on the other side of the wall, none of this ever disturbed me in the slightest. If anything, my ability to do so is improving because, with age, one grows slightly deaf. Unfortunately, that also means I scarcely hear the kind of music, from Gregorian through Bach and Schubert to Rachmaninov, which I like to have wafting around when I work.

My supervisors were Professors Donald Cameron Watt and James Joll. Joll was mainly an intellectual historian who had written about the role of intellectuals in politics. Watt was an expert on international relations and, specifically, the origins of World War II. I dealt mainly with Watt, a big man who would talk down into his tummy so that I could barely understand what he was saying. At first much of what I could understand sounded very critical; whenever I found him too discouraging, I would run to Joll

Prof. D.C. Watt, at about the time I met him. Note the typical late 1960s tie.

for comfort, which he gladly gave. Thus one professor did the actual work of supervision, assigning me books to read, reading drafts, correcting them, and making suggestions for further research, whereas the other kept up my spirits. Whatever the disadvantages of the arrangement, for me it worked just fine. Many years later I told Watt how much he had terrified me at first. He answered that, given what he had been told about the budding genius from Jerusalem, he was equally terrified of me. If not strictly true, at any rate it was nice to hear.

Watt also asked me to take part in one of the seminars he taught, but I did not find it very good. Once, stimulated by a glass of sherry, I even had the effrontery to complain about it to the head of the school. To my great good fortune, he let it pass. The group, which was made up entirely of graduate students, met every two weeks for an hour and a half. Each time somebody would present a paper, and we would discuss it. I do not remember that I gave a paper. Nor do I remember that there was a program—although, thinking about it, there must have been one—or a reading list. As a result, the course was not well organized. We moved from one unrelated topic to the next. The most memorable thing about it was Watt's ability to sleep through the seminar. Here he was, looking like an overgrown teddy bear, nodding away and even snoring softly. Yet always at the right moment, he would wake up and ask the sort of penetrating question that left his audience gasping. I and others to whom I have spoken have often wondered how he did it. But I never succeeded in imitating him.

The subject of my PhD was the same on which I had been working for years, namely German strategy during the year between the fall of France and the beginning of the attack on the Soviet Union. In part, the decision was the product of fear. It was only many years later that I felt sufficiently sure of my professional ability to move from one subject to the next as the spirit took me without worrying too much about the amount of work it meant. There was, however, a change of attitude on my part, and this came about mainly under the influence of Dr. Geoffrey Warner. Warner, several years older than I, was working as a reader at the University of Reading. Having already published a book on Pierre Laval, the French prime minister during the Vichy period, he was working on a subject somewhat similar to mine, i.e. the *guerra parallela* (parallel war) Mussolini planned to wage in the Mediterranean while his dear friend Hitler was finishing off Britain. Warner was very generous, allowing me to use the Italian material he had collected and was available nowhere else in Britain.

He also spent many hours discussing things with me in his office or at his home.

Until then, I had assumed that studying history was about learning stories, correcting them—if there were "problems"—and retelling them. Some stories were important, others less so. Some were exciting, others, like the one which detailed the exact rank Cato had carried at Cynoscephalae, less so. Depending on the context, different historians might tell the same story in different ways from different perspectives. This was called "interpreting," the best and most sophisticated thing anyone could do. I remember how, visiting a club in Montmartre in 1966, I was disappointed to learn that the stripper who waved her breasts in front of my face was also "interpreting" a dance.

A good story was true and accurate and integrated as many other stories as possible. If you were really up to date, you would base it not just on old books but on some sophisticated tool like radioactive carbon dating or air photography. But a story it remained. The reason for telling it, if any, was to fill "gaps" in existing knowledge. The fact that those gaps only existed in the minds of a few professional scholars was ignored. My discussions with Warner, who initially knew much more about my subject than I did, taught me otherwise. I soon realized that he saw events in the Mediterranean in one way and I in a different one. To resolve the issue, we took quotes from the German and Italian archives and threw them at each other for hours on end. Though nothing was ever said explicitly, somehow the process made me realize that the essence of studying history is not to tell stories. Rather, it is to ask questions and find answers.

At that time I was already the proud owner of an M.A. *summa cum laude*. Nevertheless, whether through the fault of my teachers at Hebrew University or my own, it had never occurred to me to look at things in this way. Though it took me time to realize the full implications of my conversations with Warner, the impact was overwhelming. Until then, I had always been worried that my work might not be original, given that each story I picked up seemed to have been covered already by so many different historians. Shifting the emphasis to questions enabled me to evade that problem. After all, the number of questions is infinite. No two people will ever pose the same question in exactly the same way, let alone give identical answers. As the Dutch historian Pieter Geyl used to say, this is precisely what makes history interesting.

Much later, when it was my turn to teach, students used to come to me with similar problems. In response, I explained the way I saw these things. I also prepared a short guide on how to do a seminar paper, which also applies to writing an article or even a book. The opening sentence read as follows:

"The purpose of a paper is to answer a question that the author finds interesting. A good paper is one that defines the question exactly and answers it adequately."

I have never seen any reason to change those words.

The fact that the objective is to answer a question does not mean that all questions are born equal. To quote a Dutch proverb, a single fool can ask more questions than ten wise men can answer. The artistic touch consists of finding a question that is neither too easy nor too difficult, neither too close to our putative readers' mind as to appear trite nor too remote from it as to make them yawn, or, worse still, take up arms against you. Quite often, the very best questions concern things that are, or are supposed to be, well known. For example, one day in class we were discussing the possibility that Jordan might become the Palestinian state since the majority of its people were already Palestinians. Suddenly, a young student raised her arm and asked, "How do you know?" Good questions are like good tunes you have heard but cannot quite remember; once they have been raised, they simply refuse to go away. She spent weeks doing what she could to find an answer by reading, talking to experts, searching the Internet for additional information, and discovering the hard way that the question is by no means as simple as it sounds. In return for her paper, I was happy to waive the final exam.

The shift from stories to questions also helped me in another way. It solved, or at least got rid of, the nagging doubt whether we historians were making "progress" as natural scientists did; in other words, whether we deserved our daily bread or were just lazy dogs endlessly rehashing our predecessors' work. Being familiar with the likes of Thucydides, Sallust, Caesar, and Josephus, I was under no illusion that either I or anybody else stood the slightest chance of improving on them. This was true in respect to the method we used; it was even more true in respect to the sheer ability to analyze events and to make them come alive. Now I realized that it did not matter. The reason was that, living in a radically different world and studying history from a radically different angle, we could ask questions they never did.

In my view, the historian's ability to ask new questions and to answer them more than justifies his existence. Though I prefer our methods to theirs, the same is also true of other social scientists. In 2012 my wife Dvora and I went to the visitor center at CERN near Geneva, which, incidentally, is one of the worst arranged I have ever seen. Somewhere on the wall there was a sign—or was it a virtual sign?—with the questions that form the organization's mission: Who are we? Where did we come from? Where are we going?

Thus any inferiority complex I may once have had *vis a vis* the natural scientists has long evaporated. They do their work; I do mine. Though our methods are as different as different can be, my contribution to understanding the way the world has worked, works, and (perhaps) will work is not a whit inferior to theirs. This is not in spite of the fact that the questions I ask are influenced by my environment, as they are bound to be, but *because* they are. Studying history makes one feel like a man who is carried along by the current of a river. Encountering new and unexpected objects, he is constantly forced to reassess whatever he has seen before. Thus we make "progress" whether we want to or not.

At our very first meeting Watt told me to limit myself to 100,000 words. "What you cannot say in 100,000 words," he added in his characteristically blunt way, "do not say." I thought then—and I think now—that this was very good advice to give a young scholar and that those who write more should be punished for their pains. Possibly because he was a superb supervisor, harsh and critical at first but generous and very supportive later on, and possibly because I was well prepared by years of preliminary work, the thesis itself only took me eighteen months to write from start to finish. Nowadays I often feel sorry for my younger colleagues. Instead of writing down their ideas on a page or two, which is what Schapiro and Watt asked me to do, they have to submit research proposals that can be as many as twenty pages long. Instead of working with a single supervisor, they have entire committees breathing down their necks.

As they say, a camel is a horse created by a committee. Each committee member wallows in his or her self-importance and feels duty bound to point out defects only he can see. Each of them is, or pretends to be, terribly busy and can only be bothered so often, and then only with proper advance warning. Once warned, he is as likely as not to be away on sabbatical or something. Each absolutely must get a copy of everything, neatly printed and neatly bound. After all, it will not do to present a professor with anything less. The students spend years wrestling with what is meant to be not a *magnum opus* but simply a claim to become a junior faculty member. By the time it is finished, so, in many cases, are they.

I found, as I have often done since, that the hardest parts are the beginning and the end. You start with great confidence in yourself, forging plans, gathering material, and writing down your precious ideas. Then, as you go along, you find that things are more complicated than you thought and that much of what you thought you knew was really the product of oversimplification and ignorance. Your confidence gone, you wrestle with that finding for several months. You read, look for clues, break your head (sometimes, literally so; people in this situation have been known to do strange things) and, when things do not seem to go well, take a walk. This is the period of incubation, and there is no escaping it. Discussing your problems may help. So may engaging in some totally unrelated task or simply breaking away and taking a vacation.

My own breakthrough came in October 1970, about a year after I had started work and after having spent a week touring South Wales in the company of my brother, who had come over to see what Britain was like. I remember how impressed we were with the miners' cottages in the district to the west of Bristol. Garlanded with flowers, to us young Israelis they looked as if they were fit for millionaires. Yet this was precisely the period when one coalmine after another was being shut down until, nowadays, there are few if any left. We also visited the fortresses built by Edward I, played tennis, walked, and swam in the sea, which was as cold as any I can remember. I am always reminded of a story told of, or by, James Watt. Apparently, he solved the problem of building an efficient steam engine, with which he had been wrestling for months, while on an absent-minded Sunday stroll on Edinburgh Common.

At first, not even recognizing the idea for what it is, you may well dismiss it as you have so many of its predecessors. Gradually, though, you will find that it eats into your soul, crowds out its competitors, and takes you over. You find yourself thinking of it when you get up in the morning, when you take your meals, brush your teeth, sit, stand, walk, and sleep. Sometimes, I am afraid, you think of it even as you are making love. The consequences are predictable and become worse with age. Here is one of the many advantages women enjoy over men.

Now and then, losing patience, you try to create a shortcut. Knowing full well you are not ready, you sit down and force yourself to write. But the only result is nausea, and you soon give up. Then

all of a sudden, things start changing. You feel that this or that just
might work, and you write it down. Another line, another idea, is
added. At first things go slowly and haltingly. Each morning you
wake up with a sinking feeling that what you did the day before may
have been—probably was—absolute rubbish. Fear that the recently
found inspiration will disappear causes you to work more than you
should and places you on edge.

Gradually, almost without your noticing it, your self-confidence
increases. A back wind starts blowing, and you find yourself carried
aloft. There follows the kind of creative period when you cannot stop
pouring out your soul. Even reading becomes a chore. With so many
of your own ideas competing for attention, the last thing you want is
to allow intruders to enter. It is a joy to be alive. You work as though
possessed. In fact you *are* possessed. Yet, paradoxically, the living is
easy. You seem to have all the spare time in the world, and you feel
free to take off at any moment to mow the lawn or wash the dishes.
If you have never gone through the experience, and also if you have,
take time to listen to Beethoven's 9th *Symphony*. It was Rachel who,
during our stay in London, brought it to my attention. For that I
am eternally grateful to her. Since then, I have always thought it is a
faithful record of one person's emergence from depression into light.

That stage, however, is not the end of the story. It is true that
creation, if one feels it is successful, ends with an explosion of joy so
intense one is scarcely able to contain oneself but feels like dancing
over hill and dale. In my experience, however, before the end, there
is almost always another period of great uncertainty and doubt. One
knows one has the knowledge to complete one's work. One can
see the goal ahead; one strives for it with all one's might; yet one
is unable to reach it. That is how Moses must have felt when he
stood on top of Mount Nebo and looked out over the Promised
Land. Instead of granting him a last favor, the Lord made him die.
However, that may also have been the greatest favor of all, given that

an achievement and the elation that goes with it is almost always followed by a disappointment to match.

Early during my stay in London, I worked Saturdays as well. Soon, however, I decided that, having moved to a country where everybody worked five days a week, there was no reason why I should work six. On the weekends Rachel and I explored. Having skimped on lodgings, we were able to run a little used car; this was at a time when most of our Israeli contemporaries could only dream of such a thing. The first time I drove on the left, I was absolutely terrified, but later I adjusted. In the eighteen months we owned it, our Hillman Imp tore the cable that linked the gas pedal to the carburetor. Next, it broke a clutch, blew a gasket (which caused it to overheat and stall in the midst of the lions' cage at Windsor Safari Park), lost its brakes, needed new shock absorbers, and finally had to have its gearbox replaced. Yet never have I enjoyed a car more; our baby son Eldad, whom we used to lift in through the rear window as he sat in his pram, knew that to get in, he had to bow his head. Used to Israel's semi-arid landscape, we found the pleasant green fields of England breathtaking. This remains true, yet I would not exchange the vistas of my own country for anything. Where else can one take a walk and feel that the terrain has remained unchanged since King David did the same 3,000 years ago?

My Italian trip apart, London enabled me to have my first encounters with world-class art—the kind of blessing that, in the little, isolated, poor Israel of the time was almost entirely absent. We visited all the important museums, parks, gardens, or whatever they were called—most of them more than once. And we probably did not leave a country house within seventy or so miles unseen. Richmond House, Zion House, Windsor, Hampton Court, the various Rothschild Residences, Blenheim Palace, Sissinghurst Castle, Longleat, Woburn Abbey (where I once helped chase a baby hippopotamus that had escaped from its pond), everything was grist to our mill.

To top it all, we went to the "proms" at the Royal Festival Hall, where we heard some of the world's best symphonic orchestras. In the summer we attended open-air concerts at Kenwood, my favorite location of all. There, the ducks waddled among the rows of deckchairs standing on the grass. I remember listening to a spirited rendition of Tchaikovsky's *Capriccio Italien* and, at the end of the season, to Handel's *Music for Royal Fireworks*. It was the only time in my life when I attended concerts on a regular basis, and one I still remember with profound emotion. *Pace* the myrmidons of the free enterprise school, a government which, by subsidizing such events, enables penniless students to enjoy them cannot be entirely bad.

Even more important was the growing realization that there is more to history than books. I learned that every object, however humble, has a tale to tell. This is how people used to live, eat, dress, sleep, perform their ablutions, work for a living, amuse themselves, carouse, and make love. Doing so both reflected and affected their attitudes, their feelings, and their thoughts. I remember spending hours at the British Museum's collection of ancient Greek vases, many more of which were on display then than now. I also recall inspecting one of the first water closets installed in an English home—I think it was Osterley House near London—which made me wonder what people used to do earlier.

Some of the things they did, as shown e.g. in a seventeenth-century painting by Pieter de Hooch of a Dutch family at a bowling party, were so familiar as to fill one's eyes with tears. Others seemed strange, foolish, or repulsive. Yet there was no doubt that the people who had created this marvelous or, less often, not so marvelous art, were as sensible and as intelligent as we are. What we are in our day they were in theirs; what they are now we shall be soon enough. Presumably, they had their reasons, which by and large were as good or as bad as ours. It is true that they were sometimes very cruel. But at any rate the organization and the technology at their disposal did not permit them to produce either an Auschwitz or a Hiroshima.

To this day, my second wife and I love visiting flea markets to look at curiosities of every kind. If we do not often buy, then this is mainly because one cannot go on filling one's home. It is much better to make presents to our children, whose homes, thanks goodness, are still fairly empty. Another minor hobby I practice is lifting my eyes from the book I am reading and glancing at the TV screen in the midst of a film. Not knowing anything about it except what I can see at that moment, I try to guess the time and place where it is set by the furniture among which people move, the clothes they wear, the cars they drive, their hairstyles, and the like. Usually, I succeed.

By the early spring of 1971 my dissertation was finished. I rented an electric typewriter to type the requisite seven copies, and by May that job too was finished. However, the two obligatory years one was supposed to spend working were not yet over, so it was necessary for us to stay in England a little longer. Rachel worked outside the home, and I spent some very pleasant weeks reading in the garden. Behind me I could hear the voice of old Mr. Caesar Levy as he listened to his own taped speeches, his favorite occupation in life. Right next to me was Eldad, now almost one year old. He sat on a blanket eating daisies; as long as he did not try to make me eat them as well, I did not mind. Once I took him for a walk in nearby Hampstead Heath, a garden-like park I often visited and which I learned to love as much as any place on Earth. It was one of those mornings that feel like creation—not too hot, very clear, with a perfect blue sky. I was pushing the pram and singing as I went. A man approached, looked me up and down, and said, "Your song is going straight to Heaven."

When the time for the obligatory oral examination arrived, Watt arranged things in such a way that the original examiner, whom he described as a difficult man, stayed at home. Instead, he asked Warner to join him, which made sure I could not fail to pass even if I had tried my hardest. At the same time it also made sure the examination was something of a farce, a fact that left me slightly disappointed. More importantly, he helped me publish my work with Cambridge University Press. There, it appeared under the title *Hitler's Strategy, 1940–1941: The Balkan Clue* (1973); if memory serves me right, I thought of the title in 1972 en route to Cyprus, as a passenger in an open sailing boat that carried twelve other young people besides me. Although the reviews were fair, looking back, I think I was lucky. Like anything else, books have their entries and exits. Had the same thesis been written only half a decade later, it might very well have been considered too specialized and too narrowly focused to see the light of print.

More remarkable still, Cambridge accepted my volume just as it was. I did not have to change a single word. Much later, this made me think about many other students, especially American ones, who have not been as fortunate as I. There seems to be something very wrong with a system which, by requiring students to follow its rules, compels them to produce work that cannot be published unless, often at the cost of much time and money, it is thoroughly revised first. Nor, as will be seen later on, do I consider this to be the only way in which academia regularly betrays the students who enter its gates.

Chapter 2

Young Historian

I got my appointment at the Department of History of Hebrew University because of a power struggle between Talmon and another professor. For some reason, Talmon had never liked me. On one occasion he made me reel off all the languages I could read. After I had finished, he told the participants in the seminar that I might end up as a successful waiter. Fortunately, the other professor, a younger man with whom I had not studied but who was head of the department, decided to show him who was boss. I well knew Talmon did not want me. On one occasion, visiting London soon after my oldest son was born, he summoned me to see him in order to tell me so. Still, I did not know how I had served as a battering ram in the ongoing power struggle in the historical teacup. I only learned of it a long time afterward and consider myself lucky.

The Jerusalem to which Rachel and I returned in September 1971 was a different place from the one we had left two years earlier. When I went there in the mid-1960s, it had been a poor, neglected town located at the apex of a triangle jutting into Jordanian territory. As people used to say, the best thing about Jerusalem was the road to Tel Aviv. The 1967 war changed this. It reunited the city's two halves, which had been separated in 1948. It broke the feeling of claustrophobia, caused vast crowds of tourists to pour in, and resulted in new neighborhoods springing up like mushrooms. It also led to a much more cosmopolitan atmosphere now that we had so many Arabs living with us.

Bit by bit, the grip that orthodox Jews used to have on the city was relaxed. Previously, on Saturday all one saw in the streets were stray cats. Now, Saturday found the eastern part bustling with life. There were even some signs that the Jewish neighborhoods might follow. Already there was an occasional act of terrorism, and already one could see the prime minister's office opposite the campus being turned into a fortress. Still, on the whole the city remained remarkably peaceful until the beginning of the Second Palestinian Uprising in September 2000. Visiting the U.S., as I began to do regularly from 1980 on, I always assured people that Jerusalem was much safer than Washington, D.C. Which, in fact, it was.

My family, soon to include a baby girl named Abigail, and I settled in one of the new neighborhoods, though still within the pre-1967 armistice line. Soon enough I went to work. Normally, at Hebrew University teachers chose their own subjects with few, if any, strings attached. However, young ones were sometimes asked to do this or that for the greater good of the department. I too was asked to do the same and, of course, could not refuse. I was saddled with a workshop about the Dutch Revolt against Spain and with a pro-seminar about Italian Fascism. I owed these duties to the fact that I knew Dutch and some Italian; the two languages, however, were absolutely the only qualifications I had.

Fascism had something to do with the two World Wars, and I enjoyed teaching the course. I translated original texts into English and read them with my students. My underlying thesis was that Fascism was an answer to a national inferiority complex. The complex had started developing in the sixteenth century when Italy failed to form a unified state as other European countries did. It was strengthened by the Italian army's poor performance in 1915–18. This idea, which I took from Luigi Barzini's *The Italians*, is one I would defend even now, though only as one part of the story which, as usual, was much more complex.

The course on the Dutch Revolt was more problematic. First, though I myself was of Dutch origins, the country's history was *terra incognita* for me. Second, instead of focusing on Protestantism and neo-Stoicism, as those who made me teach the course intended, I taught the origins of the revolt and the way it unfolded and became bogged down in the details of various military campaigns. To make things worse, I had to teach two parallel classes on the same subject. My superiors, worried about my ability to cope, may have made this arrangement to help me during my first year. I, however, hate having to repeat myself. Observing schoolteachers, I can only admire their ability to do the same work year after year without dying of boredom. This is all the more the case because the material they teach is dictated to them by officials at the Ministry of Education, many of whom have never taught a class in their lives. As for Hebrew University, one thing I can say in its favor is that, after the first year, nobody ever told me what to teach and how. At least, not successfully.

Apart from a few months when, as a fifteen-year-old boy scout, I was in charge of about twenty unruly children five years younger than myself, I had never done any teaching. It took me years to learn how to do it the way I think it should be done. Universities would do well to give young faculty a helping hand in this respect. If so, that help should come from senior faculty and not from professional educators, who, in my experience, raise obfuscation to a rare form of art. Now that I am teaching at Tel Aviv University, I continue taking my duties very seriously, feeling this is something I owe my students who, after all, pay tuition. I expect them to reply in kind and, as part of an attempt to ensure that they do, always start classes by reading the list of names even though, in truth, I do not care whether or not they miss a class. Since I rarely miss a class—my students know that, if I do, I must be on my deathbed—and since I always build in some slack, in theory I should always be able to complete my program.

In practice it does not always work out that way. The reason is that I consider it my first duty to answer every question as best I can. Both because they deserve it and to show them what, in my view, an academic discussion should be like. In such cases, to avoid leaving the students hanging in the air, as it were, I use the last meeting for a general summing-up. I always prepare my classes even if I have taught the same course before and even if, as a result of having studied the subject for years, I know it by heart. To show students I am indeed prepared, the first thing I do is pull out a sheet of paper and put it on the table in front of me. I expect it would do some good even if nothing were written on it. The desire to show students that study is a serious business also makes me dress up, if only by the standards of Israeli universities. At places where even the rector may not always wear coat and tie, doing so is not difficult.

Right from the beginning I did my best to avoid making my students memorize dates and facts. Instead, I tried to challenge them by presenting them with the kinds of questions to which I did not have a simple answer and which I myself had enjoyed answering when I took my exams. Alas, it did not take me very long to learn that the number of those who wanted to be challenged was limited to, if I was lucky, perhaps one third of the students in any single class. In my experience most of them are men. Either because they are physically smaller on average or else because they have been conditioned not to put off men by appearing aggressive, few women will speak up when the latter are present. This even applies when they are in the majority, as they often are in the humanities. On the other hand, I have noticed that, on the few occasions when I addressed classes made up entirely of women, they can be quite as lively as men. Perhaps this is an argument in favor of resegregating education.

Male or female, the rest would just sit there. They ignored my existence even as they busily wrote down—nowadays, type on their laptops—anything I spouted, an experience I found more irritating than I can say. Once addressing the Danish Command and General

Staff School in Copenhagen, I asked the students to do themselves and me a favor and to forget about their laptops. Only a genius, I said, can listen and type at the same time. "I am a genius," one student said. We all laughed, but after we had finished doing so, most of them complied with my request.

In favor of my Israeli students I will say that, having done their conscript service and being older on the average, they are less prone to behave in this way than some others I have met. Nor do they expect me to stand *in loco parentis* as American ones often do. Neither I nor anybody else at the department can even remember dealing with a student's parent. Only once did such an apparition walk into the Secretariat and introduce herself, making those of us who happened to be present think she had fallen off the moon. It turned out she had come to hand in a paper written by a student who was doing his reserve service.

I want to fill heads, not notebooks. This being academia, apart from discussion, the only way to make a head work is to make its owner write a paper. Unlike some of my own former teachers, I never told my students what to write about. The reason is that only they know what interests them and also because selecting a subject is probably the most important, as well as the most difficult, part of the exercise. Once the decision is made, I do my best to help by offering suggestions, criticizing, etc. I also take care to comment on each paper and to provide each student with a letter that will evaluate his work and explain why he received the grade he did.

Teaching is like watching one's children learning to walk. You have to give them leeway. Even though your heart trembles for them, and even though what you would really like to do is gather them up in your arms. I am sorry to say that I sometimes gave them too much leeway before they were ready, causing them to fall in mid-stride and to break their necks. Best of all is the joy of having them come back with ideas of their own. A really good student—I am not referring to the type who is only out to show what he already knows—will speak up. Meeting resistance, he will ask for a chance to present his ideas in class even if doing so involves doing extra work.

Conversely, as Nietzsche wrote, students who merely echo their teacher repay him or her evil for good. Perhaps my expectations are exaggerated. After all, most students are where they are not because they want to but because they and their parents feel that a piece of paper with the letters "B.A." or "M.A." on it is essential for getting a proper job. Others, especially foreign ones, consider their period of study as time off from serious life, for which I cannot blame them. Either way, some consider me a figure of fun, particularly when my back is turned.

Over the years I have had many excellent students. Some are enthused by the challenges I present them with. They take the bit between their teeth, research their subjects at much greater depth than I intended, and come up with answers I never dreamed existed. Some recommend me to their friends. Some go their separate ways, taking up careers in fields as far apart as diplomacy and business. Some stay in touch, and some get to the point where, since they know more about a subject than I do, I can ask them to criticize my own work. I cannot imagine anything better happening to a teacher. Thus, the present volume was reviewed by a former student, Mr. Zeev Elron. Having studied with me, he has since completed his PhD on the evolution of the Israel Defense Force (IDF) during the nineteen fifties and is working as an instructor at the Command and Staff College. Short of breaking the law, I will do anything I can to help my students to lower a bucket inside themselves, as it were, and to come up with the best they have. My only regret about not being an administrator is that I do not have grant money to distribute and cannot help them as much as I would like and they deserve.

Whether because I am known to prefer interacting with students to haranguing them or because I am uncompromising when it comes to academic quality, my classes tend to be on the small side. Not long ago I had, in my class, an air force lieutenant-colonel who was about to be promoted to a critically important post. As he himself told me, no sooner had he discovered that I made "heavy demands" that he decided to leave. I never give pep talks about the importance of education, etc. Instead, for many years I used to make sure that participants are highly motivated by starting some classes at 8:30 a.m. Given Jerusalem traffic, this obliged some of them (and me) to leave their beds at 6:30 a.m. or earlier.

Once the doors are closed, I aim for perfect freedom. Every meeting opens with a brief summary of the last one. That often leads to unexpected exchanges as students, having had time to digest what they had learned, come up with new ideas. Next, there is often a presentation by a student, though I have learned that it is better not to try this method with freshmen. If, during the discussion that follows, a question is too difficult to answer at once, I may ask students take out pen and paper, take a few minutes, and jot down their thoughts. Another technique is to tell them you are going to give them *your* answer and to ask them what they think of it. As far as time allows, all this is as true in lectures as in seminars. Almost the only difference is that, in the latter, students are supposed to come prepared. To ensure they do, I have taken to demanding that, after reading the assigned material, they formulate some questions and address them to the student who will speak in the next meeting. They must also give a copy to me so that I can respond in writing, as I always do.

I do my best, though I do not always succeed, never to say a harsh word to anybody. Once, as we were discussing Thomas Hobbes' view of the state of nature, I told a student who said that there were more important things than personal security that he did not know what he was talking about. I regretted it immediately and do so still. Normally, the strongest expression I use is "I disagree." As my reward, the students soon start doing the same. I have even been told my classes are the only ones in which there are no bad questions, which I took as the greatest compliment of all. The discussion can become too animated. Once we were studying Marx when the window of the room opened and a girl climbed in from outside and dropped to the floor. She had come from the class next door, and she asked us to lower our voices so they could hear themselves think. Having finished laughing, we gladly obliged.

Since my visual memory is bad, I have trouble remembering faces. Here and there, though, a student stands out, leading not only to a fascinating intellectual exchange but enabling me to look into his or her personality as well. This can lead to surprises. Once, discussing commando operations, I learned my class included a member of a super-secret air force unit who had spent years doing commando work in Lebanon. Something I said about members of such units sometimes being issued stimulants to keep them awake caused him to boil over with anger; later, we clarified the misunderstanding and made peace.

Another outstanding student beside Elron was a nineteen-year-old immigrant from Russia, Alexander Epstein. At the time we met he had a willowy body and glasses so thick I could barely see his eyes. He kept saying, "Yes, Professor," and, "No, Professor," in a high-pitched voice. I thought he was the most servile student I ever met. He would clasp his hands like a Buddhist monk when talking and would leave my office walking backward. Once, having arrived late and knowing I would not allow him to come in, he sat down on the floor outside. When he wanted to say something, he stuck his arm round the corner and through the door. This, of course, caused the class to roar with laughter and me to invite him to enter.

Then, this fellow turned out to be a pacifist, and a very combative one at that. Believing himself a conscientious objector—I am not sure he still retains that persuasion—he refused to be drafted and spent many months corresponding with every IDF command echelon. Finally, with a little assistance from me and a few other faculty members, he took his case all the way to the Supreme Court. His Hebrew was defective, but he turned even that into an advantage;

representing himself, the substance of his plea was that, since Israeli women can obtain exemption on conscientious grounds, the same should apply to him. So effective was his appearance that, had the judges not told the IDF lawyer to spare himself an adverse ruling by having the plaintiff declared physically unfit, he would have won his case. An accidental meeting I later had with the head of the IDF's manpower division revealed that he, the general, was familiar with every detail of the case. Since then, Epstein has mastered English as well as Hebrew, received his PhD in near record time, and launched what will surely be a brilliant academic career.

Yet another student was Yuval Harari. Like Epstein, he was small of stature, but the similarity ended there. Like most others at Hebrew University, the course, whose title was "Modern Strategy," lasted an entire academic year and was made up of twenty-six meetings. During all those meetings, Harari just sat there, never once opening his mouth. A more marginal, not to say autistic, student one has never seen. Two months later I got his paper, which dealt with the art of command in the Middle Ages. I only had to read a page or two to know: a genius. Since then, this guy has received his PhD from Oxford University. He has also published four books—of which the last, *Sapiens: A Brief History of Humankind*, has been translated into forty languages and made its author world famous. I flatter myself that I have helped him a little and wish him all success in the future, too.

As a teacher, something else I like to do is organize field trips. At the History Department we had a long tradition of two- or three-day tours, and at one point I assumed responsibility for them. With the help of an assistant or two, each year I selected a different theme: be it ancient history, Byzantine history, Crusader history, military history, or whatever; in practice, Israel being as small as it is, we often visited the same places repeatedly. I used to go from class to class advertising the coming event. When I considered it necessary, I put on some appropriate gear to attract attention. Once, I appeared with plastic armor, *pickelhaube* and sword, making teachers and students roar with laughter. I booked hostels, rented buses, and collected money. Later, I learned my method of doing so was strictly illegal, but there were never any complaints. I also had maps and blueprints of the sites we were about to visit printed.

We had excellent guides, several of them world-class experts in their fields. The most prominent one was general (ret.) and prime minister-to-be Ariel Sharon. He joined us to explain the 1948 battle in which he had been wounded and gave one of the best talks I have ever listened to. Usually, I was able to manage things in such a way as to treat the participants to some extra. Be it a refreshing swim in the Sea of Galilee; or a hat with a logo ordered especially for the occasion; or a restaurant meal; or a bottle of wine to be consumed in the evening as everybody gathered for an impromptu seminar. Twice we went abroad, once to Jordan and once to Istanbul. All the trips were a great success, and I received many letters of thanks. Later, various factors caused interest in the larger tours to decline. However, I still take students to see the Israeli Armored Corps Museum at Latrun not far from Jerusalem. They enjoy it, and so do I.

These joys notwithstanding, there are a few things about teaching that I find exasperating. The worst is having to listen to students' excuses. You assign a paper—wishing to make people think rather than simply memorize facts, all my exams are of the take-home type—asking that it be handed in on such and such a date. However long or short the time, you can be sure that, a few days before it runs out, the telephone will start ringing or, nowadays, emails arriving. One student has just had a very bad flu. Another's grandmother has died. A third absolutely must attend his sister's wedding, which, he is sorry to say, takes place in Timbuktu. Some of the excuses are probably true; others false. I cannot say I care. I deal with the requests as best I can, granting one, refusing another, and not-so-secretly wishing that those who make them go to Hell.

Once I came across some students who said they had been given university-issued certificates to the effect that they were slow learners. I answered that, as an employee at the university, I would respect the latter's wishes and grant them the extra time they were asking for. However, I added, it seemed to me that making use of such a certificate was the most humiliating thing in the world. It also represented a fail-proof way to be rejected by any future employer. My appeal to their pride worked. One even thanked me.

As an aspiring faculty member I had always known I would teach. Though I did not really understand what it meant, I thought I was ready to do so. But nothing had prepared me for the loneliness of academic life as I experienced it. Like most middle-class youths, I had spent my life being told what to do, when, and, to a large extent, how. The more so because my mother always insisted on maintaining a very tight domestic schedule. Make sure you reach school at eight o'clock, which meant rising at seven so as to bravely wash your face, comb your hair, and eat your soft-boiled egg. Make sure you have done your homework by day so and so. Read your assignments, prepare to sit for your exams, write your papers, submit your thesis, and, in general, do as your parents, or your teachers, or your professors, told you to do.

Now, at twenty-five, I was the youngest lecturer (the lowest rung on the academic ladder, roughly corresponding to the American adjunct professor) in the entire country. For the first time there was nobody to tell me what to do, and a terrifying experience it was. To be sure, you had to present yourself in class at such and such hours and spend ninety minutes teaching each one. However, even if you included preparation, reading papers, office hours, etc., once you got the hang of it, doing so only took up about a day and a half per week on the average. At that time Israel was still on a five-and-a-half-day working week that started on Sunday morning and ended shortly after noon on Friday. What would I do with the other four?

Looking for an answer, at one point I read Erich Fromm's *Escape from Freedom*. It told me why, in the author's view, people had become Nazis. But it did not solve my problem.

Our departmental secretary, Ms. Yaffa Razin, was married to a famous professor of biology. From her I learned that, in the natural sciences, people worked in the lab, going there each morning and returning in the late afternoon or evening. In the humanities and social sciences things were different. Originally, most of us did not have an office. Even after we got one, the force of habit proved strong, and we continued to work at home, as I myself have done during most of my career and as I am doing right now. Some people filled some of their time by forming clubs and meeting to discuss one another's work. However, I have always liked to work alone and hardly ever show my work to anyone before I think it is quite finished. It is history that interests me, not the chit-chat and cups of coffee that surround it as they do so many other activities.

Others still did administration. For some reason I could never understand, they love nothing better than meetings during which they discuss such vital questions as whether a seminar paper is an extended pro-seminar paper or whether, to the contrary, a pro-seminar paper is a miniature seminar paper. Partly because their decision-making authority is very limited, partly no doubt out of sheer boredom, they keep repeating themselves, rehashing the same issues every few years, and going around in circles.

That is why I could not force myself to take an active part in the meetings, let alone accept the offers of participating on this or that committee, running this or that institute, which, especially at the beginning of my career, sometimes came my way. I have absolutely no interest in any of this. My colleagues soon found out and left me alone. I understand that General Eisenhower, who for a time served as President of Columbia University, saw academia in a similar light. They always tend to turn mice into mountains.

Other people still filled their time by engaging in politics. No doubt remembering what the Romans had done to the Greeks, my revered teacher, Alexander Fuks, once participated in a hunger strike to protest against the 1974 Egyptian-Israeli Separation of Forces Agreement. I, however, do not feel I am suited for the wheeling and dealing and vote canvassing that politics involve. Unlike some of my colleagues, I have not meant most of what I have published to carry a political message. My overriding aim is to find out how things work, not to push some agenda. When one is there, it is always secondary. The most I have done is to participate in an occasional demonstration, sign a petition, or listen to some public figure holding forth in an attempt to obtain my vote.

Most of the demonstrations were in favor of Arab-Israeli peace, or the rule of law, or the separation of religion and state, or capitalism with a heart. Much later, after my second wife and I left Jerusalem for Mevasseret Zion a few miles to the west, she and I also demonstrated for the right for our community to remain independent of Israel's capital. In our eyes, it has long become a hotbed of fanaticism, sectarian violence, and economic backwardness. Finally, some people solved the problem by taking up a hobby. However, the one thing worse than a Calvinist home is a Jewish-Calvinist home. I have always felt that a hobby, or any other activity besides work, might be enjoyed only after work had been well and truly done.

So who would tell me what to do? When would I get up? When would I stop working, telling myself that enough was enough? How much time should be devoted to work, and how much to other activities such as running—my long-time recreation, and one that, ere my knees gave way, I loved very much—taking care of household problems, and looking after my children? What should I do first, what last, and how could I be sure any of it was not being wasted but was leading anywhere? To be sure, the working lives of most people are not exactly fun and games. Some would even argue that we academics do not live in the "real" world. In a sense that is true enough. Still, they do not have to face these questions on their own but can, to a large extent, trust their employers to do so for them. As for me, it took me years before I found the answers. Or, at any rate, gained sufficient confidence so that it no longer mattered.

Since then, I have realized that having no boss and being in control of my own time are rare privileges very few people share. By now, if I *had* a boss, I would not have known what to do with him. Nor would he have known what to do with me. While I cannot speak for others, for me this fact had a very important impact on my professional career. This is particularly true in comparison with military life as I have known it. No two lifestyles are as different as academia and the military. Had I been forced to live in a closed community, to wear my place in the pecking order and my achievements on my chest and shoulders, to have my life regulated by standing orders, and to respond to emergencies as soldiers often do, then it is very doubtful whether I could have developed into a scholar, let alone a scholar with independent views.

My upbringing apart, there were other reasons for my obsession with work as well as my tendency to go into depression when it does not go well. First, I have never found anything more interesting than history. As a result, when I am doing anything else, up to a point I am bored by definition. Second, as a young faculty member, on pain of losing your job, you only have five or six years to get tenure. Therefore, as a young faculty member, you have only one overriding concern: publish or perish is the name of the game. Sometimes this is literally true, for cases have been known when someone, having failed to make it and thinking that as many as twelve or fifteen years of his life have been wasted, put a bullet through his head.

The transition from the hothouse of school to the rigors of the labor force is hard for anyone who has to make it. Still, academics may well have a harder time than most. For me personally, it was as trying a time as I have ever gone through. Nor did I go through it without it leaving some permanent scars on me. Now that I think of it, perhaps one reason why I write this is to help others in my position or, at any rate, to make them realize they are not unique.

✳ ✳ ✳

I too wanted to get tenure as soon as possible but had no idea as to how to go about it. Though my thesis had skirted the border between political and military history, I was not yet quite sure that the latter was indeed my chosen field. This was all the more the case because, having been made to teach it, I was becoming seriously interested in Fascism as well. In fact one of the first articles I published after returning from London discussed the origins of the Italian racial laws of 1937–38. My idea was

The army in which I did not serve; a 1950s IDF recruitment poster.

that Mussolini, so long as he opposed Hitler, had resisted the latter's racial doctrines and even made fun of them. Having allied himself with Germany, though, he could no longer afford to do so. On pain of being regarded as inferior, he had to invent a pedigree that would show that Italians, though scarcely Nordic, were quite as good as Germans. Of course I knew that the department of which I was now a member had ancient historians, medieval historians, and modern historians. But I did not want to be one of them. I looked for a field that would be mine, and mine alone, and military history qualified.

Owing to my cleft palate, I never served in the IDF. Dr. Muggia, who had examined me for my mathematical talents, was a self-taught expert on manpower classification. One thing he had done, on the request of Moshe Dayan, who was then serving as deputy chief of staff, was to design the first tests for aspiring air force pilots. Later, he used to do his reserve duty at a Tel Aviv enlistment center, so my parents asked him to see what he could do. He came back with the answer that the IDF would take me, but only if I would sign the necessary forms and absolve them in advance from responsibility for anything that might happen to my face. This generous offer I declined, but doing so was not easy. Some of the first Hebrew songs I, a four-year-old boy from the Netherlands, learned had to do with soldiers and how wonderful they were, especially in the eyes of girls who, in the lyrics, were told not to be shy around them.

Furthermore, my hometown, Ramat Gan, was studded with monuments to those who had died in the 1948 war. I remember how I used to contemplate them in awed silence even though I only half understood what it was all about. Later, my friends and I used to collect spent cartridges, which could still be found lying in the fields, and used them as whistles or put them on display. At the end of each year of high school the town mayor, a Mr. Krinitzi, would come to congratulate graduates and would tell them it was now *their* turn to become soldiers and heroes.

Both the media and the public positively adored the IDF; this was an adoration which, in the years immediately after the 1967 war, grew into adulation. Influenced, not to way brainwashed, by our seniors, we youngsters looked up to it as if it were the greatest organization since God had created the world. The highest compliment one could pay to anyone was that he was a "fighter," an expression we used in the original English. The best one could say about anything was that it was "like a military operation." Absurdly enough, this even extended to military operations. To wear a uniform was to be a demigod. Boys—not, if memory serves me right, girls—who did so at the ubiquitous Friday night parties were much in demand, particularly if they also carried an office's insignia on their shoulders. By contrast, not to have served was to be excluded from conversation and branded as an outcast. Later in life it could also lead to problems finding a job in the public sector.

More immediately, my rejection meant I had to get special permission to get a driver's license. Doing so was a humiliating experience that hinged on the IDF informing the authorities that I had not been disqualified for mental deficiency. I also lost my high school friends at a single stroke, a fact I still regret. Entering the university, I found myself in the company of students all of whom were considerably older and more experienced than me. Aged 21–22, some had already commanded a platoon or else been in charge of a tank. The girls, too, were older and more experienced, leading to more than one misunderstanding. Later, I learned that one or two of them may have been put off by my non-Hebrew sounding name; in Israel at that time, dating a *goy* was not something everybody did.

I had always been a loner, but now the situation made my social life even more restricted than usual. I spent most of my days on campus, where I often sat down with others to discuss the world over a cup of coffee. However, in the evenings I was almost always alone. Perhaps it was loneliness that made me spend as much time and effort long-distance running as I did. Up and down the hills of Jerusalem I went. I trained for the marathon, dreaming I might one day reach the Olympics. I never got close to that goal; still, such exercise does teach you what determination means.

My interest in athletics also led to the first of two occasions when I came under fire. It happened on April 6, 1967, a Friday. I traveled to kibbutz Gadot in the Upper Jordan Valley where a marathon race was to be held on the next day. Having hitchhiked the last part of the way, I arrived just as the Syrians on the Golan Heights opened artillery fire. We all ran for shelter and, having gone underground, waited as the explosions thundered and the earth shook. Emerging two hours later, we found that only one woman had been wounded. To have somebody deliberately trying to kill you was a strange experience; yet

I cannot recall that I felt afraid. Rather, we young visitors from Tel Aviv and elsewhere thought it was great fun, particularly in hindsight. Understandably, this feeling was not shared by the kibbutz members, whose homes were demolished by no fewer than 240 rounds. The race was canceled, and, it being the Sabbath when there is no public transportation, I had to hitchhike all the way home.

In the years since then I have often asked myself whether the fact that I was disqualified from serving in the military had anything to do with my decision to study the history of that military. The answer, as always, is probably both a yes and a no, or, to be precise, a no and a yes. Long before I knew that I would never serve, my imagination was fired first by the wars between the Greeks and the Persians and then by World War II. I also remember reading various books on military affairs. One of the earliest was an abridged version of Napoleon's memoirs. I received it from Ms. Muggia. It was a strange gift to come from that aristocratic, rather sickly, woman, who spent practically her entire life reclining on a couch. Another, which I actually read while in the hospital for an operation, was Jean Latréguy's 1960 novel *The Centurions*. The former turned me into an admirer of the French emperor, some of which admiration I still retain. The latter made me wish, for a time at any rate, that I could become a centurion myself. Up to a point, my dissertation was but a logical extension of these interests.

Still, as my article about the Italian racial laws shows, I had not firmly made up my mind. At one point I even considered entering another field altogether and writing a history of family, love, and sex in utopia; in other words, of imaginary solutions to problems that have always preoccupied humanity and always will. The idea came to me from reading Mary Berneri's *A Journey through Utopia* (1948), a book that tackled its subject from a left-wing socialist point of view and that I have long admired. The reason why nothing came of it was that I happened to start my research with Plato. The latter, I soon found out, had covered the subject much better than I, or anybody else, could; compared with him, all the rest were second or third rate. Nevertheless, I believe that the fact that the IDF did not want me did play a role in my decision. If I understand him correctly, the same was true of the late John Keegan, a great military historian and, during his last years, a friend.

Thus my contacts with the IDF are more limited than most. Nevertheless, no one can live in Israel without being deeply aware of war and all it entails. I personally have been lucky enough never to have witnessed a terrorist act. But several of my acquaintances were killed or injured by them. During the outbreak of the Second Palestinian Uprising, we could often hear the guns firing at targets in Bethlehem. Of course this awareness includes fear—nobody who, in the midst of what seemed the most profound peace, suddenly heard the air-raid sirens announcing the outbreak of the 1973 war will ever forget the trauma. As we say in Hebrew, our generation is "scratched" like some old-fashioned vinyl record.

Nor are we unfamiliar with the pain and the sorrow. However, it would be hypocritical not to mention, too, the sense of national purpose and the unique elation only war and victory can bring. To know what I am talking about, one must have experienced it. For weeks after our great victory in the June 1967 war, we Israelis seemed to be floating in the air. The more so because the first thing any visitor from abroad wanted was to hear about our heroic deeds.

Like everybody else, I too have tried to understand what was taking place as best I could by following the media, talking to people, and listening to officers and colleagues at conferences. The fact that, in some ways, I was handicapped by my lack of military experience scarcely requires being pointed out. In any case, it often *is* pointed out. Usually, behind my back. On the other hand, the same lack also constituted an advantage. It has probably prevented me from being caught up in the olive-green machine as so many others have been. It helped me develop a point of view that is uniquely my own. Perhaps this explains why, to my knowledge, I am the only Israeli whose books on military history have been translated into twenty languages.

To take the idea one step further still, I think it would be true to say that there exist two kinds of military historians. To wit, ex-generals and would-be generals. Of the two, the latter are usually better. The difference is that, for an ex-general, to start writing military history almost always implies a sharp drop in status. In the past generals were often grandees in their own right. Others, having served their country well, received a so-called donation from the state, which enabled them to set themselves up in the style of country gentlemen. But nowadays they are little more than uniformed civil servants who depend on their salaries and their perks like anybody else.

His pension apart, a general who retires loses all he has. One day he is in charge of thousands of men and, nowadays, women, who listen to him and do whatever he tells them. He even discovers he has a much better sense of humor than he ever suspected. On the next, he must evacuate the nice house he had on base as well as surrender the official car with its driver and flag. On his way toward oblivion, he may even find himself carrying his own books to his car. This is something I have seen with my own eyes, and a sad spectacle it is. All he is left with are his medals, his memorabilia, a word-processor (or, before processors, a typewriter), a few books, and, if he is lucky, an assistant or two. By contrast, we civilian military historians start with nothing. Driven by the fear that we may also end with nothing, we must work our way up by our wits. Our motivation is stronger because it is all we have.

Given this dilemma, perhaps the ideal solution is the one presented by Thucydides. Thucydides was an Athenian general who at one time commanded troops. However, after the Battle of Amphipolis in 422 B.C., he was cashiered and spent the next twenty years in exile. As he says, this gave him "rather exceptional facilities for looking into things." The result was a book, as he also says, written not for his own time but for all times. Another is Julius Caesar, a superb general who must have written the *Bellum Galicum* during some period when he had nothing else to do. Others still are the Maréchal de Saxe, who claims to have written his *Reveries* during ten feverish nights; and Helmuth von Moltke, who was able to write and think because, during the first decades of his career, Prussia was not involved in any wars.

The best example of all is none other than Clausewitz. To be sure, Clausewitz was a professional military man. Having started his career as a cadet at the age of 12, he ended up as a general. But he was an underemployed general whose superiors did not trust him to teach, let alone command. All they did permit him to do was to look after the administration of the Kriegsakademie, a job he disliked and which only took up a fraction of his time. Time after time he tried to obtain other posts, among them that of his country's ambassador in London. Having failed, he spent the mornings working in his wife's drawing room and evenings talking things over with his former superior, August von Gneisenau. Thus he was simultaneously in the army and out of it, which is probably the best vantage point from which to study any organization.

I have always suspected that, had he had the chance to try, Clausewitz would have made a lousy commander of troops. The same is true for me. For one thing, the kind of power that comes out of lording it over people has never appealed to me. I much prefer to hammer the facts of history into their place and, following the example of Christopher Marlowe's Faust, feel like "a God on Earth" while doing so. Nor is this the only reason. As Keegan pointed out so eloquently in *The Mask of Command*, a good commander cannot afford to have his men suspect that he has doubts, second thoughts, afterthoughts, or, perhaps, any kind of thoughts. I, however, have always been afflicted with thoughts. As a child, I used to worry about the remote future when the sun would burn out and the Earth cool down. Not only are many of my thoughts so contradictory and so confused that even I cannot make sense of them, but I am not very good at putting on a mask and hiding them.

The last-named problem links up with the fact that, to be a successful commander in war, one needs the kind of intelligence that is sometimes known as "Machiavellian." As Sun Tzu said, all war is based on deception. You must read your enemy's mind, trick him, and outwit him, all the while pretending that you are the most straightforward person in the world. Dayan, who had so much of it that people sometimes feared he might strip them of their socks without taking off their shoes first, called it "astuteness." Successful lawyers must also have it. For good or ill, I do not.

The way I see it, military history is simply my particular field, which is as valid as any other. From the Australian aborigines to the "fierce people" of Ecuador, to say nothing of many more "civilized" societies, hardly any society is so small, so isolated, and so saintly as to do without the use of force or at least the threat of it. This is true for external defense as it is true for maintaining internal order; history without military history, meaning the history of the way organized violence has been used to gain political ends, is inconceivable.

On the other hand, I have the years I spent in Britain, as well as the infinite cultural treasures that country has to offer, to thank for the fact that I never made the mistake of confusing military history with history as a whole. Doing so is a common error, particularly with young people about to enter the field or with officers who enter it after a long period of service in the forces. To the former I talk, pointing out that there has never been a good military historian who was only a military historian and encouraging them to broaden their interests. The best of them take my advice; the rest tend to disappear without a trace. For the latter, I am afraid, it is often too late. Officers necessarily spend much of their career mastering their profession. For them to strike out in directions where they have no special expertise may simply mean forfeiting whatever comparative advantage they have; in this sense they are damned if they do and damned if they do not.

Nor did the fact that I chose military history as my subject ever turn me into a militarist. Growing up in a country where the annual military parade, held on Independence Day, was *the* most important public event of the entire year, I enjoyed watching it as much as the next Israeli kid. I also eagerly participated in the kind of paramilitary activities that formed part of the high school curriculum. As an adult, though I am a citizen of a country that used to worship its army, I never thought of things military as the supreme good. I did not even think of them as good in themselves. At best they are a regrettable necessity and one which, if we are very lucky, will one day be dismantled. Once, having said so in public in what must have been too provocative a manner, I came close to being beaten up. I was only saved by a squad of my friends, who organized quickly to prevent disaster.

This was 1976, and the meeting took place in London, where my family and I were on sabbatical. Deeply offended, the chairperson asked the Israeli ambassador to respond. He rose to the occasion and gave an impromptu speech, telling some two hundred people how crazy I was for refusing to regard the IDF as sacrosanct and for suggesting that there would never be peace in the Holy Land unless we talked to the Palestinians. Looking back, I think the incident indicates how crazy *Israel* used to be. Yet the prime minister at the time was not some right-wing Likud member but Yitzhak Rabin. Nor can I say that, speaking of the Palestinians, we have made much progress since.

Unlike some of my colleagues in the field, particularly those who cater to the popular market or serve or have served in the military, I have never collected militaria. Neither insignia nor ancient weapons nor model aircraft grace my shelves. At one time I thought I would start a collection of plastic tanks, but nothing came of it. Almost the only object of the kind I own is a small paper knife with a hilt shaped in the image of Frederick the Great. And even that I bought mainly because it reminds me of a very pleasant year spent in Potsdam. It is true that the room in which I work used to be crammed with dust-gatherers. Some were presented for having spoken at numerous military institutes of higher learning around the world, this being a cheap and easy way to reward the likes of me. Others I got as souvenirs from individual officers I worked with or taught. At some time, however, I grew tired of them. Now all I have is a beautiful painting my wife made.

Just as I do not care for militaria, I never developed a liking for wargames. Some games, such as the ones my children used to play on their computers, require too much manual dexterity for me to master. Like many other adults, when I try to play them, I tend to get nervous and may, unless I am careful, end up with a bad case of computer rage. Others, such as the ones that are played with little cardboard markers on a large board full of hexes, I consider both too complicated to master and, owing to the snail-like pace at which they proceed, inexpressibly boring. Others still, such as those that involve carefully painting miniature plastic soldiers (as well as miniature plastic horses, miniature plastic guns, and miniature plastic field-toilets) and moving them around some table or floor, I consider childish.

Almost the only wargame I have ever played is chess, and then only occasionally and only at a very elementary level. As I shall explain later, what I did find very interesting were the different ways these and other games—beginning with the Roman *ludi* and proceeding through chess to football all the way to computer games—relate, or do not relate, to real-life war. I wanted to know what they succeeded at simulating, what they did not succeed at simulating, and why. In addition, I wanted to know who played them, what for, in what ways, and the like. Often, to answer a question, I write a book. This time the outcome was *Wargames: From Gladiators to Gigabytes* (2013)

Once I had decided in favor of military history, I quickly discovered that, in my home country, hardly anyone had the slightest use for it. This, after all, was 1971–72. The IDF was on top of the world. As far away as New York, shirts were being sold with the logo "Israeli tankman" on them. The IDF's commanders were Minister of Defense Moshe Dayan, whose contempt for academia was notorious, and General David Elazar, who since leaving high school, had never attended anything more advanced than a one-year command and general staff course. The last thing Israeli officers thought they needed was civilian scribblers to teach them their business. I even remember going through an IDF publication that used the term professor as a synonym for idiot.

So much did the IDF despise higher education that it did not even have a war college. An experimental institution of that kind had been set up in 1963. Three years later Yitzhak Rabin, who was then serving as chief of staff, said officers were reluctant to waste their time in it—which may well have been true—and shut it down. Nor did Israel have a single civilian institute of strategic studies. Strange as it sounds, the term "strategy" itself only came into common usage after the 1973 war had robbed the IDF of some of its glory. Until then, all one heard about were "fighting" and "stratagems."

At a deeper level, the very success of the IDF militated against any interest in military history. The reason was that, as long as one can feel the wind blowing in one's back, one always expects the future to be much better than the past. That past, in turn, appears almost ridiculously puny when compared to the present. As Dayan once put it, a single IDF squad was capable of carrying out all the deeds of Hashomer, the Lilliputian early twentieth-century Jewish paramilitary organization that served generations of young Israelis as their inspiration.

Normally, it is only when they feel they are in a deep crisis that people will stop, look back, and try to understand how they got there and what went wrong. A clever historian can exploit this fact in his favor by causing the publication of his work to coincide with some deeply felt crisis. Better still, he may first invent a crisis and then convince everybody that it really exists. An excellent example of the genre is Oswald Spengler's *Decline of the West* (1918–20), an arrogant, confused tome that owed its fame almost entirely to its excellent timing. And, in the politico-military field, Paul Kennedy's *The Rise and Fall of the Great Powers*, which is a work I greatly admire. Predicting the decline of the U.S., it was published in December 1987 just as the stock market crashed. The rest is history.

I was just a young historian, and I did not yet know how important crises are. Two years after my return to Jerusalem, the October 1973 war broke out. Whatever else, for me it provided an opportunity to visit the Sinai battlefields, where I was a guest lecturer on behalf of the IDF. I climbed over captured tanks and on one occasion watched an Israeli aircraft being shot out of the sky. (The pilot bailed out and was captured.) Most of the time, though, the troops, who were at the end of their tether, and I simply lay down on the sand and slept.

Later, I flexed my military-intellectual muscle on the pages of the *Jerusalem Post* weekend magazine. The magazine editor, Jacob Reuel, was a man of scholarly tastes who took a liking to me. Had he been twenty years younger, he might not have gotten the job he held but found himself in charge of some obscure intellectual periodical. For several months I wrote longish articles about what I thought the lessons of the war were or ought to be. They had titles such as "Broken Chariots" and "This Arrowless War." The former referred to a book on armor with the title *Brazen Chariots*. The latter, to the fact that, compared to the 1967 war, the one in 1973 was much less mobile and only saw limited operational maneuvering. Firepower, in the form of anti-tank missiles operated by the Egyptians, seemed to have triumphed over maneuver, a situation many compared to the Battle of Crecy in 1348.

My articles followed a simple recipe. Take newspaper accounts of recent events. Mix with a little Basil Liddell Hart, a little John F. C. Fuller, and a little Alfred von Schlieffen to lend weight to what you have to say and to make it look authoritative. Add a reference to the Blitzkrieg and another to Napoleon, shake well, and there you are. In any case I was a rank beginner, and there was very little else I knew.

At the time, the *Jerusalem Post* was a rather staid paper loosely associated with the left-wing centrist Labor Party. Almost the only Israelis who read it were elderly people who, like my parents and their friends, did not quite feel at home in Hebrew. As a result, except for a few readers' letters, idle telephone calls, and one invitation to lecture at an old people's home in Haifa, the interest I raised at home was close to zero. The same was true with regard to my scholarly publications. To this day, only one of my books has been translated into the language of the country where I live and work.

However, the lack of domestic interest did not matter much. The reason is that, at Hebrew University, Hebrew-language publications do not count; among ourselves we used to joke that, had God applied to us for tenure, he would have been denied it because he had not written the Bible in English. Even my then four-year-old son Eldad realized how inferior Hebrew was. Wishing to do me a favor, he once "wrote" an article for me in "Angleen." As to run-of-the-mill IDF officers, with them the problem was exactly the opposite. Having scarcely known a moment of peace since the country was born, they received their spurs not by studying but by chasing Arabs over the hills, as the saying goes. One could hardly expect them to read, let alone do so in some esoteric language a toddler found interesting.

Abroad, it was a different story. Several foreign journalists asked to interview me. But I, not yet knowing how to deal with the media, blew my chance. A few ambassadors and military attachés asked me to dinner. What was more, they invited me to dine at the Tel Aviv Sheraton. At the time, so poor was Israel that entering the gates of the Sheraton was beyond the wildest dreams of the likes of me. In the Israel I grew up in there were just two kinds of cheese, white and yellow. Perhaps I may be forgiven for considering the invitation a great honor and stuffing myself on the kind of food I had rarely seen before.

In particular, I was lucky to catch the eye of Professor Walter Laqueur. Laqueur, who was born in 1921, is an Israeli who spent much of his life in Britain and the U.S. He has written or edited dozens of books and keeps moving in the gray area between—often first class—scholarship and journalism. Visiting Jerusalem soon after the war, he summoned me to his home. It was our first meeting, and he asked me to do a short piece for a book, *Confrontation*, he was writing about recent events in the Middle East. I think he offered me 50 British pounds. Until then, I had hardly earned a penny from my academic writing, so it was no wonder that I was in Seventh Heaven.

Laqueur must have been happy with what he got, for later he asked me to do a study of the military lessons of the war to be published as a monograph by the Center for Strategic and International Studies at Georgetown University. Lacking sufficient information, I found it very hard to write, but in the end I did so. Later, I was delighted to hear that Henry Kissinger had ordered a copy. Even though, as Laqueur hastened to add, it was most unlikely that the great man would actually read it; between negotiating for an Egyptian-Israeli Separation of Forces Agreement and getting married, presumably, he had better things to do.

More importantly, these were the years when belief in *détente* was waning. Sparked by the 1973 war, when the superpowers got the world as close to a nuclear crisis as they had done at any time since 1962, the so-called "Second Cold War" was getting under way. In the USSR Leonid Brezhnev was approaching the peak of his power, sending his troops to cover a Cuban landing in Angola and to help the Ethiopians wrest the Ogaden Desert from Somalia. Finally, he occupied Afghanistan. From there, it was rumored, he might one day continue toward Iran and the Persian Gulf.

By contrast, the U.S. Armed Forces had just been defeated in Vietnam and suffered the loss of Cambodia as well. As I have explained above, people start taking an interest in the past when things go wrong. An armed force that has suffered defeat will want to reform itself and, to do so, will look for intellectual guidance. Previously, the buzzword had been systems analysis. Having been introduced into the military by Secretary of Defense Robert McNamara and his "whiz kids," that discipline was just then going down in the world. It was, indeed, being blamed for the defeat. Particularly between 1975 and 1985, about the worst thing one could say about anybody was that he (no shes, at that time) was a systems analyst. And, supposedly, too dumb to recognize the limits of that discipline.

By contrast, military history, which previously had been almost as neglected in the U.S. as in Israel, seemed to provide an answer or at least an approach that might lead to an answer. For about ten years the Pentagon bookstore, which I got to know well during the nineteen eighties, could not have enough of it. The reader who has followed my argument so far may easily guess what happened next. For good or ill, the 1991 Gulf War restored the U.S. Armed Forces' self-confidence. It convinced them that they were the most magnificent in history and had nothing to learn from anybody, least of all a bunch of civilian scribblers who had never even been *over there.*

As a result, their interest in military history dropped like a stone. Its place was taken by newfangled disciplines with mysterious names, most of them originating in business administration. Among the earliest was something called TQM (Total Quality Management). It claimed, if I got it right, that the armed forces are a corporation and the enemy is a "client." As a client, he has to be "serviced," in

other words, killed as quickly and as efficiently as possible. This was
about as transparent as pea soup. Before long, it was replaced by
other, even less comprehensible, doctrines, such as ISO 9000, lean
manufacturing, and six sigma. I, however, did not mind. By that
time I was already beginning to move to greener pastures.

* * *

In the mid-nineteen seventies, needless to say, I had not the
slightest notion of all this. As in the writing of the present volume,
one idea led to another. I simply went for what, at any moment,
seemed to me most important and most interesting. This happened
to be the history of World War II and, specifically, that of the Africa
Corps. While in high school, I had done a so-called "final paper" on
that corps. Absurdly enough, doing so absolved me from having to
matriculate in Hebrew literature. In 1974 I got a hold of the micro-
filmed documents available at the General Services Administration.
Using them, I examined the corps' logistics in an attempt to discover
what role they had played in Rommel's ultimate defeat. I found the
subject absolutely fascinating. Almost for the first time, I was able to
observe the mechanics of a military machine in motion and to study
the way its parts related to one another.

Since I was in need of a research-project in order to obtain a grant
for spending a sabbatical year in London, I decided to expand the
chapter into a book. After much trial and error, I settled on its
title, *Supplying War*. When I started, I thought that doing studies
of unrelated campaigns taken from different periods would be easier
than writing the history of logistics from A to Z. That proved to be
the case. Besides, by using case studies, I would be able to look at
each campaign in considerable depth. Hopefully, I could combine
the approach of Fuks with that of Talmon and reach conclusions that
would be both accurate and of some significance.

The London we returned to in the summer of 1975 looked poor

and grimy, the pound having sunk from 2.40 to the dollar six years earlier to 1.60. However, the National Health Service was as good as ever. We, though we were foreigners, had a first-class surgeon operate on our daughter for free. The same applied to the research facilities the city offered. By way of the British Council, which had given me the grant I wanted, I was loosely associated with the newly established Department of War Studies at King's College. Its head, Professor Lawrence Martin, had been asked to keep an eye on my work. He, however, said I was a mature scholar, and we seldom met. If that is delegation of authority, then I am all in favor of it.

The department did give me an office, but it was such an un-pleasant, out-of-the-way place that I only took one look at it and never returned. Most of the time I worked either in some library or archive or at home. I did not even have a room of my own but typed away in our bedroom while sitting at our landlady's old dressing table. Looking back, I cannot understand how I did it. The lodgings were the same as in 1969–1971. However, the couple that had been smoking marijuana was long gone. As a result, we were able to occupy three rooms instead of two.

Once again, skimping on lodgings permitted us to run a car, though it was a much better one. Once again, we spent practically every weekend visiting country houses and museums. The military ones included the British Army Museum, the Imperial War Museum, the RAF Museum, and the cruiser *Belfast*. If I cannot claim to have hands-on military experience, at least I know enough about weapons to identify them when I see them. Traveling to Scotland, we visited Alnswick Castle, Sterling Castle, and Edinburgh Castle, where we admired the giant fifteenth-century bombard. Still, my interests were not satisfied. I spent a Saturday watching a horse race, another attending a motor race, and another swimming in Loch Ness looking for Nessie.

I believe one should try everything once. To date, that includes eating worms (in South Africa, where they are considered a delicacy by some tribe or another), deep-sea sailing, white-water rafting, watching a monster truck competition, bungee jumping, ballooning, taking snuff, and smoking a joint. Once, I tried horse jumping. Amadeus, the horse, preferred to eat the flowers that decorated the obstacle to leaping over it; given the danger involved, I suppose he did me a favor. Eldad, now five, and Abigail, three, went with us. Sometimes we took along the daughters of a Japanese family we had made friends with. Perhaps it was my preoccupation with military history which caused Abigail to develop an interest in the "Red Soldiers," as she called the guards at Horse Parade, Buckingham Palace, and Windsor Castle. One evening, knowing there would be many such magnificent creatures around, we took her to a performance of Tchaikovsky's *1812 Overture* in the Royal Albert Hall. She, however, fell fast asleep, and not even the booming cannon could wake her up.

As I started work, I noticed how little had been written about my subject. As far as I could make out, previously, the only army ever to take an interest in the history of logistics had been the Austrian-Hungarian one. Between 1866 and 1914, for some mysterious reason I have never understood, its officers published a number of monographs about the subject; those apart, the only publication I could find dated to the nineteen-thirties. Accordingly, I had to gather my material in bits and pieces, putting together whatever published and unpublished sources were available. One place I visited was States House, Medmenham, where the famous pundit Basil Liddell Hart had spent his last years. At that time he had been dead for about five years, but his widow Kathleen still lived there. Though she suffered badly from arthritis, she was very kind and invited me to lunch. In the afternoon I spent some hours working in the barn-like structure that served him as an archive; unlike me, he never threw away a single scrap of paper he had written or received. I found a few interesting items. To be allowed to quote them, I had to sign a long form that ended with the words "your humble and obedient servant."

Another place I visited was Freiburg im Breisgau, West Germany, where I worked in the Bundeswehr's Archive and its Military-Historical Research Office, the Militärgeschichtliches Forschungsamt. I spent most of my time in the former. It was located well away from the center of town. There was not a restaurant for miles around. To eat in the cafeteria, you had to order your meal days ahead. Even so, the food you got was absolutely lousy. Accordingly, I did without lunch as I spent two weeks plowing through thousands of pages of German army documents. It was not as bad as it sounds, and I soon learned to recognize those I needed by the kind of paper they were typed on. The reading room was on the tenth floor. Looking up, or rather down, one could see a barracks where French recruits were being put through their paces.

The original idea was a modest one, namely to examine the logistics of a few campaigns, to compare them to one another, and to see whether I could explain the direction in which things had developed over time. I did that, discovering—contrary to anything I had read—that the great turning point was 1914 when, for the first time in history, armies consumed greater quantities of fuel, spare parts, and ammunition than they did food and fodder. As a result, instead of taking their supplies from the surrounding countryside, they needed extensive lines of communication stretching back dozens and sometimes hundreds of miles. As a result of that, instead of starving when they were staying in one place, they started running out of supplies when they moved from one place to another.

More important than these technicalities, which only interest a few specialists, the book reexamines military history from a point of view which, though everybody knows that armies march on their stomachs, had been thoroughly neglected. That, probably, was the real reason behind its popularity. As for me, I took several years to realize what I had done. In fact it was only brought home to me by my reviewers. If my colleagues sometimes complain that reviewers do not understand the "larger purpose" behind their books, with me things have often worked the other way around. Since then, several other histories of military logistics have been published, at least one of them by a very senior officer who has moved more supplies in an hour than I have in my entire life. None, however, was as successful as mine.

In a radio interview, famed German author Thomas Brussig (*Heroes Like Us*, 1999, a hilarious satire directed at the late unlamented German Democratic Republic) was asked whether, having produced that masterpiece at the age of 30, he did not fear he might never produce another. He said he recognized the problem and was psychologically ready for it. *Supplying War* was also written when I was 30, and many people regard it as my best book. Unlike Brussig, whose courage I admire, had I known it at the time, I might have despaired. In the event it took me so long to understand the truth, if the truth it is, that my understanding did not hold me back. Now, it no longer matters. The real reason why I keep writing is that to stop doing so is to die.

By the time *Supplying War* was finished, though not yet published, I got tenure on the strength of my earlier work, including my published PhD thesis, a few articles, and the monograph on the 1973 war. As with my original appointment, Talmon did what he could to put difficulties in my way. Four years later he was dead; though not all my colleagues went to his funeral, I did. Thirty is a surprisingly early age to get tenure, and this is even more true today than it was then. As in so many other fields, it is a question of inflation. Most of those who wrote the *New Cambridge Ancient History* during the 1930s only had their master's degree, a fact that did not prevent them from producing a monument of scholarship. My own supervisor, D. C. Watt, never received a PhD. Neither, I believe, did James Joll; nor, except for an honorary one, did A. J. P. Taylor. Nevertheless, all three were outstanding scholars who would have done honor to any university that might have employed them.

Since their time, even in England, things have changed. Nowadays, anybody who does not have at least a PhD does not stand the slightest chance of entering the hallowed halls of academia. Even then, it is still necessary to do a so-called "post-doc." As the demands for more and more advanced degrees pile up, the age at which people get tenure rises until, at my own university, it is well over forty. Until one gets it, one is constantly threatened with dismissal, making one feel and act like a fish in a frying pan. Worse still, worrying about the future makes people focus on short-term projects. It shrinks their horizons just when they should be flexing their intellectual muscles. By the time they finally get the security they need to think, many are beyond help.

I was lucky to get tenure as early as I did. It did not make me take things easy as some of my colleagues did. To the contrary, it helped me focus on the things that really interested me, and I have continued to do so ever since. As it happened, the mid- to late-nineteen seventies was precisely the period when the welfare state began to be challenged by aspiring politicians such as Margaret Thatcher and Ronald Reagan. Watching the lives of other people, my stepson Jonathan included, I realize the immense privilege tenure entails in a world that is growing increasingly competitive and, as far as the salary-earner is concerned, increasingly insecure. Even in Japan, lifetime employment is fast becoming a thing of the past.

What my life would have been like if I had to spend it as most people do, I cannot imagine. Obviously, I would have had to manage as best I could. Still, I suspect that fear of the future—in plain words, constant worry as to how I would support my family—would have had a paralyzing effect on my ability to do useful work. The more so because the fruit of that work is often years in the future, and the more so because there are quite a number of times when it never leads anywhere at all. I justify my privileges by quoting H. G. Wells, who said that it is good for society to have some people who can do what they want. Whether the reason is that they have independent means, which is what Wells meant, or that the conditions under which they are employed do not allow them to be fired, as at a university, is immaterial. The end result is, or can be, largely the same.

Even more important than the economic security that tenure provided, which is quite modest, is the academic freedom that came with it. In theory, that freedom is available to anyone from the youngest student up. In practice, since people who stray off the accepted path are no more liked in academia than elsewhere, it starts when they can no longer get rid of you except through a long and complicated process, one that may rebound against them and lead to hostile headlines. Had I not possessed this freedom, I could not have done my work which, as in the case of any scholar or scientist, consists of asking questions I consider useful and interesting and trying to answer them as best I can. Whatever others think of the matter, to me not being able to speak my mind is a fate almost worse than death. If the price of being a loose cannon is that nobody listens to academics, then it is well-worth paying.

In favor of Hebrew University I want to say that, in my view and that of some others to whom I have talked over the years, during most of my career, it allowed its faculty more academic freedom than most. Unfortunately, as far as I am concerned, that is no longer the case. I shall return to this subject later on in this volume.

Once I got tenure, one of the first things I did was to switch from writing academic articles to writing books. My main reason for doing so was rooted in considerations of cost-effectiveness or, to put it plainly, effort spent for money earned. As a young scholar, and often as a senior one as well, you may consider yourself lucky if the periodicals to which you submit your work do not ask *you* to pay them for doing you the favor of publishing your work. This is a result of publish and perish, and one of the least desirable ones at that. Where the demand exists, the supply will follow, to the point where you may be asked to present a paper at a conference and to defray the organizers for the cost of permitting you to do so. When it comes to *chutspe,* there are no limits; in contrast, a book may earn you some money.

These considerations apart, writing many articles on many different subjects is a waste of time and effort because, for each one, you have to build a fresh infrastructure of background knowledge. It makes much better sense to spread the overheads and to write a book. It is true that doing so is harder than writing an article and requires a different technique. On the other hand, once you get used to it, writing one 300-page book is much easier than writing 12 articles each 25 pages long, or so it seems to me. As a result, I only do articles for special purposes, as when a friend who is planning a collection on such and such a subject asks me to contribute. Another objective may be to ventilate some thought I may have. Another still, to advertise a book I am writing or have just finished writing.

Seen from the point of view of pure scholarship, writing articles in scholarly journals is very good exercise for young academics who want to cut their teeth and who, doing so, often produce excellent work. That apart, the effort that is put into them is largely wasted. The only people who read them are those who are planning similar articles on similar subjects in order to get promoted. In a sense, whether or not anybody actually reads them is irrelevant. What matters is less what you have to say than the number of citations you get. Those citations themselves may serve those who sit on the various committees as an excuse *not* to look at the articles in question; after all, counting things is much easier than trying to understand them in depth.

Worse still, the switch from reading to counting means that those in charge of your career abdicate their responsibility. They transfer it to some computer program written by God knows whom, God knows where, for God knows what purpose, on God knows what principles. The strangest thing about it is that, even with all this equipment, the "process" of promoting a Hebrew University faculty member takes anything between 18 and 30 months. I find all this very unsatisfactory. As this and other facts indicate, apparently, universities have not yet discovered that time is money. I am aware that, in some places, only articles in refereed periodicals, rather than books, count toward promotion. I know of one scholar who has signed a contract with Oxford University Press to do a book on a subject that is as novel as it is intriguing. Instead of completing his 700-page manuscript, though, he feels he must first fill his quota of articles; to repeat the above-mentioned joke, obviously, those who devised the policy would have no room for God either.

Since almost all articles are ephemeral, I believe scholars in the humanities and social sciences should be judged on the strength of the quality of the books they write and on practically nothing else. The number of conferences you have attended is irrelevant, given that most conference papers are even more ephemeral than articles in scholarly journals. So are the departments you have headed, the number of students you taught and the way they rated your teaching skills, the amount of grant money you have raised, and the learned societies of which you are a member. Not to mention any kind of volunteer work and community service you may or may not have done. Such things may testify to you being a well-rounded person, but they say nothing about your academic abilities and achievements.

Looking back, who remembers that Max Weber was a great lecturer whereas Karl Marx was not? Nietzsche claims to have been an excellent teacher, but it was not his teaching that brought him his fame. Nor is it clear that his students shared the high opinion he had of himself. Instead, they seem to have regarded him as a rare bird, which he certainly was. In our own day, did Samuel Huntington, or Paul Kennedy, or Thomas Piketty ever sit on a committee? If so, who cares? The same is true of any other number of scholars. Their light is shining, but almost exclusively to the extent that it has been enshrined in their books.

As to deciding what to write about, plainly, your books should deal with the subjects which, at the time you start working on them, are the most important and most interesting you can think of. Or else why bother? For me the method of writing books and making them as readable as I could worked. I became an associate professor at 36, still well ahead of the age at which most people nowadays get tenure. Though my parents had always felt that aiming so high smacked of *hubris* and sometimes berated me for it, becoming a professor had been my goal in life since at least the last classes of high school. So gratified was I by my newly acquired title that I spent days muttering to myself. I put the term through every possible Hebrew declination, inventing new ones as I went along; I professored, you professored, I am being professored, are you professoring, she should have been professored, and the like.

By contrast, when my professorization to full professor came six years later, it made little impression on me. I owed it to the above-mentioned Ms. Razin. Like so many secretaries, she was the real power in the department. The reason was that she was always there whereas chairpersons only came in spurts, so to speak. Besides, they only remained in office for three or four years whereas she looked as if she had been born at her desk. Like many others on the administrative staff, she became a good friend, and I used to give her a copy of each of my books as it came out. She, in turn, gave them to her husband, Professor Shmuel Razin, who besides being a biologist is also a highly educated man of many different interests.

Purely by accident, Shmuel was on the relevant interdepartmental committee. When it came to deciding my fate, he was the only one who had read all my books and was therefore able to call the shots. Send your bread over the water, as the Biblical dictum goes. I suspect that some people rather regret the fact that I was professored. Others would like nothing better than to get rid of me entirely and have done whatever they can to reach that worthy objective. I, however, already had greener pastures to graze in.

Chapter 3

Defense Consultant

My studies so far had caused me to take a strong interest in the World War II German Army, which many considered among the best in history. Therefore, when Edward Luttwak visited Israel in the autumn of 1978 and asked to speak with me, I was ready with an idea. At the time, Luttwak, who as best I can gather is a Romanian-born, Italian-bred, British-educated American-Israeli (or Israeli-American) was thirty-five and thus three years older than me. He was the well-known author of *The Grand Strategy of the Roman Empire* as well as, together with the late Professor Dan Horowitz of my own university, *The Israeli Army*. Both of them were excellent volumes as good as any military history published in the twentieth century. Even better was *Coup d'Etat; a Practical Handbook*, which was published in 1969 and translated into no fewer than nineteen languages. Visiting the British Military Academy at Sandhurst in the autumn of 1975, I was told that no other book was so much in demand among the young Commonwealth officers who were being trained there. For all I know, it might well have been true.

I had met Luttwak before, in 1972 I think. But at that time I had no idea who he was or, more important, how famous he was about to become. He may not have known himself. Apparently, the only one who did know was his wife, Daliah Yaari, a very fine woman whom I have since come to like and esteem. In 1978 he was working as a consultant to the U.S. Department of Defense (DoD), having set up a partnership with Steven Canby, a reserve lieutenant colonel (Army) with a Harvard PhD in economics who was making a name for himself with his articles about light infantry tactics.

At the time the U.S. military was just beginning to come to terms with the Vietnam War. They were seeking to leave that experience behind and to return to real soldiering, by which they meant preparing for a war against the USSR in the so-called "Central Theater," i.e. Europe. Congress, on its part, had lost faith in the military and was hiring new staff to upgrade its ability to supervise them. All this soul-searching caused the so-called "defense community" to expand and the consulting business to boom; retired officers, businessmen, academics and journalists cruised around the Pentagon like sharks looking for blood. People spoke of the "Beltway Bandits," and not without reason. Driving along the highway in question, one could see the shiny new buildings that taxpayer money had enabled them to build for themselves.

Israel, by contrast, hardly had a "defense community." All it had were officers. The latter had been pulled down a peg or two by the events of October 1973. Nevertheless, they still considered themselves the sole experts on their subject as they looked down on everybody else and disdained theoretical study as the reconstructing of the IDF and, to a growing extent, skirmishing along the Lebanese borders claimed their attention. I myself did not even know an apparition

Andy Marshal, head of Net Assessment at the Pentagon, with whom I worked for about ten years

such as a defense consultant existed, let alone dreamed of becoming one. Luttwak said he had been impressed by *Supplying War* and by some other work I showed him. Now he wanted me to work for him. The first step in the process was to prepare a research proposal for

Andy Marshall, the legendary head of the Office of Net Assessment, Office of the Secretary of Defense, who was about to visit Israel and whom Luttwak described as a "big player" in the field of intelligence. As it turned out Mr. Marshall, as everybody called him, did not come to Israel, but I prepared my proposal nevertheless.

As usual, the underlying idea grew out of my previous work. *Supplying War* included several chapters on the German army. Studying it, I had been struck by the ideals it claimed to uphold and the splendid way in which they were expressed, the best-known one being Alfred von Schlieffen's "accomplish much, make no waves, be more than you seem." Going on from there, I wanted to know why the World War II Wehrmacht had been such an excellent fighting organization. Both on the offensive and on the defensive, it had killed several enemies for every one of its soldiers who was killed. Its victories, particularly those of 1940–41, were legendary. Most impressive of all, it kept on fighting with undiminished ferocity practically until the bitter end. This inquiry, I vaguely thought, might provide some insight into the problems of the current Western, and particularly American, armed forces which, considerably outnumbered, were preparing to fight the Red Army along the Iron Curtain.

Much later Luttwak told me that, when he received my research proposal, he at first considered it feckless but decided to submit it nevertheless. It may have been true, or perhaps it was merely his way of putting me in my place. In any case, whether because he was persuasive, or because Mr. Marshall had a keen nose, or through sheer luck, it got through, and I was now a consultant working for C&L (Canby and Luttwak) Associates, and, through them, for the DoD. Note that, my 1975–76 sabbatical apart, until then, I hardly had the wherewithal to do research abroad. Hence it was a marvelous opportunity such as few other Israeli scholars at the time enjoyed.

Making use of it, in the summer of 1979 I went to Freiburg for the second time. The problem of lunch still persisted. Yet I found it a wonderful place. People who produce so much excellent wine but drink it all themselves, which is why it is not too well known outside the Breisgau, cannot be all bad. From then on I became convinced that, as far as cleanliness, good order, public transportation, cultural facilities, and the oh-so tempting opportunity to get out into the countryside and to take a walk are concerned, there is nothing like a medium-sized German town.

As to work, it is a different proposition. A town can be too quiet to stimulate one's brain, particularly if it is populated by Germans who have the annoying habit of limiting their professional interests to the subjects on which they are, or think they are, experts. I prefer one that is both calm *and* centrally located. London in the late nineteen sixties and early seventies was ideal. Here was a place that was as central as central can be. Once, walking in Kew Gardens, I took time and discovered that an aircraft came to land at Heathrow Airport every fifty seconds. As a result, it was full of people from the most varied backgrounds while also in possession of all the research facilities that only a world-class city can offer.

Yet, since work started at ten and ended at four with a two-hour lunch in between, it was anything but frenetic. Taking the ferry from Calais to Dover, the first thing one did upon arrival was to reduce one's driving speed by fifteen miles an hour. Foreign visitors often commented on the relaxed atmosphere. At first they would find it unsettling, as Rachel also did. But later they would adjust and learn to enjoy it. Jerusalem too used to be very good, at least until the Second Palestinian Uprising tore into its living fabric. Since then, it has become a hotbed of fanaticism which I try to avoid as much as I can.

The staff of the Forschungsamt, particularly Professor Manfred Messerschmidt, Professor Wilhelm Deist, and Dr. (as he then was) Hans-Erich Volkmann, were very helpful. The time I spent there taught me the difference between British, Israeli, and German cultures, which is as follows. In Britain, if you worked in a magazine library and wanted to enter the stacks, you would never dare ask (in

1969 as a young student, I asked for permission to work in the British Museum Library; obtaining it was one of the most humiliating experiences in my life). In Israel, where respect for the law is not highly developed, you would hardly even bother to ask but go straight ahead. In Germany, once they get to know you, you ask for permission and receive it a few minutes later. Personally, I prefer the German way to both the Israeli and the British ones. It seems so much more sensible.

This being a Bundeswehr installation, each Wednesday afternoon all the employees spent a couple of hours doing athletics; it helped keep one's mind fresh. Still, the first weeks in Freiburg were very hard. For one thing I was very lonely. Though I did have some acquaintances who were very kind to me, there were limits to how much I could impose on them. Drinking beer in a *Kneipe* while trying to chat with strangers has never been my style. I spent most evenings reading in my hotel room till I fell asleep. Some Sundays I took bus tours into the surrounding countryside. Known as the Black Forest, it is very beautiful; however, since all the other passengers were decades older than myself, the pleasures were doubtful. Whatever others may feel in the matter, I hope I shall never repeat those periods when, having left my family behind, I spent months on my own doing research in foreign countries.

To make things worse, my work was not going well. True to my Marshall-imposed mission, I had come to study the German army. But the more I studied it, the less I understood. To be sure, I learned how the Wehrmacht had gone about its business. Their doctrine put much emphasis on the offensive and little on organization. They trained their enlisted men, the Landser as they were called, in one way and their non-commissioned officers in another. They had so and so many officers per unit. Their headquarters were structured thus and not otherwise, and they did not appoint "political" officers— meaning, officers specifically charged with troop-indoctrination— until very late in the war. But what did it all mean? I remember sitting in the reading room of the Forschungsamt and feeling like the embodiment of black despair. I was more than a month into the job, and all I was doing was scribbling notes without the slightest idea where I was heading. At one point I even started dividing the number of D Marks I had spent by that of record cards I had filled. *That* is how crazy the situation made me feel.

Salvation came from an unexpected direction. Before leaving Israel, I had already decided that, for comparative purposes, I would also look at the official history of the U.S. Army in World War II. Those volumes, though, were available at Hebrew University, and, accordingly, I did not propose to spend my expensive time in Germany reading them. However, feeling stuck, at one point I decided to do so nevertheless. After all, I was wasting my time in any case. I rose from my seat and approached them. Located in the reading room, they had been looking at me for weeks, silently reproaching me for neglecting them.

No sooner did I turn to look at them were my eyes caught by the countless tables they contained. Clearly, what was being described here was a military system very different from the one I had been studying, which put far less emphasis on statistical data. At one point, indeed, I had read a German staff document that explained why such data, and the machinery needed to process it, should not be utilized to excess. The way the Wehrmacht's officers saw it, mechanization could threaten both the commander's authority and unit cohesion. In fewer than fifteen minutes, I *knew* I had found the clue and that my work would be well and truly done. The excitement grew and grew to the point that, when the time came for my youngest son, Uri, to be born in November, I kept talking about the project to Rachel right until the moment she was taken into the delivery room. Then I had to leave because the other two children needed looking after.

What I had not clearly realized until then was that one very important road toward understanding—whatever that may be—lies in making comparisons. Comparisons are to the social sciences, history included, what experiments are to the natural ones. They enable one to delve under the surface and get into the guts, so to speak, of the things that are being compared. For the effort to bear fruit those things must be different from one another, but not too different. For example, there is nothing to be gained by comparing two identical pens. To illustrate the point, I used to hold out two such pens to my students. Nor is there much to be gained, say, by comparing a pen with a pineapple. However, compare a fountain pen with a ballpoint, or else a pen with a pencil, and you may arrive at some insight that is interesting as well as useful. These general principles apart, there is no way of saying in advance which comparisons are going to be fruitful and which ones are not. Choosing them is an art, not a science; quite often, the outcome is a surprise. Jonathan once told me how impressed he was by a visiting scholar who drew up a detailed comparison between the Roman and Inca Empires, something that never would have occurred to me to do.

Fighting Power, to quote the title of the book on which I was working, was different from anything I had done before. Previously, I had been an academic who was trying to find out "the truth" about the past. Now I still remained an academic who was supposed to find out "the truth" about the past; at the same time, though, I was supposed to produce something my employers at the DoD would find useful. My knowledge of the U.S. armed forces as they were in 1980 or so was extremely limited. Even so, it was obvious to me that the principles developed by the German army over hundreds of years and then applied, in modified form, at the hands of a ruthless totalitarian regime neither could nor should be applied without further ado in a totally different environment. In 1939–45 the Wehrmacht executed over 10,000 of its own men. If that was what it took, then clearly it was going much too far. The trick was to find out what worked, for whom, under what circumstances, and why. Once this had been done, it would be up to others to see what could be done with my findings.

In April 1980 I went to the U.S. for the first time. Arriving at Dulles Airport, which at that time was not nearly as large or as busy as it is today, I was taken back by practically everything I saw. It started with the strange vehicles that took you to the main terminal. Next, there was the rental car I took. Since I had preordered it, they just threw the keys at me and let me look for it myself; cars, in other words, were a self-evident necessity and not objects to be approached with some reverence as was the case in Israel. Next came the near impossibility of finding a socket that would fit my electric razor and the difficulty of having breakfast on Sunday morning. In the whole of Washington the only restaurant that was open was the one on the upper floor of the Air and Space Museum; as a result, crowds started gathering around it long before the opening time at 10 A.M. I also remember how bewildered I was by the tremendous variety of food that even the most humble coffee shop seemed to offer. Each time you asked for something you were confronted with God knows how many different choices. Each answer you gave only led to more choices. All of them reeled off so fast, and in such a monotonous voice, that you could barely understand what they were.

I stayed at a hostel run by Quakers not far from Dupont Circle, which, considering my subject, was a strange choice. The objective of my visit was to complete my research, and I spent some time at the General Archives at Suitland, Maryland. One day I missed the shuttle back to Washington, D.C., where Luttwak had invited me to deliver a lecture. I was terrified that I would be late, and, having no idea what to do or even how far it was, started walking in what I hoped was the direction of town. I recall passing houses built on lots that had no fences to separate them, or perhaps I should say that, since there were no fences, there could be no question of any lot at all but only of a meadow on which houses had been scattered as if by some giant's hand. It was the first time I had seen a real-life American suburb, and I thought the wide-open spaces gave it a strange, almost surrealistic, appearance. Since then, I have learned how much truth there was in that impression. In any event I made the lecture on time, though how I managed to do so I can no longer remember. Such were my earliest encounters with the "otherness" of American life, a subject to which I shall return later.

Another thing I did in Washington was to present my work to Mr. Marshall. Luttwak invited me to his home and spent three hours giving me the most thorough grilling I have ever undergone. After all, I was going to represent his company. He did not want me to screw up. He must have been happy with what he heard, for we went to the Pentagon, where I repeated my performance. In the event, *Fighting Power* became a great success. The Marines in particular loved it. They called it "The Blue Book," after the color of the binding and saw it as a battering ram against their traditional rival, the U.S. Army. They asked me to do a similar study on them, but I, suspecting there was no new ground left to discover, declined. The book helped initiate, or at any rate justify, the so-called COHORT System, which was then being introduced into the army in order to increase unit cohesion by making individual soldiers serve together for a longer time. As usual with the U.S. Forces, administrative efficiency came before anything else, and it was not long before COHORT was dismantled. I, however, had made my name and was able to suggest my next proposal to Mr. Marshall.

Apart from introducing me to the world of defense consultants, *Fighting Power* taught me other lessons. The most important one was the role of quantification. I myself had been educated in the humanist tradition. However, by the nineteen seventies that tradition seemed to be dying. Instead, the decade saw the rise of something called Cliometrics. As so often, historians were jealous of the natural scientists who, having landed on the moon, seemed to be racing ahead. Their success, as everybody knew, derived from the fact that they used *computers*. Computers were wonderful new machines that did whatever wonderful things they did at wonderful speeds in wonderful ways few people (except for the wonderful programmers who ran them) understood.

One thing was as clear as sunshine: namely, that no study in any field could be any good if it did not make use of computers. To use computers, it was first necessary to quantify the material, if possible with the aid of as many differential equations as possible representing as many variables as possible. The outcome was a flood of bad history. Indeed, it was so bad that few people tried to understand it, and even fewer succeeded. Fortunately, Cliometrics proved no more than a passing fad. By the mid-nineteen eighties it had largely disappeared into the limbo from whence it had come and where, by right, it belongs.

I, however, was writing the history not of a single person, or even of a group of persons, but of two vast military organizations— the German and the American—which had fought each other over several years. During World War II about 18,000,000 men passed through the Wehrmacht and Waffen S.S. The figure for the U.S. Armed Forces was not much smaller. This created a problem. Suppose I wrote 300 pages, and suppose that, to support and illustrate my claims, I would use three examples per page. The total number of examples in the book would therefore be about 900, against well over 30,000,000 men who had passed through both organizations combined. Clearly, this was nonsense; using such methods, I could prove anything, and so could anybody else. Clearly, the only way to bring out the differences between the two armed forces, the ones that presumably explained the German Wehrmacht's superior fighting power, was to rely on statistical data. Besides, ignorant as I was about the mentality of the U.S. military, I knew they adored such data. Fortunately, both considerations reinforced each other and pointed in the same direction.

Though I never used equations, the above considerations caused *Fighting Power* to become the only book I wrote that is based almost entirely on statistical data (it has about 100 tables and figures). This approach made it look very much like a staff study, which caused one very renowned publisher to turn it down. Given that it has since been translated into several languages and that, over thirty years later, it is still in print, I'd like to stuff it down their throats. Though no mathematician, I had been interested in numbers from childhood on, collecting them and playing games with them. Now I believed they proved the points I was trying to make as, up to a certain point, they did; still, later I began to develop my doubts. Even assuming the figures themselves were okay, which was not always the case, all too often you could change what they meant simply by distributing them in a different way.

Suppose, for example, you had a survey that divided soldiers into five groups according to the state of their morale. Now change the number of groups into four, or three, and add the figures in the groups you had deleted to those in the groups that remained. By such methods you could get practically any result you wanted. And you could do so, moreover, without falsifying or even misrepresenting any of your data. Thus figures did not really eliminate confusion and provide objectivity, as the advocates of Cliometrics claimed. Quite often, they provided the appearance of objectivity without the substance; in other cases they were merely nonsense on stilts. Later, I discovered that Darrell Huff in *How to Lie with Statistics* (1954) had said the same thing much more elegantly than I ever could. No wonder that book became a favorite of mine.

Fun and games aside, the question as to how many numbers are enough—as Aristotle once said, to each subject its own degree of precision—remained and could not be avoided. I am no admirer of the kind of history that, to convince the reader that it is as precise as the natural sciences, floods him or her with numbers. Mathematics apart, I am not even sure those sciences themselves are as precise as they claim to be. Precisely that point, incidentally, was addressed by a book on the topic that was presented to me by my then nine-year-old grandson, Orr, who thought, rightly as it turned out, I might find it interesting. Still, when one deals with more than one individual, sometimes even when one deals with a single individual, numbers often represent the fastest way of gaining insight and passing that insight on to the reader.

For example, if you want to understand this country or that, you could do worse than start by noting how many square kilometers it has and how many people it contains. Add its per capita GDP, the percentage of its economy made up of industry and services rather than agriculture, and the number of computers per household. Check the way these data have changed over the last quarter century, and you are in a position to say some important things about the country in question as well as about others about which you have similar data. True, the country's real "essence," if there is such a thing, is still entirely unknown and, perhaps, unknowable. Certainly, it is unknowable with the aid of numbers alone. The bottom line is that, as the U.S. Marines might say, what you need is a few good numbers. Just what "good" numbers are I cannot tell. All I know is that when I see bad ones, I usually recognize them.

Another problem that *Fighting Power* made me confront was that of writing "contemporary" history. When I entered Hebrew University, the prevailing idea was that history had ended in 1914. Anything written about the years after that was not history but journalism, an inferior field better left to hacks. Nor were these ideas limited to Jerusalem alone. In 1966, when Walter Laqueur and George Mosse started the excellent *Journal of Contemporary History*, they felt the need to justify themselves by writing an introduction. In it they explained that "up to date" did not necessarily mean the opposite of "serious." Most of the facts, they claimed, become known almost immediately.

By the time I did *Fighting Power*, having already written my monograph about the 1973 War, I was inclined to agree. So were most of my younger colleagues at the History Department. Yet I confess that

I did so with a certain uneasiness of mind. First, it could certainly be argued that, whatever the situation in other fields, in that of military history some things were deliberately kept secret. And with very good reason An excellent example was Ultra; the famous and highly successful World War II code-breaking British operation whose very existence was only made public thirty years after that conflict had ended.

Second, when writing contemporary history, one does not know how things end (if they ever do, but that is another matter). Not knowing how they end, one cannot say which ones are important and which ones are not. This lack of perspective all but guarantees that almost all that is written today will be irrelevant tomorrow. As a look at yesterday's newspaper will show, often the more up to date any piece of information, the truer this becomes. Yet here I was, a young and supposedly serious scholar, trying to use history as a guide not only to the present but to the future as well. It is a task which, however often I have engaged in it since, still makes me shiver.

Though it makes me shiver, it is also inevitable. As a student at Hebrew University and, to a lesser extent, the LSE, I had the lesson that the goal of study was to gain objective knowledge hammered into me. The way my teachers saw it then, and many of my colleagues see it now, allowing the present to interfere with the past means introducing factors that were not obvious during the period you have chosen to study. As with Heisenberg's Law (which says that we shall never see the elementary particles since our very attempt to do so will cause them to change) doing so all but guarantees that our understanding of that period will be distorted. As to trying to look into the future, since every historical event is unique, the very attempt to do so contradicts the nature of the discipline and should be rejected. I understood their position and respected it. Somewhat later I also read Karl Popper, who had written *The Poverty of Historicism* specifically in order to tell the likes of me how right they, the critics of historicism, were.

But once I had become a defense consultant, following their advice was a luxury I could not afford. Here I was working for a senior defense official whose job was to provide advice to some of the most powerful men on Earth, men whose mission in life it was to save the world from the Evil Empire and who, in trying to do so, had it in their hands to unleash forces that would determine the life and death of hundreds of millions. History was of use to them, and hence to me, *only* to the extent that I mixed the present with the past. To bleat that it should not be done, or could not be done, or that I could not do it, simply meant passing the job to somebody else, who, I consoled myself, might have even less ability and fewer scruples than I did.

Thus, more by accident than by design, history became, for me, a dialogue between the past and the present. I try to use the present as a source of fruitful questions about the past. Conversely, one important reason—though certainly not the only reason—for studying the past is in order to use it for shedding light on the present and, as far as possible, a little on the future as well. As Theodore Roosevelt once said, the more you know about the past, the better prepared you are for the future. To my mind, not only is understanding the past an essential tool for looking into the future, but it is also the only available tool. Take away our knowledge of the past, here understood as everything that took place more than a minute ago, and all that remains are religion and magic. From the little I know about those two disciplines, and those who practice them, they seem to provide an even less adequate basis for prediction than history does. I am reminded of what Churchill said of democracy. It is the worst regime, except for all the rest.

To put it in a different way, anybody who has ever planned for the future or invested in it, and who was not content to do so on the basis of pure guesswork, necessarily brought his or her past experience to bear. Yet the only people who can claim any expertise on the past are those who have studied it. Thus, to argue that historians alone should not be allowed to do so is patently absurd.

Largely because modern armed forces spend so much of their time preparing for their profession rather than exercising it, the problem with using the past as a guide for the present and future is more acute in the case of military history than in that of any other kind. Clausewitz had something to say about the matter, as did Liddell Hart in *Why Don't We Learn from History?* Rooted as it is in a late-nineteenth century positivist outlook, and one that is only half-digested at that, the latter book is not one of my favorites. Still, I do agree with the author that, if you want to use the past as a guide to the present and the future, the first thing to do is to seek the truth about it. Quite apart from the practical difficulties involved, which can be quite formidable, this is not as trivial a point as it might seem. Though it is true that many people see history as a science, others see it as a branch of literature or art and are prepared to take liberties with the truth in order to achieve the effects they are aiming at.

Of course it is true that art can and should be used to present science in as coherent and as elegant a way as possible. My colleagues tell me that this even applies to the natural sciences. There, too, a good solution artfully presented has a better chance of being accepted, or at least considered, than a good one clumsily explained. Mix art with science, stir well, let them stew, add salt and/or pepper to suit your taste, and decorate with a leaf or two. Seriously, though, if your goal is to tell people what the future may be like and, therefore, what they should do in anticipation of it, then only the kind of history that aims at truth—and, to that extent, is "scientific"—is of any use. Period.

Second, you must assume there is more to history than simply telling what happened next. What you are looking for is regularities. If the same causes do not always, or at least usually, lead to the same effects, then "understanding," let alone using whatever you think you have "understood" for looking into the future, is impossible by definition. This, after all, is the method economists use. To the extent that economists can claim any scientific basis for their work, they too must start by studying the past in order to find regularities in what happened. Assuming they have found any, they too use those regularities to try to look into the future, predicting or trying to predict such things as consumption, inventories, prices, employment, growth, money supplies, and interest rates.

The regularities economists look for are less complex, more reliable, and more subject to modeling and quantification than those historians use—or so economists fondly believe. Still, the essence of the process is the same. In a sense, economists are nothing but historians of a rather specialized kind. To wit, they are historians who deliberately leave out non-economic factors, and, by doing so, distort reality to an extraordinary degree! I would go further still and argue that, in their quest for regularities, historians resemble not only economists but natural scientists, too. What is a "law of nature" if not a distillation of regularities repeatedly observed?

Thus the principal remaining difference between history and the natural sciences is that the events that form the subject matter of the former cannot be reproduced in the laboratory. Since the same applies to economics as well, we historians are in good company.

At this point, the question whether the regularities apply to all societies or differ from one society to the next can no longer be avoided. It is a basic belief of most natural scientists that the laws of "nature," whatever that may be, apply everywhere, at all times. In fact anyone who challenges them on this point may bring out a stream of invective. In contrast, it is claimed, the regularities unveiled by historical study and social science, assuming they exist at all, vary from one civilization to the next and are, in this sense, not regularities at all. But is this difference real? I can certainly think of some regularities, such as the fact that women have children and raise them during the first few years whereas men do not, that are the same for all civilizations at all times and places. Nor are the economic, social, and psychological implications of this fact as trivial as some feminists would like them to be.

Conversely, though I am not a natural scientist, I think I can think of worlds in which some of the ordinary laws of physics and chemistry will not operate in the same form. For example, imagine a distant planet populated by forms of life based not on carbon but on an element that we do not know. It can only exist, say, under tremendous pressure found in black holes, giving it all kinds of strange qualities we cannot even imagine. What will the resulting creatures be like? Will they thrive on X-rays? Will they obey the laws of "life" as we know them? Will they, indeed, represent "life" at all? Precisely what *is* this life we are talking about? Assuming, for a moment, we do not know the answer to that question, how dare we talk of regularities that govern all of it? Of course I admit that the regularities of social life are less precise and harder to establish than those of the natural world. That, after all, is one reason why I decided to study them in the first place. However, the more I think of it, the less convinced I am that the presence or absence of regularities does, in fact, constitute the real difference between them.

Finally, there is the problem of free will. In recent years it has become fashionable to speak of "strategy." Originally, strategy was a military term referring to large-scale operational plans. Now it is something even viruses use to survive and replicate themselves. Whatever the psychology of viruses may be, I am not aware that dead matter makes conscious decisions, a fact that greatly facilitates the work of the chemists and physicists who study it and try to describe its behavior.

Those scientists are lucky. When it comes to human affairs, economics specifically included, people consciously adopt this strategy or that in the hope, which may be true or false, of obtaining this outcome or that. As a result, the problem of free will can never be eliminated. All we can do is try to attenuate it. The standard method for doing this is to focus not on individuals—those short lived, infinitely varied, capricious beings—but on large groups of people. After all, physicists who study what happens when a container full of gas is heated are not expected to predict the behavior of every single molecule but only to average that of all of the molecules. To demand that historians do more seems grossly unfair.

Fundamental as these propositions are, they merely represent the assumptions which, it seems to me, must underpin any attempt to look into the future (or, if you will, to become a defense consultant). As to the actual way in which one should proceed, at bottom I can only see three possibilities. The simplest, and perhaps most superficial, way of using the past is to apply the regularities you have found in the past to the present and the future. In such and such a civilization, such and such factors led to such and such an outcome. Provided you have identified the factors with sufficient care, and provided the civilization is still more or less the same, you therefore have at least some basis for thinking that the same will happen again. For example, military history teaches that large-scale airborne operations against an intact enemy, unless they are supported by ground forces, usually fail. A simple lesson, to be sure, yet one that was ignored time and time again.

On a more advanced level, another way to proceed is to identify a trend and to project it into the future. Inside and outside my own field of military affairs, there is probably not a modern historian who has not tried this game on occasion, and the same is true of many more who are not historians but tried to play it as if they were. Taking point A, so and so many years ago, as their starting point, they use it as a base for more or less learned, more or less successful, predictions. For example, one may trace the figures to conclude that the future will see more people visiting shopping centers and fewer going to church, or, perhaps, things will develop the other way around.

The difficulty with this method is its unreliability. As one limerick puts it, "A trend is a trend is a trend/the question is, will it bend/or be pushed off course/by some unforeseen force/and come to a premature end." As often as not, to assume that things will continue moving in the same direction as they have been doing is to court disaster. This is even more the case in military studies than in watching the NASDAQ. The reason is that, since our opponent is a free actor and capable of learning, the key to victory lies in never doing the same thing twice. Of course, this is itself a logical contradiction, but not one I am going to explore here.

A third method, and one that to some extent takes these difficulty into account, is to rely on dialectics. The idea that history does not unfold in a linear way but obeys the laws of dialectics is commonly associated with the above-mentioned German philosopher, Georg Wilhelm Friedrich Hegel. However, it can be traced back as far as Heraclitus around 500 B.C. Starting from intellectual history, which was his first specialty, Hegel thought in terms of a thesis, an anti-thesis that grew out of it and contradicted it, and a synthesis that combined both. The synthesis itself turned into a thesis and so on until paradise was regained and/or mankind became re-united with God. In so far as I think that the end of the process will at the same time signify the end of mankind itself, I disagree with his analysis. In so far as it seems to fit the way history unfolds, I think there is a great deal of truth in what he said and that the process is at work always and everywhere.

Suppose you want to use this logic for looking into the future. In that case, you must first establish in what direction history—or, more practically, the part in which you are interested—seems to be moving. Next, you must ask yourself what might constitute its opposite and whether you can discern signs of it emerging from the shadows. Thus, relying on dialectics is the exact opposite of extrapolating trends. Instead, the assumption is that any trend is pregnant with its own opposite, so to speak.

Not only do dialectics provide the best available description of the way things change over time, but they also apply to the way we *think* about those things. When it comes to driving history forward, human ideas are as powerful a factor as any. Anyone who does not take this fact into account does so at his peril. Considering the problem from the standpoint of dialectics, I tend to agree with something Nietzsche wrote in *Ecce Homo*. The fact that everybody believes in something does not prove it is true. To the contrary, that is a good reason to question whether it will remain true for long or if it ever was true. Hegel himself said that the owl of Minerva only flies at dusk.

I well know that none of the above three methods is "scientific" in the strict sense of that term. Not only are all three problematic in themselves, but it is first of all necessary to decide which one to apply to what problem. Nor is that all. Even if you succeed at discerning what will happen or the direction in which things may move, there still is no reliable way to find out *when* they will and how fast, or slowly, the processes you have identified will unfold. Working as I did for the Pentagon, I learned that, over there, the critical time is always four years away. Assume it is three, and people will say that it is too late to do anything. Assume it is five—meaning, that whatever is going to happen will happen after the coming presidential elections—and nobody cares. Seriously, for all the problems that the three approaches raise, they are the best I can do. I challenge anyone to do better. Certainly, they are preferable to crystal ball gazing and incantation, which seem to be the only alternatives.

Nor, as a look at the daily weather forecast will show, are historians necessarily less successful than natural scientists at predicting the future. One very important method natural scientists use to hide their ignorance is statistics. Some tell us that a person who smokes increases his chances of contracting cancer by X percent. Others say that the chances of the Earth being hit by an asteroid within the next century are such and such. By using this technique, they are sure to have right on their side both if the prediction comes true *and* if it does not. I am reminded of a story told about a former Israeli chief of staff, General Rafael Eytan (served 1978–82). Preparing some air force operation, he asked the planners what the weather forecast was. They told him there was a 20-percent chance of rain. Wrong, he said the correct answer is 50 percent. Either it rains, or it doesn't.

Other scientists still say now one thing, now its opposite. For example, few people remember that, as late as the 1970s, the drug Ecstasy was supposed to be good for you. It was, in fact, widely used to combat depression. During the same decade, what worried scientists was not global warming but something known as the "Global Weather Conspiracy," which, if it were not restrained, might lead to a "New Ice Age." For decades now we have been told women should exercise just as men do; recently, all of a sudden, we start hearing the opposite.

Even the difficulty social scientists face in separating cause from effect is far from unique. It is matched by the inability of natural scientists to decide whether it is carbon emissions that cause global warming or global warming that is accompanied by growing concentrations of carbon gases. Briefly, it is not true that many natural scientists are very good at predicting the future even in their own relatively simple fields. Conversely, historians have no monopoly either over nonsense or over the kind of methodological errors that lead to it. The real difference lies elsewhere. When natural scientists expose their predecessors' errors, people say that the discipline in question is making progress. But when we in the humanities and social sciences do the same, this is taken as proof that our fields are without predictive power to begin with. Surely there is some trick involved. How do they do it?

Like a natural scientist, a historian who tries to predict the future may get it right for the wrong reasons. For example, I once wrote a study in which I recommended that America's war colleges be consolidated so as to bring together officers from all four services and to make sure they understand one another. This was 1988, and I did not know—although, with the wisdom of hindsight, perhaps I should have known—that the USSR was about to disintegrate and that the Cold War was about to end, let alone that cuts in military expenditures would soon cause the militaries of most countries to implement exactly that measure not only at the war college level but further down as well. As I am writing this in early 2015, I think the only major exception is the United States.

Finally, historians also resemble natural scientists in another way. Even if they do get it right, they cannot necessarily make people act on their vision, no more than even the best map can force travelers to use it to get from point A to point B by the shortest route instead of getting lost. This was brought home to me very forcefully in the autumn of 2000 when I was visiting Stockholm for the second time. I had just finished a talk about the future of war, my usual subject at the time, when a civilian approached me. He said he was a defense official and that he had attended a seminar I had given on a similar topic back in 1994. At that time we had discussed the future of the Swedish army.

Being a guest, I never pretend to know the requirements of my hosts better than they do. At that time, however, I did argue that there would be no room in future warfare for any number of tanks, so buying new ones was a waste of money. Now my interlocutor told me that the Swedes had not taken my word. Instead, they had consulted some other experts, including Israeli ones. Everybody but me told them that a modern army without tanks was not an army at all. They went ahead and spent a billion dollars to buy German Leopard IIs. Six years later, those tanks were rusting somewhere in the snow. The moral of the story is true (for them) but sad (for me). Had the Swedes paid me $100,000,000 for my services, they still would have saved $900,000,000.

* * *

To come back to *Fighting Power*, the book that for the first time caused me to think about these and similar methodological problems, some years after it was published in the U.S. it was translated into German, courtesy of the Forschungsamt. Long before, I had been made aware of the problems that might follow when I had a glass of wine with the then director of the Militärarchiv, Dr. Julius Stahl. Stahl, who was then in his early sixties, was a veteran of World War II, in which he had lost an arm. Like other former Wehrmacht officers I met, he found it hard to accept that the cause for which he had allowed himself to be shot to pieces had been criminal. We were not even five minutes into our conversation when he burst out, "This was 1941! We were marching on Moscow! A thousand kilometers! On foot! It was fantastic!"

I did not think then, and I do not think now, that Stahl was particularly militarist, let alone that he was a right-wing extremist hankering for the lost glories of Nazi Germany. I have often heard non-German officers say similar things. The most notable one was Ariel Sharon. By his own testimony, he loved every moment of the 1973 Arab-Israeli War. Dayan, too, had something to say about the matter. So did Robert E. Lee, Winston Churchill, and George Patton. Many of them regard the wars in which they took part as the greatest times in their lives. Once, when I asked a class of American Gulf War veterans how many of them would have missed it for their lives, every single hand stayed down. As the examples of both Dayan and Stahl show, very often, this even applies to those of them who have been mutilated. Still, listening to a former Wehrmacht officer express the same sentiment about the war in which he had participated was not exactly congenial. The abhorrence National Socialism has created is the cross Germans will have to bear for many, many years to come. Nor, as an Israeli and Jew, am I sorry to see them bear it.

The term *Fighting Power* was my translation of the German *Kampfkraft*. Between about 1917 and 1945 *Kampfkraft* was a normal part of German military terminology. It was used to express the value of a unit in a way that took into account more than bean counting alone; now that the German army hardly fights or suffers losses any more, it has been largely forgotten. Alerted by my experience with Stahl, I wrote a new preface for the German edition. Its purpose was to make clear that my praise for the Wehrmacht's military excellence was not meant to absolve it of its responsibility for participating in every kind of war crimes.

Unfortunately, some people on the extreme right of the German political spectrum refused to listen. Either they argued with me, disputing what I had written in the introduction, or, which was worse, they quoted my findings to show what a wonderful organization the Wehrmacht had been. For some time both groups even sent me some of their publications for free. To add insult to injury, one of them was called *Neue Ordnung*, A New Order, a term the Nazis loved to use. A book is like a child one has raised and is now making its own way in the world. Once it has left home, there is no knowing what it will do to people and what people will do to it. All you can do is watch it from afar and wish it well.

In the late spring of 1980, it was clear to me that I had broken the back of *Fighting Power*. Saying that I live for my work would be going too far. Still, it is true that, without work, I cannot live; as Aristotle put it more than two thousand years ago, happiness is purposeful work. Each time the end of a project draws near I seem to be looking into a black hole. On the strength of my plan for *Fighting Power* I had obtained a fellowship from the Humboldt Foundation so as to spend a year in Freiburg (actually we went to Lahr, some thirty miles to the north, to live with the Canadian army and their English-language schools). However, by the time I was able to take up the fellowship the book was more or less complete, and I needed something else to keep me busy.

One evening I visited a friend, Professor Amnon Sella, and poured out my troubles. Sella is an expert on the Soviet/Russian armed forces, and anything he does not know about them is not worth knowing. Now he suggested that I should do a history of C^3. I had no idea what C^3 was and asked him to explain. It turned out that C^3 was Pentagonese for command, control, and communications; later, wishing to make the alphabet soup even less transparent, they added computers and intelligence and created C^4 I. I raised the idea with Mr. Marshall, and he snapped it up. At that time, I could do no wrong.

About a year later I started tackling the subject in earnest. I had spent the months in between writing a short study—also for Mr. Marshall—on Bundeswehr manpower systems and making corrections to *Fighting Power*. To some extent, doing so was an excuse for *not* thinking. Once you are on top of a subject, you tend to fall into a rut, coasting along comfortably without too much effort. Getting out of the rut takes time and energy. It is much easier to go on tinkering with what you already have; your excuse, of course, is that it is not quite finished yet. Heaven forbid that I disparage the process of revising and polishing. I know it is indispensable, and also that it can easily take as long as the writing proper does. Still, I learned that there are times when I, and presumably many others as well, will do anything but think. Strange as it sounds, even writing, instead of expressing a thought, can be a substitute for it.

In the early summer of 1981 my family returned to Jerusalem whereas I went to Washington, D.C. to work in the Library of Congress. My youngest son Uri was 20 months old. So offended was he by my sudden disappearance that, when I came back to him, it took weeks before he would look at me again. The change from a large, comfortable apartment in Germany to a rather dilapidated utility flat came as a tremendous shock. It was my first extended stay in Washington, and I found the climate was not at all to my liking. To make things worse, the restaurant food I ate proved to contain too much animal fat for my taste. In fact, before I found a place to live where I could prepare my own, it made me feel sick.

To complete my misery, my fear of the new project proved to be well founded. I soon got stuck; such was my despair that I wanted to give up and return home. I called Luttwak, my direct employer, and almost cried over the phone. He was very good to me, gently explaining that what I was trying to do was important and that I should therefore stick to it in spite of all the difficulties I was experiencing. Since then, my relations with Luttwak have had their ups and downs. But I shall always remember how, when I really needed him, he was there for me, even if he himself does not.

The turning point came one day when I was working on Napoleon's command system. All the books which had been written before me and that I had consulted were unanimous that the emperor left his principal subordinates very little freedom of action. I, however had already done some work—though hardly anything had been written down as yet—on command systems before the French Revolution. Comparing the emperor with the likes of Frederick the Great, rather than Helmuth von Moltke or some twentieth-century commander, it turned out that the standard interpretation was wrong. He was no tyrant who kept his commanders dancing on a string. On the contrary, he was the greatest military decentralizer who ever lived.

It was precisely Napoleon's readiness to let those commanders operate independently that enabled him to revolutionize strategy, indeed, almost to invent it *ex novo*. As he himself put it in a bulletin published soon after his victory at Ulm in 1805, he was waging war with the troops' legs instead of their bayonets. As had been the case with *Fighting Power*, it only took about fifteen minutes for the miracle to happen. I just *knew* I was on the right track. I also knew that, though almost the entire book remained to be written, in a sense all that remained for me to do was to fill in the details. This, in fact, proved to be the case. It was only when I came to the last chapter that I got stuck again. By then I was prepared for this to happen, though, and I did not let it affect my mood too much.

Once again, the two months I stayed in Washington, D.C. made me wonder about American life. Though I have spent most of my

life in Israel, my own background is European. The more often I
go back to that continent, the more clearly I realize it. Of course
it is true that the U.S. also has its roots in Europe. Nevertheless, it
was a strange and unfamiliar place, one that was by no means easy
to understand or necessarily congenial once one did understand or
thought one understood.

Occasional misunderstandings notwithstanding, my work was
now well in hand. I no longer felt I was wasting my time, causing life
in Washington to become much brighter than it had been. The flat I
rented was located very near Stanton Square, about halfway between
the Library of Congress and Union Station. At that time it was a very
run-down neighborhood and supposedly very dangerous. Each time
my friends drove me back from some place or another they would
wait in the car until I had gone inside, locked the door, and turned
on the light. I am sure they knew what they were doing, but I myself
did not feel unsafe. Each evening I went for a walk, taking now this
route and now that and getting to know the area. Some Saturdays I
spent kicking a football with the junkies in the square. I suppose I
was lucky.

By the spring of 1982 the book was ready. I briefed Mr. Marshall
about it in his office; this time Luttwak did not see any need to grill
me first. Over the years I learned to value Mr. Marshall, who is now
in his nineties, for what he was: namely, a true defense intellectual
who was always thinking about the road ahead. He was very tight
lipped, as indeed he had to be if he was to tell truth to power and if,
surrounded by people, all of whom wanted contracts, he was to retain
his objectivity as well as his sanity. Still, there was no doubt that he
was very happy with what he heard, both because of the contents of
what I had to say and because he got lots of feedback from others
in the Pentagon. The reason why he got lots of feedback from other
people in the Pentagon was that my work happened to fit very well
into the "maneuver warfare" school that was then taking its first bold
steps in the corridors of that building.

These were the post-Vietnam years. Not yet having discovered that it had actually "won" that war, America blamed the defeat very largely on something called "attrition." Rooted in the industrial superiority which, in the past, had so often enabled American forces to roll over their opponents rather than engage in elegant operational maneuvers, "attrition" stood for all that was wrong with the U.S. approach to war. Grant's Plan Anaconda, which had ended up by strangling the Confederacy during the Civil War, was attrition. Eisenhower's Broad Front in 1944–1945 was attrition. After the Inchon Landings, the Korean War was attrition, with both sides facing each other along a fortified line and the U.S. Forces blasting their opponents' "human wave" attacks with artillery.

All these campaigns were indicted in the sharpest terms. Had it been possible, no doubt those who originated them and carried them out would have been tarred and feathered. The same was even more true of the Vietnam War itself. In that war General Westmoreland had failed to develop a proper strategy to deal with the guerrillas confronting him. Not having a strategy, he was reduced to trying to kill more Viet Cong and North Vietnamese than the enemy could feed in. This was the origin of "search and destroy," a system whereby poor American infantrymen slogged across the jungle until, having stumbled onto the Viet Cong, they could call in artillery and air power to deal with them. To prove it was succeeding, he, or his superior Robert McNamara, or some bright young men at the Pentagon, had invented the notorious body count, which, in turn, produced more dubious statistics than any war before or since.

The alternative to attrition was maneuver warfare. In essence it was as old as war itself and could be traced back at least as far as the ancient Chinese commander and writer Sun Tzu. Not by accident, the latter's star rose; by the early 1990s, no fewer than four different English translations of his work could be found in American bookstores. In its modern form it had been invented by Napoleon, whose command system I had studied and whose operations Liddell

Hart had once compared to the waving of the tentacles of an octopus. Later, it was developed by the Germans Helmuth von Moltke, Erich von Manstein, Heinz Guderian, and Erwin Rommel, as well as the American George S. Patton and the Israelis Moshe Dayan, Israel Tal, and Ariel Sharon. Researching and writing *Fighting Power* had turned me into something of an expert on the pre-1945 German Army. I think that, although I never made any bones of the fact that I had not been a soldier, the fact that I am an Israeli also gave me a certain comparative advantage.

It is true that the volume I had just finished was not about maneuver warfare. In fact I had hardly yet even heard the term. Instead, it was about the history of command. My main argument was that the best command systems are decentralized. Tracing them from Greek and Roman times on, I discovered that this is true almost regardless of the kind of technology at one's disposal. Command is not simply an outgrowth of the available technology as most people believe. On the contrary, it consists very largely of using organization and training in order to find ways around the *limitations* of the technology available at any given time and place.

Like *Supplying War*, *Command in War* was written as a series of case studies, this being my way of avoiding the difficult question of a chronological organization versus a thematic one. Like *Supplying War*, it provided a new way of looking at military history though this time I fully realized what I was doing even before I finished it. Finally, and also like *Supplying War*, it was put on the American officers' professional reading list. Later, somebody told me that I was the only foreigner on that list as well as the only author to have *two* books on it.

About 1984 I was about to enter "proceedings" toward my promotion to full professor, and I did not want to take any chances. I therefore submitted my work to Harvard University Press as the most prestigious one around. They accepted, and I was very happy with the work they did. What I remember in particular was an argument we had about the title of the forthcoming book. As indicated above, I had long been an admirer of A. J. P. Taylor, whose books stand out for their fluent style, sense of humor, and readability. I wanted to make my latest volume as readable as his, and as part of this, I suggested that we call it *Command*. My point was that, though a short title cannot guarantee a good book, a good book is very unlikely to have a title that is not short. To support by case, I cited Herodotus (*The Histories*), Thucydides (*History of the Peloponnesian War*), Plato (*Georgias*), Augustine (*Confessions*), Shakespeare (almost all plays), Adam Smith (*The Wealth of Nations*), Charles Darwin (*The Origins of Species*), Karl Marx (*Capital*), and any number of others.

True, some of these originally had subtitles. But that fact merely proves that they could well have done without. Similarly, movies, both good and bad, always try to attract viewers by means of snappy titles such as *Modern Times*, or *Casablanca*, or *Star Wars*. Very few spoil the effect by having subtitles as well. For example, imagine a movie called *Shrek: The Story of an Improbable Monster*. My ideas raised hackles among my colleagues at Hebrew University and elsewhere. Following some German and French intellectual traditions, they believe a book can only be worthwhile if it is too incomprehensible for anybody to read. As to Harvard University Press, they only accepted my argument in part, and we ended up by compromising on *Command in War*.

It was during those years that I was divorced. My first marriage had always been unhappy, and the one good thing that came out of it is three children I love. In the autumn of 1982 I was teaching a course on the Scientific Revolution of the seventeenth century. As usual at the first meeting, the students did not know anything about anything. As usual at the first meeting, having explained what the course was all about, I had time on my hands. I used it for a kind of general introduction. The students were freshmen, and for some of them it was the first university class they had ever attended. I wanted to explain how the meaning of "rationality" has often changed during history, to the point where things considered perfectly reasonable at one time were no longer considered so later on, and the other way around.

Perhaps it was foolish on my part to use the following question as an illustration: "What would you say if I stripped naked right here in class?" Sitting opposite me there was a woman about ten years older than most of the rest. The way I remember it she was right in the center; the way she remembers it, she was at the back. The difference may testify to the force of her personality. In any case she was sitting very straight. "I would like it very much" she shot back, making the class explode with laughter. Later, she claimed it was the only time she saw me blush. Had the same exchange taken place twenty-five years later, it would be a fine question as to who was "harassing" whom. As it was, I thank my stars that the students were still able to take it as a joke, which it was, and that the university had not yet gotten it into its head to try to prevent two adults from falling in love. And so does she.

She was Dvora Lewy, the wife of a former student. Having decided to go and study, she asked him whose classes she should attend, and he sent her to mine. When she said the subject did not interest her, he answered that anything I taught would be interesting. Nor could he know how right he would be. Thus it all started, and we went on under our own steam. She has changed me in many ways, for the better I hope. She also brought me two stepchildren, Adi and Jonathan, the best anyone can have.

I was now part of a group known as the Military Reformers. The Military Reformers emerged during the early 1980s as a direct response to the Vietnam War. A few were military or ex-military, but most were civilian. A few worked for corporations, but most were freelancers. Their original objective was to reexamine everything connected with the U.S. Armed Forces and to fix it. There was at least one political scientist, one economist, one former fighter pilot, one engineer, one Marine Corps colonel, and one or two jacks of all

trades. Finally, there were two members of the House of Represen-
tatives, Richard Cheney and Gary Hart. The former was not yet the
arch-conservative he later became. The latter made military reform
into one of the issues on which he ran for the presidency until he
permitted his campaign to be derailed by a woman aboard a yacht
called, appropriately enough, *Monkey Business*. Looking for evidence
to back up their theories, several of them branched out into military
history. After all, where else could they go? Intellectually, they were
the most stimulating people I have ever met. they were always asking
questions, trading ideas, suggesting future policies, and trying to see
if they could agree on them.

While the thrust of their arguments was broadly similar, several
had special hobbyhorses. One was the *Schwerpunkt* (center of grav-
ity), meaning the need to find the opponent's most vulnerable point
and to concentrate all of one's own resources against it. Another was
the OODA (Observation, Orientation, Decision, Action) Loop and
the need to move through it faster than your opponent could. Yet
another was the need to take the gold-plating off weapon systems
so as to make them more affordable and more reliable or to have
armored operations proceed flexibly while bypassing obstacles, rather
like water trickling down a roof.

Though there was something called the Congressional Reform
Caucus, for the most part the Reformers never comprised more than
a loose group of eight or nine individuals armed with typewriters.
Perhaps it would be true to say that, by the time word-processors
finally began to oust typewriters around 1990, the end of their influence was approaching. In large part the reason was that their ideas,
like those of Marc Bloch, had swept the field, if not in the sense
that people understood them, then at any rate to the extent that
everybody paid lip service to them. As I can testify from personal
experience, this even applied to the most senior commanders of all.
For a number of years, a "maneuverist" was the very best anyone
could be.

One of the principal characters was the late John Boyd, who has since had several books written about him. Others were Pierre Sprey, Mike Wyly, Franklin Spinney (who once made it onto the cover of *Time* magazine) and Bill Lind. It was Lind who, working for and with the commandant of the Marine Corps, General Alfred Gray, wrote *The Maneuver Warfare Handbook*, probably the most important single text the movement produced and one that has been called "the Bible" of its subject. Last, not least, there was Steven Canby, my direct employer after he and Luttwak split up. Canby's specialty was manpower systems as well as the factors that link it to organization on one hand and tactics on the other. They are subjects about which he probably knew more than anybody else and definitely knew much more than most uniformed bureaucrats will know in their lives. I would say that Luttwak, who at one point was chosen by *Time* Magazine as one of the 100 most influential people in the world, was also a member even though it was typical of him that he would never admit a link with ordinary mortals. I, who along with Bundeswehr General (ret.) Franz Uhle-Wettler was the only non-American, hovered on the margins.

Looking back, I think that being a non-American was both an advantage and a disadvantage. It was an advantage in the sense that it kept me away from Washington, D.C. In this way I was prevented from turning into a pain in the neck, which is how many Israelis see me. Nobody is a prophet in his own home, and I am less so than most. It was a disadvantage in that it kept me away from the center of discussion and prevented me from learning the ropes. To say the truth, given my total disinterest in administration and committee work of any kind, I would probably have failed to learn them anyhow.

It was Steven Canby, a real insider's outsider who made a point of knowing everybody, who did what had to be done in terms of administration, etc. Decades after he stopped doing so for me, he and his wife Marianne still remain the best friends Dvora and I have or which anybody can have. Their house became our Washington base, as indeed it has for many others as well. Together, we took many walks along the C&O Canal or else visited Borders Bookstore, now unfortunately gone, where I looked around for new books to buy whereas he leafed through investment magazines.

Working for what I liked to call "The Pentagon," I felt big and important. In the fullness of days Boyd, Wyly and I were even honored by a sketch of imaginary terrain, used by the Marine Corps Officer School at Quantico, with features that were named after us. Still, how influential we really were is hard to say. One volume written about us, which was published by the National Defense University, credited us with initiating a serious re-examination of U.S. military thought as well as a revival of the warrior spirit, especially among officers.[2] High praise, but probably overdrawn. Another, penned by a retired Israeli brigadier general, Shimon Naveh, credited us, and Bill Lind in particular, with the invention of a doctrine that was not only the most sophisticated ever but valid for all times and places. High praise, but definitely overdrawn.

In some ways, indeed, General Naveh's volume almost amounted to a travesty of everything many of us, Lind specifically included, tried to do. Had we not emphasized that each historical period necessarily had its own way of waging war and that the style suited for one was not suited for another? Also, later, that the U.S. military was behind the times and, for all the loose talk, did not really understand what maneuver was really about? Certainly, we acted like gadflies: stinging, criticizing, and, if only by making people mad, goading them into action. Certainly, we were listened to, sometimes with respect. In a way we represented the spirit of the age, which was very much in search for solutions to the problems that had manifested themselves in Vietnam.

Though people did listen, quite often, the very fact that they did so showed either that they were in the process of being educated— in other words, attending some course, academy, school, college, or whatever—or else had time to spare. Either way, they were clearly not the most important decision-makers. If some of what we had to say reached the latter, as I know it did, then it did so by more indirect channels as the atmosphere became filled with our ideas, so to speak. In any case the military, and the U.S. military in particular, are probably too large, too complex, and too cumbersome to be understood, let alone pushed in any direction and reformed, by a single individual. By and large this is true if even one is secretary of defense. It is certainly true if that individual is just a military historian based thousands of miles away and if, in addition, he has little or no access to classified information of any kind.

As I came to realize over the years, at the Pentagon the objective of practically all decisions is to get as much money out of Congress as possible. This is true both for the military in general and for the service, arm, or whatever one works for. At least one former deputy chairman of the joint chiefs of staff told me that he owed his promotion to his success in that field rather than to his prominence as a warrior. With bureaucratic infighting playing a large role, I think that, at best, papers and studies such as I and my fellow Reformers produced were sometimes used as weapons in that fighting. At worst, they disappeared into some drawer without anybody inside or outside the Pentagon paying attention. I often heard Canby explain how much money the armed forces could save if only they would adopt his suggestions on manpower organization. They probably could. But then, to say the truth, saving the country money was the last thing they wanted; once, when I told Marshall as much, he smiled.

Nils Naastad, the impish Norwegian whom I met at the time he was an instructor at the Air Force Academy in Trondheim, put it perfectly. The generals, he said, reach "conclusions." As an "expert," your job is to "support" those conclusions. You do so by presenting them in logical order, linking them to one another, and sprinkling them with the kinds of figures and footnotes that, today, are regarded as an essential part of any serious scholarship. Cynical, but true. What he forgot to add is that quite often those most in need of an explanation are the generals themselves. Some are looking for conclusions they can present. Others do not understand their own conclusions. After all, they are extremely busy people who do not have time to read studies as I do. To paraphrase the sixteenth century saying Swiss mercenaries addressed to their employer, the King of France, *Pas des conclusions, pas d'argent.*

Partly because Mr. Marshall is so tight lipped, partly because I did not live in Washington, D.C., and partly because I do not have the antennae it takes, I myself never learned what the generals' conclusions were, if any. Of course I wanted to get whatever support for my work I could. Who wouldn't? Still, when everything was said and done, what mattered the most to me was being able to study those subjects that, for good or ill, I considered the most interesting and most important. To make sure I retained my freedom as an academic I asked Mr. Marshall for the right to have my work published after a decent interval. He agreed, and I think that was not the least of his merits.

His attitude is particularly interesting because, years later, the IDF invented something called "the classified PhD thesis." It permitted students to enter its archives and to write its history on the condition that they did not reveal their sources which, of course, also remained closed to other people. I, for my part, always told students who asked my advice that the system was absolutely useless. It was and remains my view that no academic work that deliberately conceals the evidence on which it is based can be, or deserves to be, taken seriously. Better not write at all than do so under conditions that impede or limit thought. Even Eisenhower, who ought to have known, allegedly told his subordinates that if something was secret, they had better not tell him. Some of my students listened; others did not. Among those who did, I am proud to say, are some of the very best.

* * *

Having finished my book on what technology could, or rather could not, do for command in war, it was logical to take a look at military technology itself. Besides, I was gaining in self-confidence. In 1983 I was thirty-seven years old, an associate professor, and possessed of a certain reputation in my chosen field. I felt it was time for me to tackle a really big subject and that this was better than doing case studies as in *Command in War*, *Supplying War*, and, to some extent, *Fighting Power* as well. After all, none of the great historians I admired had gained his fame by doing case studies. This is as true of Fernand Braudel and Johan Huizinga and Alexis de Tocqueville as it is of Tacitus and Thucydides. Nor did any of them try to debunk the myths created by others. To the contrary, such was the quality of their works that they themselves created and became myths. To a man, they chose what they saw as a very important, if not the most important, subject they could think of. Next, they tried to trace its development from beginning to end. They used the space in between to address as many aspects of the story as possible and, in doing so, to bring to life an entire world.

Besides, case studies got me into a problem. When I first went to study in Jerusalem during the nineteen sixties, the library there was tolerably good. Later, it deteriorated until, except when it comes to Judaica, it hardly deserved to be called a research library at all. This, of course was, long before email and the Internet. Since doing case studies meant going into considerable detail about very different subjects and periods, researching my first four books had forced me to spend long periods abroad, whether with my family or on my own.

I, however, could only take my family on sabbatical every five years at most. Even so, it was a tremendous hassle for everybody concerned. The older the children, the harder they found it to adjust and readjust. Going alone meant being alone, often for months on end. I remember how, living in Freiburg, I felt jealous of the couples entering or leaving the movie houses. My absences helped break up my first marriage—not that I was sorry about that once it had happened. And I was determined not to let that happen again. Young researchers, be warned. When previous generations prohibited scholars from getting married, they had their reasons.

Though I did not realize it at first, *Technology and War* was the perfect solution to the problem. So huge was the subject as to be capable of being done almost anywhere. Indeed, when you work on very large subjects, the question is not which sources to read but which 90 percent *not* to read; the difficulty is that, to make that decision, you must first of all decide exactly what you want to do. I spoke to Mr. Marshall, and he agreed. As so often, I started full of confidence in my own powers. Originally, I thought the question I wanted to ask was how technology impacted on war. I therefore divided war into various domains, such as command, organization, strategy, tactics, etc., and set out to explain how technology interacted with each. The outcome was a lot of uncoordinated nonsense. I myself came to understand this and suggested to Mr. Marshall that the reason for my failure was that I had not had enough time to think things through. He saw my point and generously gave me a second chance.

The second draft was as bad as the first. In fact there never was a second draft, only the first chapter in which, Clausewitz-like, I tried to set forth the theoretical foundations of the relationship between the two factors. Unable to continue with the second chapter, I spent several months adding bits and pieces to the first one, trying to convince myself that this was necessary for the sake of clarity. Finally, I sent it to Steven Canby—I who never show my work to anybody until it is as good as complete, believing, as the Hebrew proverb has it, that only an ass does so. He responded with a single word: "verbose." I saw his point and stopped; since I remember his warning to the present day, it must have done me a lot of good. That, however, still left me with the question as to how to do the job.

At that time I was going through my divorce, making it almost impossible to concentrate. As with *Command in War*, I was on the point of throwing in the towel. As with *Command in War*, I was saved by a friend. This time it was not Luttwak but Canby, who insisted that the contract, in which he had invested so much work, be honored. Gradually, I realized that, in both drafts, I had done everything wrong. Instead of focusing on history, which is my *forte* as well as my great love in life, I had tried to do analytical work. I think it was Simone de Beauvoir who once wrote that it is only one person in a million who can write philosophy the way it should be. The rest of those who try are merely third- and fourth-raters. Thinking of it, perhaps that is the reason why she herself chose literature. I had tried to write analytically and, not being the chosen one, had fallen flat on my face. To gain a good understanding of the interaction between technology and war, I had to get back to history. In fact both disciplines aimed at the same objective. The former sought to understand the nature of things by first defining them and then relating the definitions to one another so as to form an interlocking web; the latter, by watching them develop over time.

Once the decision had been made, the rest proved surprisingly easy, and indeed it took me less than a year to finish the book from beginning to end. As a German friend of mine, Prof. Elisabeth Erdmann, once told me, at the time you are working on a book you think it is the best book ever written. Unless you believe that, you are not going to be able to write. Once you are finished, and your period of Beethoven-like joy is over, you cool down. For a time, you think it is the worst book ever. Finally, you see it for what it is: a book. That is the time to consider what you have done right and what you have done wrong and to start all over again.

Technology and War earned some critical praise and was even elected Book of the Year by the American Military Institute. It was also translated into Chinese and Korean. I still think it provides as clear, succinct, and comprehensive an account of the development of technology and war as there is. This is all the more so because it does not focus on weapons alone but has something to say on the technological infrastructure, from roads to computers, that forms the indispensable background for all military activities.

On the other hand, Marshall found *Technology and War* disappointing. It did not have the sharply defined, innovative conclusions that my previous work for him did. What conclusions it did have were not of much practical use. Once, after it was finished, he hissed at me that I should have written about how to use technology "to get at them" (the Soviets). It was only decades later, when I read his biography, that I really understood what a central part of his thought that was. Looking back, I wish I had had the wit to understand it myself or else that he had told me before I had started. The outcome would have been a different volume; although, perhaps, not one that people still keep reading more than three decades later.

One thing *Technology* did achieve was a manageable outline. It was my first attempt to go beyond case studies, and a big challenge it was. Many historians, academic ones in particular, never even try. In their eyes, the smaller and the more esoteric a subject, the higher its "scientific" value. It reminds me of the joke about the German professor who spent twenty years researching who had written the poems of Homer. only to conclude that it was not Homer but another poet whose name, too, was Homer.

Seriously, though, how does one master a subject that covers 4,000 years while simultaneously examining two such vast fields as technology on one hand and war on the other? What, in any case, does "mastery" of such a subject mean? Certainly, it cannot mean the same as when you describe the (political) activities of one person during one day, as I myself had done in the very first scholarly article I ever published. Where is one to start? Where is one to end? What comes first? What comes last? Where does one draw the limits? As Chairman Nikita Khruschev once said, no soldier can fight unless there is a button to hold up his trousers. Does that mean buttons are military technology? Or simply, did Khruschev mean that the subject can be stretched *ad absurdum*?

In the end the volume was divided into four parts, each starting with a brief introduction and each made up of exactly five chapters. Of the five chapters in each part, the first four deal with various aspects of war during the period covered whereas the fifth has a more integrative character. All the parts and all the chapters are more or less equal in length. I believe that if one subject takes up much more space than the rest, something must be wrong with the way you have organized your book. It is like a painting: creating a pleasant effect by means of an asymmetric design is much harder than doing the same with a symmetric one.

Yet the fact that all the parts of *Technology and War* are of approximately equal length is deceptive. The reason is that the periods they cover get shorter and shorter: 2000 B.C. to 1400 A.D., 1400 A.D. to 1830, 1830 to 1945, and 1945 to the present; here, too, the similarity to the foreshortening technique painters use is evident. Balance and symmetry apart, the other thing to aim at is simplicity. Ideally, an outline should be so simple as to enable a reader to grasp it at a glance. You should have neither too many chapters nor those nasty beasts, sub-sub chapters. If you do, and unless you are some exceptional genius, your book is probably not worth looking at.

Since my outlines are always very carefully worked out, when I tell people that I am an unsystematic worker, they do not believe me. Yet that is precisely the case. I start with an idea, however vague. Sometimes it is suggested by others, but more often it grows out of my previous work or else out of something I have read. Often, indeed, it is born out of the feeling that, having answered one question to my own satisfaction, I have missed the boat and that the truth I am looking for lies somewhere else. If this means that the quest is endless, then it may be better that way. A world in which everything is known and understood would not be worth living in. It could even be argued that, by always making the stone that Sisyphus pushed to the top of the hill roll down again, the gods, far from punishing him, gave him a purpose in "life." At least he had something to do, which is more than anybody else in the underworld could say.

I read some books about the subject, start taking notes, and try to write a preliminary research proposal. I soon find that the questions I asked are either the wrong ones or are only part of the problem. Being easily bored, I find it hard to focus on a single question for any length of time. Instead, I tend to look now at one, now at another, in the same way as, clearing the table after a meal, I like to start now with the plates, now with the flatware, so as to observe the different patterns that emerge. Long before I have read everything I should, my hands start itching. I feel the urge to put down my thoughts and, what is perhaps even more important, to arrange those thought in some kind or order. Almost always, the result is some fragment that tries to do too many things at once, connects them in the wrong way, and turns out to be useless. I wander into paths and bypaths, many of which appear to be *cul de sacs.*

Strangely enough, real progress starts at the point where I meet resistance, in other words where I am no longer free to do as I please. At first the number of directions I can take seems endless, and everything seems equally relevant and equally important. In time, however, each fact begins to mesh with some of the others. The outcome is that I cannot simply put in what I please and take fewer wrong turns. A sort of mental sieve goes into action, weeding out irrelevant ideas and focusing attention on the rest. The point comes where each paragraph has implications for all those that precede it and follow it. The book takes over and starts dictating its own outline, as it were.

By the time I reach my conclusions the range of options will have become very narrow. In a sense, if there *are* any options left, then I have probably failed to make my case. This, of course, does not mean that it is impossible to make changes. I suppose the experience of painters, musicians, moviemakers, and natural scientists is similar.

To put it differently, writing is by no means as one sided an activity as many people think. No sooner does the text one is working on come to life than it starts fighting back. The more progress one makes, the truer this becomes. In this sense writing has much in common with a wrestling match. The sensation of power that follows a victorious outcome is also similar.

Since it is not I but the wrestling match that really gives the book its shape, at the time I start I seldom know where I may be heading. Not knowing where I may be heading, I cannot explain it to others or systematically search for the sources I need. They, too, are as much an outcome of the wrestling match as a prerequisite for it. It is true that one can no more write history without sources than one can make bricks without straw. However, in my experience once you know what you are looking for, the sources will usually come crawling out of the woodwork.

In other words, it is not so much the availability of the material as the questions you ask of it that matter. Once again, this is an insight I owe to Geoffrey Warner who, even as he let me use the sources he had gathered, reached quite different conclusions. Another source was Elisabeth Erdmann, who used to say as much. The disadvantage of my method, if it deserves the name, is that I can only produce a proper research plan at a relatively late point in the process. More than once, applying for a grant, by the time I got it the project was already more or less finished.

Another disadvantage is that, in spite of several attempts, I have never been able to work with assistants. I always do my own research, fact finding, typing—even if it involves re-typing an entire book, as happened with the present volume after I accidentally erased it and was left with a printed copy only—picture finding, caption writing, indexing, and proofreading. Some people think doing so is a waste of time and employ armies of researchers to do these and other jobs. I myself think that the time I devote to these activities is, on the whole, well spent. Some I even enjoy. For example, producing a good index is by no means as routine or as easy as many people believe. Of course I could appoint assistants and make them run errands for me. As long as I stay healthy, though, I feel that doing so almost amounts to abuse, and I just cannot make myself do it.

If anything, the unsystematic way I work was reinforced by the switch to word-processing that, for me, took place in 1985. Arriving in London in 1969, one of the first things I did was to spend 40 pounds on an Olympia typewriter of which, at the time, I was very proud. Having pounded on it for twelve years, by the time I wrote *Command in War* it was in ruins, and I felt rich enough to change it for a second-hand IBM Selectric. Switching to a word processor—an Apple IIe—meant that I could now introduce as many changes as I wanted without having to recopy the entire page or use scissors, scotch tape, and a stapler to move paragraphs about. Since the same applied to the table of contents, the machine also made the process of planning a book easier or, at any rate, less costly. By so doing, it strengthened my tendency to forge ahead and to worry about the outcome later.

The computer also changed the way I worked in a more fundamental way. Previously, I used to separate research from writing, first collecting my material on record cards—the "black" part, as some called it—and then writing the book. Word-processing made it possible to combine the two phases. One reason for this is that almost any information one needs is always at one's fingertips. Another is that any material one collects can easily be moved from one place to another and, like some mythological creature, assume whatever shape one wants. Mastering the technical side of operating a computer was relatively easy. However, doing the same with regard to the new working methods it made possible was much harder and took me a couple of years. Some people, particularly older ones, never adapt and stay with their pens. As for me, I have almost forgotten how to handwrite, particularly in English.

The fact that a book is written with the help of a word-processor rather than a pen—or, for that matter, a quill—does not, of course, mean that its quality is higher. One reason for this is that editing has become so easy that you are in constant danger of overdoing it. The main reason, though, is that a computer can do anything except help you think. However good the equipment, you still need to go through an incubation period, complete with the crises that tend to come after you have started the book and as you are about to end it. Having said this, I must add that, now that I have long gotten used to word-processing, I cannot remember what life without it was like. Some years ago I happened to take a look at a manuscript copy of *Fighting Power* that was stored in some library. I could hardly believe my eyes. Did I type all this? Where did I find the stamina? Didn't it break my back? In fact, thinking of my days in Lahr, it *did* break my back. Yet *Fighting Power* is by no means a long book.

On Luttwak's advice I took on literary agents, Mr. Gabriele Pantucci and Ms. Leslie (they are a married couple) Gardner of Artellus Ldt, London. Over the years I have had nothing but good experiences with them. They are the kind of agents who understand the problems an author has while he is trying to write a book, which requires a warm heart as well as a cool head. They gave *Technology and War* to the Free Press, the first time I worked with a commercial publisher. My editor was Ms. Joyce Seltzer, who later moved to Harvard University Press. An extremely hard worker, she corrected the manuscript and sent it back for me for approval; opening the parcel, I found that, wielding an unmerciful pencil, she had struck out entire pages. I contacted her angrily, asking her how she dared tamper with the work of an important historian such as me. She told me—I think it was over the telephone—that I should take a look at what she had done and would see that she was right.

I did take a look, and I soon discovered she had done two things. First, she eliminated the equivocation. Had she been less polite, she

might as well have told me to cut the cackle. As a young student in
academia, one of the first things you learn is never to say never and
never to say always either. On the ground that life is complex (which
it is) and that academia requires precision (which it does), everything
must be hedged. It must be surrounded by qualifications, fenced-in
by cautionary phrases, and protected by clauses that will meet every
possible objection in advance. In short, it must be made as sticky and
opaque as a cup of tea with twenty spoonfuls of sugar in it. To call
a spade a spade—forgetting that, under some circumstances, a spade
may not be a spade after all—is worse than a crime. It is a mistake
and one that instantly identifies those who commit it as amateurs. A
decent academic text will take care not to do any such thing. As a
result, quite often, you may plow through the book from cover to
cover only to be left wondering what on earth the author wanted to
say.

Second, Joyce got rid of many paragraphs that dealt with philo-
sophical and methodological issues. Take the question of whether
war drives technology or the other way around. The problem itself is
surely important and has, indeed, given rise to quite some literature
written by people from Leon Trotsky down. However, a detailed
inquiry into the ways of solving it (if, indeed, it can be solved at
all) will only interest a few people. On this, too, Joyce was perfectly
right. Seeing that methodology is one of the factors that supposedly
separate them from ordinary mortals, academics often make a fetish
of it. In theory, it is a necessary condition for systematic thought. In
practice, too often people delve into it when they have nothing else
to say.

The outcome is the typical social science book. First comes a long
and learned explanation about why everybody else who tried to tackle
the subject got it wrong. Next comes an explanation of the author's
approach—the more complicated the better—and why it is the only
correct one. This tribute having been paid, the body of the book is
written as if all these explanations did not exist. I counter by telling

students that, when you enter a restaurant to have a meal, the last thing you want is to inspect the kitchen (in fact some people do want to inspect the kitchen, but I am not one of them). If you want to attract and keep your reader, there is no room for lengthy explanations of the ways, say, data can or cannot, should or should not, be gathered and classified and arranged. Explaining what you think and why you think what you think is hard enough.

This, of course, is not to say that methodology is not important, only that it should not be allowed to become uppity and to lift itself from a means into an end. Modesty becomes methodology as it does a woman. Ideally, it should be so perfectly embedded in your narrative as to be identical with it, so to speak. If, writing for academia, you feel that you absolutely cannot do without a detailed explanation of the methodology you have used or intend to use, then the best thing to do is stuff it away in some appendix. There, it can stay within reach of anybody who wants it or needs it, but doing no particular harm to anybody else.

The worst of all crimes, in my view, is to demand that doctoral students expound their methodology before they even start working on their thesis and before they have even had the opportunity to get their teeth into it by properly thinking about their subject. For myself, I was fortunate to do my thesis in the country I did, at the time I did, and under the supervisor I had. Had D. C. Watt asked me to explain my methodology at the outset, I would probably never have even started my thesis. As it was, his demand that I write down a list of ten "new ideas" I hoped to introduce was bad enough. The more so because, having read them, he told me they were not as new as I had thought. Others coming after me have been less fortunate. No wonder that, at Hebrew University and several other places, students are expected to take as long to submit their research plan as I did to complete my entire dissertation.

When I myself started guiding graduate students, I kept these considerations in mind. At our first meeting I ask the student to tell me what he or she would like to write about. Next, I send him or her home with the request to write three, or four, or five, pages on what he or she thinks he or she will do. I advise the student to divide his or her thoughts into the following, more or less fixed, parts. First, explain what your prospective title is. If at all possible, do so in six words or less. Second, explain what you envisage the final product to be—an article, a chapter in a book, a monograph, a book—and how long you expect it to be in terms of pages or, now that we all use computers, words. Third, explain what your research question(s) is or are. In other words, what exactly it is that you would like to know.

Fourth, explain in what order you are going to tackle your research question(s) by drawing up a provisional list of contents. III and IV are the most difficult parts. On the other hand, if you do them properly, you should be able to use them, in only slightly modified form, as an introduction to your work. Fifth, explain the kinds of sources you intend to use and provide a bibliography and/or list of sources arranged in such a way as to fit both the nature of the subject and the sources themselves. I hasten to add that none of what I say is binding and that they can introduce any number of changes later on. The main point is for them to provide me, and themselves, with an outline of their thoughts. Had it depended on me, three or four or five pages are all I would require. Incidentally, during all the years I worked for Mr. Marshall, he never asked for more. I still consider that one of his principal merits.

At about the same time Joyce taught me about methodology I also started my great war against footnotes. As a young student of the humanities, one of the first things you learn is that footnotes are very important even though, to say the truth, not many people bother to read them. As a young student of the social sciences, you also learn that footnotes are very important even though the kind of footnotes you are expected to put into your work is somewhat different. The difference is that historians care who wrote the sources they cite, where, when, and why. Social scientists often don't. For them, (John Nobody, 2003) is no different from (Adam Smith, 1776). Nor does it matter whether the source they are quoting is (Aristotle, 350 B.C.) or (Aristotle, 1999). Some of them, I suspect, do not even know that by the time the latest edition of his work came out, its author had been dead for some twenty-three hundred years. Nor is there any reason why they should, given that, after all, their job is not to find out what happened and why but to fit it into "models," "structures," and "paradigms."

What both disciplines have in common is that they use footnotes to certify that a given piece of work is, in fact, "scientific." The more footnotes you have, the more "scientific" your work. Perhaps, to help scholars, there should be established an IFF (International Footnote Fund) modeled on the IMF (International Monetary Fund). I see it as a sort of global bank located in a place such as Washington, D.C., New York, or Geneva. Members will promise to put in so and so many footnotes per year. In return they will receive special footnote-drawing rights (SF-DRs).

Nonmembers will be able to buy, lease, or borrow footnotes for so and so many cents each. Organized groups will get a discount, as in amusement parks. The footnotes themselves could be divided into first class, second class, and so on, and a separate tariff established for each category. Another possibility would be for the Fund to provide them with a certificate of authenticity. For a detailed proposal see Heinrich Heine, *Das Buch le Grand* (1827). With the aid of the Net, organizing the fund should be easy. Or else, thinking of Google Scholar, it already exists.

I, too, peppered my books with footnotes. Like many other young students, I used to count them with considerable pride. Not only did I want to see how many I had, but I also wanted to know how many there were per page. Nowadays, my own students sometimes ask me how much is enough. As a rough and ready guide, I tell them that two and a half a page is a fair number. Whereupon they gasp at my sophistication. As Heine also says in *Das Buch le Grand*, the more obscure the material referred to, the better the footnote.

The best footnotes of all contain material that is "unpublished" or "archival." Accordingly, I loved writing things like "Captain von und zu Verschwind to Lieutenant Colonel Suchmir, 6.8.1941, OKH [Oberkommando des Heeres]/Genst.d.H [Generalstab des Heeres] /Org.Abt. [Organisationsabteilung] II, Nr. 10962/41, Gkds [Geheime Kommandosache], GMR [German Military Records] T-706/0001131." Looking back, heaven knows where I found the patience. Before computers came to the rescue, each time you typed in a mistake, you had to redo the entire page. How the German soldiers who originally typed the documents managed to do so in their freezing, stinking ratholes is a greater miracle still. To misuse a phrase Voltaire once wrote about a false account that Frederick the Great gave of the Battle of Sohr (1743), turning it from a defeat into a victory by a stroke of the pen, *Voila ce que peut faire la discipline militaire*. Most mysterious of all, my editors at Cambridge University Press, instead of balking at this rubbish, agreed to print it. Perhaps they were even more scientific than I.

Technology and War was the first of my books that did not have any footnotes. In part, the reason was that I wrote it on my new Apple IIe—which, since it did not have an automatic renumbering command, turned the task of revision into a nightmare. In part, the reason was that the subject was too large. For each sentence it would have been possible to bring not one reference but twenty or more. As with the mythological hydra, each source only pointed the way to many others. Had I read everything available on the subject, the project would still be going on today. As I said, instead of always searching for new sources, my difficulty was how to decide which ninety percent of the available ones *not* to read. In the end, at Joyce's insistence, I substituted a bibliographical essay. Doing so is a quick and easy method of displaying your knowledge while at the same time putting down your competitors; whether it added to the book's quality, though, I doubt.

Yet the above difficulties only formed part of the story and not necessarily the most important one. Years ago, in class, somebody, who may have been a follower of Popper, said that the purpose of studying history was to disprove myths. I answered that, in my opinion, that was wrong. To be sure, disproving myths is a fine occupation for young historians eager to hone their skills and to make a name for themselves. In fact one of my own earliest published articles carried the subtitle, "the destruction of a legend." But mature scholars should aim higher. Much higher. Instead of disproving myths others have created, they should try to produce work so good as to *become* myths.

This line of thought explains why, at the age of forty-something, I was developing an obsession—one which, in retrospect, seems almost megalomaniac—with my books' ability to withstand the proverbial hand of time to the point where, dedicating *Technology* to Dvora, I did so *eis aeona*. To obtain an idea of how it was done, I spent considerable time and energy looking at some "timeless" books and analyzing them for eternality. Not surprisingly, the precise nature of the latter quality escaped me then and continues to escape me now.

However, I did make some interesting discoveries. The most important one was that hardly any of them had footnotes. Thucydides has no footnotes. To pile insult on injury, he says that the speeches, which many think are the best part of his entire work, are for the most part pure invention. That should certainly make some of us reflect on the nature of historical writing. Polybius, Sallust, Caesar, Tacitus, and Josephus do not have footnotes either. Nor do Augustine, Machiavelli, Locke, Voltaire, Rousseau, Carlyle, John Stuart Mill, Darwin, and, in my own field, Clausewitz. To say nothing of Nietzsche; like Heine, he would have laughed at the idea.

Probably the reason why these and so many others dispensed with footnotes was that they were not modern academics. Not being modern academics, they did not try to be "scientific." They did not have to compete for tenure by having their work evaluated by a committee, one whose members, instead of reading it, count (or rather, since the actual counting is done elsewhere, take note of), the number of times it is mentioned in scientific journals. Huizinga, who *was* a modern academic, in the introduction to *Homo Ludens* warns the reader not to expect documentation for every word. Another very good contemporary example is Humphrey Kitto's *The Greeks* (1951). So good is it that it sold over 1,500,000 copies. In the military field there is Michael Howard's *War in European History*. It is a real *tour de force* that, in my view, puts everything else he has written in the shade.

The more I reflected on the matter, the more it seemed to me that footnotes are characteristic of the mediocre book. The best books do not have them. But neither do the worst ones. Had *People* magazine tried to document its claims by this means, no doubt it would have gone bankrupt in less than a month. In a certain way, footnotes represent a compromise. If you think something is too important to be skipped altogether, but not important enough to be mentioned in the text, you can always put it into a footnote. Understood in this way, footnotes, far from being the mark of good scholarship, are merely a sign of indecision and, perhaps, cowardice.

The same is even truer of the kind of marginal notes that contain additional information. If, in the English translation of Michael Foucault's famous *Discipline and Punish*, practically all the footnotes have been omitted, then it is largely the author's own fault. Ink, paper, and typesetting are, or were, expensive. One cannot blame a publisher for failing to include material the author himself evidently considered second rate. Needless to say, this line of thought did not endear me to those of my colleagues with whom I discussed it, some of whom seem to believe footnotes are the pride of creation.

To repeat, normally the very best books are those that do not have footnotes. Nor would such a book be at all improved if it were provided with them. Imagine the Bible sprinkled with brackets, or little numbers, or a variety of other signs. Each one reminds the reader that this or that fact or idea had come not straight out of God's mouth but from such and such a source or else adds some kind of information that did not seem worthy of being included in the text itself.

I, too, hoped to write such a book. If it would not be one that would last forever, then at any rate it would be one that would fuse the argument and the evidence on which it rests so tightly that, like a creeper on an oak tree, they would become indistinguishable. Not to put too fine a point on it, I wanted what I wrote to be so good as to be almost self-evident. Agreement was to be achieved by persuasion, not by piling on authorities many of whom owe their presence on my pages precisely to their obscurity. This was the guiding idea behind *The Transformation of War*, a book I shall discuss in the next chapter. In my defense, all I can say is that I am willing to try anything.

With the general exception of the present volume, as well as one or two others that were commissioned by publishers who explicitly asked to have no footnotes, all the books I have written since *Transformation* have them. In part, the reason was that I was entering new and unfamiliar terrain such as women's history, American history, Israeli history, the history of conscience, and the history of equality. Academics tend to be suspicious of those who know too much or pretend to know too much. Accordingly, it was essential to show readers that I had done my homework and knew my stuff. In part, I found the task of doing without them—not of leaving them out, of course, but of writing a text so good as not to require them—beyond my capabilities.

To adduce but one example, I did not want to share the fate of Dorothy Dinnerstein in *The Mermaid and the Minotaur* (1976). The book, which earned considerable fame, is a diatribe whose purpose is to show that for mothers to look after their children is bad for both. In her introduction Dinnerstein, who died in 1992, says that, rather than providing footnotes, she hoped to write in such a way as to speak directly to every reader's heart. Instead, all she succeeded in doing was to show how much she herself hated the idea of sacrificing her glorious career. Assuming she followed her own advice, rather than stoop so low as to raise her children, she wrote two books about them. What this implies about her own mother, incidentally, is anybody's guess.

Chastened by her example, I climbed down from the heights, and indeed some would no doubt say I never reached them in the first place. I returned to common, or garden-variety, history. Eternity is a hard master; therefore, on the whole, it has been a happy decision. Still, I must confess that, on occasion, I rather regret the sensation that only striving for the ultimate heights can bring.

Chapter 4

Breaking Free

By the mid-1980s my published work had made me quite well known (Luttwak, in his inimitable, way, once told me that "you are the best, but only because there is nobody else in your lousy field"). Accordingly, I was delighted, but not entirely surprised, when I received a letter from Harvard University suggesting that I put up my candidacy for a chair in a new organization they were about to set up. The institute, or center, or school, or whatever it was called, was supposed to specialize in military history, strategy, and international affairs. Harvard wanted it to become the most important of its kind in the Western World, and my job would be to make it so.

The post would mean administration, maintaining contact with Congress and other government organizations, fundraising, and the like. Hence I knew at once it was not for me. Besides, it would mean leaving Israel for the U.S. on a permanent basis, something I, the son of Jewish parents who went through the Holocaust, have never seriously considered doing and would not advise my children to do. Still, since they had invited me, I decided to go over and have a look. The campus is beautiful, and the surroundings are civilized. Nevertheless, it was dislike at first sight. I gave a talk to graduate students, all of them from upper-middle class families and all of them behaving like dressed-up penguins. They were polite and intelligent but did not seem to have any purpose in life except, in a lackadaisical way, to advance themselves. Nor, given the way American society is built, was there any reason why they should. The thought of having to spend my life as a teacher playing the clown to such people, many of whom obviously had more money and came from a more snobbish background than I, did not please me. The dislike was mutual, and I never heard from them again.

In 1986–87, instead of going to Harvard, my wife and I went to NDU, or National Defense University, in Washington, D.C. Of course we had been to the U.S. before. Still, we found it quite hard to adjust. Even our bitch, Sandy, took months before she felt sufficiently sure of herself to talk to American dogs; once, she got lost, something that never happened before or after, and we spent hours looking for her. Later, we started enjoying American life, and I have many fond memories of it.

Academically, though, the year was not a success. In theory NDU is the equivalent of Harvard, the most important center of military learning in the world. In practice I found it problematic. The main reason was that the faculty, consisting of colonels, is barely distinguishable from the students, who are lieutenant colonels and, unless they really go wrong, are scheduled to become colonels in two or three years. Worse still, the students include a number of "under the horizon" colonels who, for some reason known only to the gnomes at manpower, enter the university at a later point in their career. With the result that, in their case, the difference between them and the military members of the faculty is exactly zero.

Second, even the younger students were lieutenant colonels in their early forties who had already commanded a battalion or equivalent. People who have reached such an age and such a position cannot be made to behave as if they were eighteen-year-old freshmen attending courses and discussing "issues." As to writing, they well know that their papers will be read only by some professor if, indeed, they will be read by anyone at all. This is all the more so because that professor has no influence on their careers and because the reason why many of them entered military life in the first place is precisely that they did not want to spend their lives writing at some desk. The fact that I was slightly younger than my students did not improve things. In the military, where rank and age go closely together, this was a considerable handicap, and I am grateful to my students for never rubbing it in on me.

What made things even worse was their habit of piling up the paper. I had an office in the basement where nobody could see me, the kind of place a visitor usually gets. Arriving in the morning and switching on the light, I would find perhaps three inches of paper with everything that had happened at the university and that I was supposed to know. I would spend thirty minutes going over it, occasionally reading an item that caught my interest but mostly trying to decide which ten percent to read and which ninety percent to throw away. The next morning would bring more paper, and the process would repeat itself. Somewhere in the building there must have been an army of Stakhanovites who operated the photocopiers. After a few days, there would be a pile three inches thick containing all the stuff I had decided to read, at which point I would throw *it* away and start all over again. In the end, I seldom read anything I got. The only purpose served by the torrent of paper that reached me, and presumably everybody else as well, was to reduce the time I had for doing serious work.

As an academic in the humanities, I had always been a loner, spending my time either doing research in the library or archives or writing at home. At NDU, however, I discovered I was expected to be in the office, or, better still, pretend that I was around and might enter my office at any moment. Those who were absent from the building did not count. Those who were at their desks, attending their own business, also did not count. What you really needed was to have a "busy schedule," which showed how important you were and how many people you met. To create the impression that your schedule was indeed a busy one, you had to leave the door to your office open. If it was closed, then that was a sign you had not shown up for the day and were probably taking it easy. But taking it easy was a sin almost as bad as murder. An open office door did not mean you had to be inside. To the contrary, the whole idea was for the office to be empty. An open door leading to an empty office meant that you were somewhere else in the building, meeting important people and, hopefully, helping make important decisions. With some of those people you might actually have lunch.

The logic came straight out of *Catch 22*. Following it, everybody at NDU pretended to be studying very hard but, in fact, was doing very little. I doubt whether, from beginning to end, even one of the students I taught read an entire book. A friend who is in the know has told me that by now it is impossible to make them read two pages. It was not that they did not have their reasons. For one things, they were made to spend far too many hours in class, listening to endless lectures. For another, both they and the faculty were supposed to play sports. At the Militärgeschichtliches Forschungsamt, which is also a military installation devoted to study, sports were something those who wanted to did once a week in a friendly way. I myself always found that running got me into a sort of trance that could be very useful in freeing the mind; some of my best ideas came to me when, my brain filled with dopamine, I was going along. Then, having calmed down and taken a shower, we would all go for a glass of beer.

At NDU, nor only was any form of alcohol strictly out of bounds, but sports were taken very seriously. At 1145 hours—presumably selected because it is about the lousiest time in a lousy climate—all work ceased. Men and women went to play softball, to exercise at the gym, or to do whatever. I myself took a six-mile run, never mind that much of it was over paved roads and thus as bad for the knees of us forty-year-olds as bad could be. My companion on these runs was an air force colonel who was later promoted to brigadier. Slightly older than I, he was married to a much younger woman; perhaps this explains why he always insisted on going all out and arriving just ahead of me.

Having exercised, everybody would shower. Their shaved chests were another peculiarity of American life that never ceased to surprise me. Next, they would eat a light lunch. Partly because they were military and supposed to work very hard, partly because most lived in Northern Virginia and hoped to beat the traffic, it was not unusual for people to rise at 0530 hours and to come into the office at 0700. By the time they had finished lunch, they were too tired not just to work but to think. They, and of course I, spent the rest of the afternoon nodding away, waiting for a decent opportunity to go home.

In time, the weird atmosphere got on my nerves. Not being a regular member of the faculty, I enjoyed more freedom than most of the rest. To keep up appearances, I made an arrangement that I would show my face twice a week and be free to do as I pleased the rest of the time, which meant either going to the Library of Congress or working at home. Doing so, I discovered that the area in and around the beltway is not very conducive to scholarship. As I said before, in my view a good place to work in should both central and quiet. As the most important capital city in the world, Washington was definitely central. But it was anything but quiet. In Freiburg, as an acquaintance once pointed out to me, the world only reached you in a somewhat dampened form. In Washington it was screaming at you sixty minutes an hour, twenty-four hours a day, seven days a week. So much happens all the time, all of it terribly important and terribly urgent, that one cannot hear oneself think.

Nevertheless, and perhaps because I was doing very little *real* work, it was during my stay at NDU that I began to notice that something was very wrong with military history as I had studied it thus far and also with whatever understanding of war I had gained thereby. It came about roughly as follows. In the spring of 1986, shortly

before leaving for my year at NDU, Harvard University Press asked
me whether I would like to review a manuscript that Luttwak had
submitted to them and they were about to publish. I agreed and
found myself immersed in what was to become *Strategy: The Logic of
War and Peace*. I thought then, and I still think now, that the first
chapter, in which the author tries to explain the qualities that make
war unique among human activities, was brilliant. In fact it is one of
the best pieces of military theory I have ever read.

As I went over it, though, I found myself in disagreement with
one important point. Time after time, Luttwak would suggest that
this or that quality was essential to war and unique to it. Each time
this happened I would underline the relevant sentence and write in
the margins, "and games as well." Of course, many games resemble
war in that they have two opponents who play against each other
and try to defeat each other. To this extent, the logic that Luttwak
exposed and called "paradoxical" applied to both. The difference is
that games have rules that define them whereas in war the rules, if
they exist at all, are of a different kind altogether. Within a year
or two this line of thought was to bring me into a head-on clash
with Clausewitz and the whole of modern strategy. As I discussed
the matter with Luttwak, though, I had no idea where my marginal
comments would ultimately lead.

At NDU, my sense that there existed a deep, hitherto rather neglected, link between warfare and games was reinforced. This, after
all, was the most important military school located in the capital
of the most powerful nation in the most powerful alliance in history. Every few weeks a meeting was held, attended by some twenty
lieutenant colonels and a few faculty members. The theme of the
gatherings was always the same: what should we, kindly freedom-
loving Americans, do in case the wicked, but unfortunately strong,
Soviets launched an offensive on the nice, but unfortunately weak,
Europeans? A desultory discussion would ensue, with one person
around the table suggesting this and another that. However, it

was only a question of time—usually, a fairly short time—before somebody raised the issue of nuclear weapons, asking what would happen if one belligerent used even one of the many thousands each was training on the other. Scratching their heads, those assembled in the room would look around and agree that, since escalation was almost certainly inevitable, such use would spell the end of the war. And, of course, of the discussion, too.

In February 1987 the class, me included, went to Colorado Springs to visit NORAD (North American Aerospace Defense). I remember the date because it straddled St. Valentine's Day, which upset quite a few of the participants in the trip. I was the only non-American in the group. As such, I was also the only one not permitted to enter the famous war room with its gigantic screen. It shows the deployment of America's nuclear forces around the world. My protests that it, or replicas of it, had been shown in countless films, including *Dr. Strangelove* and *Wargames*, were to no avail. At the time email did not exist, and even fax machines were very rare. So perhaps they thought I might go to the nearest phone, call the Soviet Embassy, and tell them the current location of the bombers and naval task forces so that the Kremlin could start World War III by delivering a knockout blow.

As my escort, I had a young female lieutenant. She showed me such fascinating tidbits as the springs on which the installation rested, the emergency diesel engines, and the place they stored the food that was supposed to last those who worked there for so and so many months if nuclear war came. I soon lost interest and asked her to take me outside. High up, on the flank of Mount Cheyenne, there is a parking lot overlooking the prairie. It may have been the contrast with the claustrophobic feeling inside—created by the surroundings as well as the ubiquitous signs, "the use of lethal force authorized"— that did the trick. Sitting on a stone, waiting for the others to come out, I had what I can only call a mystic experience. I seemed to breathe in America, oh land of spacious skies. The result was a sense of freedom I, coming from little, crowded Israel, can only envy. Many years later, talking to an American woman who had been there, I learned she had felt as I had.

More to the point, my abortive visit to NORAD reinforced my doubts about the nature of nuclear strategy. The purpose of the installation, which has cost billions upon billions of dollars and which is probably the most heavily fortified one on Earth, is to serve early warning in case nuclear-tipped intercontinental missiles are launched at the U.S. Thanks to an inconceivably complex network of satellites, radars, communication links, and computers, it is able to do to with about half an hour to spare before the missiles arrive and Armageddon strikes. I think I can honestly say I know more about nuclear deterrence theory than most people do, yet when everything is said and done, I must wonder about the purpose of it all. Suppose I, as a private individual, had been told that I was going to die in an earthquake half an hour hence and that there was absolutely nothing I could do about it. How useful would that information be to me? How much would I be prepared to pay to have it? Any amount? Nothing at all? Would I even *want* to know?

Here, then, was the great paradox. Clearly, nuclear weapons were the most powerful ever built by far. Precisely for that reason, the efforts of NORAD and the money invested in it appeared, in one sense, both futile and wasteful. Three decades later, I still do not think that anti-ballistic missile defenses are likely to change this situation in any meaningful way. The irony was even more evident back at NDU. There, the very mention of nuclear weapons invariably put an end to any attempt to understand how a nuclear war should be fought. The same, incidentally, was true for the so-called "technothrillers" that were being published at that time, such as John Hackett's *The Third World War* and Tom Clancy's *Red Storm Rising*. Both envision foreshortened repetitions of World War II. And both come to an end almost as soon as nuclear weapons enter the picture.

At the time, 1986–87, the Cold War was still as omnipresent as ever. Everybody agreed there would be a "first strike" and, rising phoenix-like amidst the ruins, a "second strike" to retaliate for it. After that, however, all that would be left was something known as "broken-back warfare." It would be waged by starving men wielding sticks and stones in a freezing, radioactive desert. No wonder each time somebody brought the matter up, everybody else in the room hated him. Conversely, one could discuss warfighting only as long as one put on an act of make-believe and pretended nuclear weapons did not exist.

By then I had read enough Huizinga to realize that make-believe is an essential element in many forms of game or play. At a more mundane level, I had often played with my children by pretending to be a dinosaur, rolling my eyes, waddling around with bent knees, making what I hoped were dinosaur-like noises, and preparing to swallow them alive. Watching his or her offspring as they are half-terrified by the experience and half-driven into laughter by it, no parent can overlook the element of pretense involved. Indeed, the whole point of the game is that it is hard to say where reality stops and pretense begins. Combined with what I had learned from Luttwak, discovering this second link between war and play made me wonder what it all meant.

Meanwhile, my year at NDU was drawing to an end. One morning, on the wall next to my office, there appeared a map. It was filled with colored pins departing students used to mark the places they were going on their next assignments. Some went to Greenland, others to Argentina, and others still to Japan or New Zealand. To me, coming from little Israel, it presented a most impressive lesson in the meaning of global power. At the graduation ceremony we listened to an address by the Chief Navy Chaplain. Among other things, he said that the U.S. was the only country in history that had been founded expressly in order to realize the ideal of freedom and justice. A student of mine was standing right next to me on the grass. He turned to me and asked if I thought that was correct. I answered that, however strange the interpretation Americans sometimes put on their ideal and however much that ideal may have been corrupted in practice, what the chaplain was saying was quite true. Nothing that has happened since then has made me change my mind.

Having returned home, what gave me the decisive push was the outbreak of the first Palestinian Uprising or *Intifada*, in December 1987. The uprising took the IDF by surprise. Twenty years had passed since the June 1967 war. Though there had always been some resistance, only a few days previously the Israeli official in charge of "coordinating operations" in the Occupied Territories had characterized Israeli rule over them as "a great success." The Minister of Defense was Yitzhak Rabin. He grossly underestimated the importance of what was going on; instead of orchestrating a response, he went on a visit to the U.S. to haggle over the price of some F-16 fighter-bombers.

From then on the IDF never recovered its equilibrium. Over the next few years it used the most varied methods to deal with the uprising, from beatings to curfews and from house-to-house searches to roadblocks. It also put into use some esoteric devices such as a telescopic rod for pulling down Palestinian flags and a converted half-track that, like a shotgun, fired gravel at demonstrators. To no avail, as one wave after another of highly motivated Palestinian youths armed, for the most part, with sticks and stones took over. Since then, some periods have been more violent than others. But only a fool will believe that, as long as Israel retains Palestinian territory, things will definitely quiet down.

Until then most of my work had dealt with large-scale conventional warfare, the reason being that neither I nor practically anyone else doubted that such warfare was the most important of all. My only real attempt to grapple with what people at the time called guerrilla, or low-intensity warfare (the term terrorism was only beginning to come into vogue), was a chapter in *Command in War* that analyzed the American experience in Vietnam. Instinctively, I knew that what was happening in the Occupied Territories was more like Vietnam than like the 1956, or 1967, or 1973 wars (which Israel had won). Since it was so much like Vietnam, Algeria, or any number of similar conflicts, there was clearly no way Israel was going to win. What I did not even begin to understand was the logic of the thing—in other words, *why* the IDF would not be able to put the uprising down. The more so because it was a thousand times more powerful than the Palestinians. As of 2017, the balance remains as skewed as it has ever been.

By that time I had been working with Mr. Marshall for close to a decade. Not only had he been very generous, but on no single occasion did he put any pressure on me to modify my conclusions. In fact, so close mouthed was he that I was never able to learn what the conclusions he wanted were, if any. Having decided that I wanted to do something on the relationship between war and games, I approached him with a research proposal for a study to be entitled, tentatively, *Games of War*. Later, I learned that a book with that title was just coming out. However, having read it, I did not let that fact disturb me unduly. The book in question did not so much try to understand war as a game, which was what I had in mind, but made an attempt to describe the kind of wargames played at the Pentagon in order to test scenarios, devise policies, and the like. Even with this limited purpose in mind, I thought it had been written by someone who did not really grasp the subject and, instead of analyzing what wargames could or could not do, told stories about them. It robbed me of my title, but that was all.

What I was thinking of was a two-sided study that would do two things at once. Going into much greater depth than the book just mentioned, it would explain how games could be used to simulate war and have been so used since time immemorial. At the same time, it would explore war *as* a game. Somehow the two equations—a game = war and war = a game—had to be linked to what was happening during the *Intifada*. However, at the time I had no idea how I was going to create the connection. Perhaps it was the vagueness of the research proposal I presented him with that made Mr. Marshall refuse to award me a contract. Or else he did not like the idea of me taking up games, a subject about which, I later discovered, he knew much more than I did. However, it is also possible that he was disappointed with some of the other work I did for him. I was never able to find out. All I know is that, from 1992 on, he rejected every proposal I submitted to him. Be it on the future of the air force, or Syrian counterinsurgency in Lebanon, or information warfare, or anything else.

After ten years of working for him, not getting another contract was a serious blow. Throughout the nineteen eighties I derived much of my status, both at Hebrew University and elsewhere, from the fact that I was active as a "consultant" for the largest and most powerful defense establishment in the world. It didn't matter that I was but a cog in an inconceivably vast machine and that my real influence, like that of my comrades in arms, was, to put it mildly, by no means always apparent. Now that it became increasingly clear that my salad days were drawing to an end, my self-esteem suffered. Nevertheless, after some time had passed, I came to regard his refusal as a blessing. However much freedom I had enjoyed in my writing, I was beginning to try to guess what he *might* want me to write and dress up my research proposals accordingly. It is the essence of commercial life that, once you have succeeded in landing a contract, you immediately start looking for the next one. Had our relationship continued, it would no doubt have turned me into a Marshall-watcher; albeit probably not a very successful one. Looking back, I consider myself lucky for having had the experience of working for him and also for having regained my freedom at the time I did and in the way I did, gradually and without any open conflict.

While this was going on, I was slowly beginning to break with Clausewitz. Like everybody else in my generation who took an interest in war, I had been brought up on the knees of the great philosopher. His thought not only determines the way we wage war but even, to a considerable extent, our understanding of its nature. By and large, this is as true of those who did not read him, the vast majority, as of those who did; perhaps more than most, I was aware of my debt to him and remain so to the present day. In so far as he emphasizes the two-sided, interactive, nature of war as well as the role that chance plays in it, Clausewitz is well aware of the game-like element it contains. Still, in the end he sees war as a very serious activity directed toward a very serious end. To quote my late senior colleague, Professor General (ret.) Yehoshaphat Harkavi, war is not a fart.

Now, however, my interest in the game-like aspects of war was beginning to pull me in a different direction. I started asking whether it might not better be understood as an irrational activity that either has no end or is an end in itself. Also whether, like many other games, it might not contain an important element of make-believe. Furthermore, Clausewitz made me reflect on the meanings of "strength" and "weakness." Had he not written that, in war, the best strategy was always to be very strong? If he were right, then the question arose why my own country, one of the most powerful armed forces, organized and trained and equipped with everything modern technology has to offer, was unable to cope with a handful of insurgents, people who never had more than pistols, hand grenades, homemade rifles, and, later, improvised explosive devices filled with nails.

In this way, though it took me a long time to realize it, reading Clausewitz actually started producing a link between the two phenomena that puzzled me: namely, the relationship between war and games on the one hand and the future of the Palestinian Uprising on the other. This was 1987–88, and I still had a very hard time clarifying my questions to the point where I would be even vaguely capable of expressing them in an orderly manner, let alone answer them. To sort out the confusion, I decided to teach a seminar on the history of wargames. As Alfred Mahan found out when he was planning *The Influence of Sea Power on History*, the best work ever written on the theory of naval warfare, teaching a subject has the very great advantage in that it compels you to think about what comes first and what comes last. Another advantage is that it enables you to discuss a subject again and again until, having answered all the questions and read all the papers, it becomes like putty in your hands. To reach this point, you need a sounding board. Had students not existed to act as one, they would have to be invented. I even began to suspect that one reason why they *have* been invented is precisely to help us professors think. Be this as it may, I always found that teaching, so far from interfering with my research, helped push it along.

The seminar turned out to be a memorable one on several counts. First, it served as smashing confirmation of the fact that war is in fact a game. In no other course I ever gave did the (male) students ever wax so enthusiastically. Trying to reach the blackboard in order to illustrate their thoughts, some of them literally jumped on tables, almost causing the latter to overturn and injuring themselves. Second, it enabled me to bring along ten-year-old Jonathan, he who fifteen or so years later asked me to write this book, to demonstrate to the participants an early version of the computerized wargames that were then beginning to be sold. He did so with great success, helping open an animated discussion on the nature of war and the extent to which certain parts of it were capable of being simulated.

Even more interesting was the fact that, from the point of view of the person who sits behind the screen, whether or not the blips he sees and tries to manipulate represent "reality" does not matter. One could indeed argue that a push-button warrior would be well served if he were deliberately made to think that what he was doing had no link to the real world. Doing so would reduce his anxiety level as well as any moral scruples he might have and enable him to focus on his work; such a scenario was explored in Orson Scott Card's excellent science-fiction volume *Ender's Game*. To this extent, much of modern warfare, especially that which takes place at sea, in the air, and in outer space, has already turned into a game, as those who spend tens of millions of dollars developing and buying simulators realize full well.

Third, the seminar caused me to cut the subject in half. It happened one day when, for some inscrutable reason, most of the students failed to show up. Not wanting to upset my carefully constructed program, I spent an hour and a half idly explaining what I thought I was trying to do to the two who did. I started with the problem of wargames—their origins, history, the ways in which they resembled and did not resemble war, what one could and could not do with them, and so on. Next, I passed to the question of real-life war *as* a game. Somehow, my ruminations on that subject must have struck a chord, for one student, Mr. Oz Fraenkel, raised his hand.

At the time Fraenkel was in his late twenties and had already accumulated considerable experience as a journalist. Now he made a comment on something that was puzzling him. The wargames played by Jonathan, or for that matter in the Pentagon, were no doubt interesting and might even be essential for training, modeling, planning, and forecasting purposes. Still, compared to the other half of my subject, i.e. war *as* a game, they were small, almost trivial. It was like studying an elephant and its tail, all the while pretending that the two were of equal size and importance. Given this discrepancy, he could not help wondering why I wanted to combine both in the same book. By that time I had already spent considerable energy researching the problem. Instead of jumping at Oz's suggestion, I resisted it. It took me weeks to grasp what he was saying, let alone to convince myself that he was right.

In retrospect, abandoning one half of my subject was a great leap forward. At the time I did not realize this but felt like a man who, having lost a limb, continues to suffer from phantom pains. When the seminar ended, I invited the students to a party at my home. One of the students, a Ms. Varda Bach, had unsuccessfully tried to teach me Bridge. Now she came up with a cake in the form of a chessboard, complete with all the figures. It was great fun; but it also underlined the fact that I had still made precious little progress. Teaching a seminar on Clausewitz the next year, I kept mulling over the subject, no doubt to my students' despair. Instead of presenting them with a clear thesis they could understand, discuss, and write down, I kept straying into stranger and stranger places. In particular wargames, though they had been thrown out through the door, refused to disappear. Instead, they kept coming back into my mind by way of the window.

Just how I reached the ideas underlying *The Transformation of War* I can no longer recall. The riddle of what used to be known as inspiration and is now called creativity has preoccupied others beside me. So confused and inscrutable is the process that any attempt to remember and rationalize it for other people to understand can only lead to distortion. On the other hand, should you try to document it as you go along, then you will probably find yourself doing nothing else. Unless you are Virginia Woolf, thinking about what you think and do not think and should be thinking will make you end up even more confused than you are. What I do recall quite vividly are the frustration, the pain, and the despair which were among the most intense I have ever known. Having abandoned the warm security of Clausewitz, I felt as vulnerable as a snail that has lost its shell. For a time my attention was distracted by the need to complete other work, namely *The Training of Officers*. Once that had been accomplished, the anguish returned.

Repeatedly, I made notes, filed them, and, returning to them after a few days or weeks, found them useless. Repeatedly, I produced drafts, got stuck, and put them aside. I drew up outlines only to realize that they were too simple and, paradoxically, too well organized to contain my contradictory thoughts. My usual obsession took over, but this time it grew and grew almost to the point of madness. Some of the madness was deliberate, if such a thing is possible at all. I tried to force myself to think "strange" thoughts that did not, could not, fit into the accepted framework. One by one, I was forced to jettison many of my convictions.

Not the least important of them was the belief, which Clausewitz promulgated and which his present-day successors have almost turned into dogma, that history changes so fast and so radically that only recent events have valid "lessons" to offer. The truth, I began to think, might well be the opposite. The main thing about the past is not its ability to tell us what to do and what to avoid. Rather, studying it is like taking a sabbatical in a foreign country, only cheaper. It can put us in touch with times, places, and thought processes so unlike our own so as to throw the latter into sharp relief: mirror, mirror on the wall, who are we if we are anybody at all? Thus it drives home, not once but time and time again, the fact that what is has not always been, nor all that can be, nor all that will be, nor all that must be. We all share a tendency to steer our lives and thoughts into a predictable groove from which, after a time, we find it hard to escape, That is why, in my view, this is the most important lesson any person can learn in his or her life. Later, reading Marc Bloch, I was happy to find that he agreed.

Then, as suddenly as always, the wave broke. It was an unusually cool, cloudy morning in the spring of 1989. At that time Dvora, who can do anything, was trying her hand as a real estate agent. So I found myself alone at home. Unable to make progress, I paced the floor of the living room, angrily muttering to myself about the fact that I did not work and could not work and would make no progress even if I did work. The next thing I knew, the earth shook, and the sky opened. I saw a chair or throne. It had the angular proportions

of sixteenth-century Spanish furniture, but its color was white. On
it was a blinding light, and it was surrounded by angels. All of them
were playing their violins with all their might; no anemic plucking of
harps, please. I am not ashamed to say that, after months and months
when I was sometimes close to eating the carpet, I sank to my knees
on that very carpet. Looking back, the strangest thing about it is that,
being an unbeliever, I am not sure what I saw or whom to thank. All
I knew, and know, and will know to my dying day, is that I wanted
to thank somebody or something. And if people call it God, then
that is fine with me.

✳ ✳ ✳

I do not wish to pretend that *Transformation* is as earth-shaking
as some other books have been. Believing that my experience is not
untypical, though, I do want to describe my experience in writing it.
As was only fitting, I called the computer files into which I typed the
chapters of the new book Genesis.

At the time, I was still using my old Apple II. Its memory was far
too small to contain an entire book, so I had Genesis I.1, Genesis
I.2, and so on stored on the old black floppy disks; looking back, I
am at a loss to understand how I ever dared entrust my work to such
fragile devices. Here and there material was lost, usually through
some stupid mistake of mine. On such occasions I used to rant and
rave for half an hour before throwing myself on the computer in an
attempt to restore the material before it faded from memory. It is
one of the most thankless jobs there is, and I hope I shall not have to
repeat it too often. In favor of the Apple II, which I still have, I shall
say it is the only computer of which I have ever heard that has never
broken down. Given a little luck, one day it will be worth a lot of
money as a museum piece.

For all my joy, finishing the book took another year. As is often the
case, good writing was like having good sex; page after page gushed

out almost without conscious effort on my part. As usual, it did not last. Twice more I got stuck, and even pouring out my heart to Gabriele Pantucci during a walk in London Regents' Park brought no relief at first. For several months I found myself grinding forward at a paragraph a day, endlessly writing sentences and striking them out. Even after the book was finished, I took the time to understand that what I had really done—at least in my own mind—was to create a new paradigm of war that stands to Clausewitz as Plato stands to Aristotle or, if you will, Nietzsche to Marx. Incidentally, the reason why I keep mentioning the names of these and other great men is that I admire them.

Nor do I apologize for what some think is hero-worship. As has been said, if no one is a hero to his servant, then the reason is not that there are no heroes. Rather, the reason is that many servants cannot see a hero even when they are standing right in front of one. Did not Pilate, confronted by Jesus and hearing Him say, "I am the truth," ask, "What *is* truth?" Studying the heroes of the spirit, I often find that they have expressed my thought much better than I can. Perhaps that is why I like to think of them as my friends. I can only hope that, had they been around, they would have agreed to be mine. In class, I like to play games with them. At the risk of becoming a schizophrenic, I pretend they sit beside me and that I engage them in questions and answers. Machiavelli in a wonderful passage describes how, come evening, he used to put on his best clothes and do exactly the same.

Those interested in what war, as I see it, really is will have to read the book. Here, I shall merely sum up what I consider to be the principal points. The most decisive factor, on which everything else depends, is the steady proliferation of nuclear weapons. Their spread is making major wars between major states, which are based on what Clausewitz called the "trinitarian" division of labor between a government that directs, armed forces that fight and die, and a civilian population that pays and suffers, fade away. The same process is overtaking the modern, conventional armed forces that have been organized for fighting it and, perhaps, the political entities—states—that have been organized for directing it.

Seeking to survive, most of the organizations in question refuse to look facts into the face. Instead, they cling to a fast-disappearing world. Even as their size is declining, they "modernize" and buy more high-tech weapons. For lack of important real-life wars, they make more and more of their personnel study "strategy." Indeed, it would almost be true to say that, the fewer wars a country fights, and the less important those it does fight, the more specialists in strategic studies it has. Nor is this surprising, given that a single attack helicopter costs as much as the annual pay of two hundred professors. To a large extent, they are playing a game of make-believe. The similarity of those games to the tournaments Huizinga describes in *The Waning of the Middle Ages* is unmistakable. Then as now, their real function may well be to act as a veneer for a deep feeling of despair.

What makes the matter vitally important is the fact that, even as the proliferation of nuclear weapons is fast consigning old forms of war to the dustbin of history, new ones have begun to take their place. The wars in question are not waged by states—at any rate, not on both sides. They are not based on the "trinitarian" division of labor states have established in their own interest. Instead of governments to direct wars, more and more we see religious leaders who tell their followers that their reward for blowing themselves up will be seventy-two virgins in Heaven and, some add, a nonstop erection to service them all. Instead of smartly uniformed soldiers strutting around, we see terrorists who do what they can to blend into the general population, lying low in safe houses, using Internet cafes to talk to one another, and flying around the world to avoid capture.

Instead of tanks, armored personnel carriers, artillery, and all the rest, we have Katyusha rockets, car bombs, and nerve gas pumped into a city's underground transportation system. Instead of convoys upon convoys of trucks carrying every kind of equipment, we see all sorts of suspect bank accounts in the Cayman Islands and women carrying drugs in their purses to pay for arms. Since their purpose was to confront one another, existing armed forces are only marginally useful for fighting the new wars. This is proved by the fact that, trying to fight the insurgents in Afghanistan and Iraq, the American ones have probably spent more *billions* of dollars than Al Qaeda ever had members. Nor will it do to ignore these developments. In the words of my friend, Bill Lind, they who put their heads in the sand will end up by being kicked in the behind.

The second, and to my mind even more important, argument of *Transformation* is that war is not primarily a rational instrument to a rational end. True enough, it may be so from the point of view of those whom Clausewitz was addressing, i.e. policy-makers, commanders, and staff officers like himself. By that, of course, I do not mean to say that those people are necessarily more "rational" than the rest of us. I mean only that, for them, to do anything but that, in their best judgment, which is in the best interests of the community they serve is criminal.

Things are different at the bottom of the socio-military pyramid. Those we meet at this level, often while they are crawling through the mud in their pain and despair, seldom know what their country's "policy" and "strategy" are all about. Nor do they care. Yet it is they who must leave their nearest and dearest, put their lives at risk, and, quite likely, die. But dying for some "rational" goal is a contradiction in terms; the reason is that dead men do not have goals, rational or otherwise. It is true that men may be prepared to die for family, country, king, class, race, and so many other things that, had all of them been properly listed and discussed, the result would have been tantamount to a history of humanity. It is equally true that doing so as a "rational" act simply does not make sense. The book of *Ecclesiastes* has the last word on this: better the live dog than the dead lion.

To put it another way, killing in itself is not war but a massacre. That is why those who engage in it, be they executioners or concentration camp guards, hardly ever gain the respect of society. It is the readiness to risk one's own life and to die if necessary that makes war what it is; as the fact that officers sometimes go into battle armed with no more than symbolic weapons proves, there are even situations where it can consist *only* of dying. However, this readiness can only well up from irrational sources, as it were. To quote Frederick the Great, whose expertise on these matters was second to none, "The one thing that can make men march into the muzzles of the guns that are trained at them is honor." In so far as no armed force can fight a war unless its members are prepared to lay down their lives, this irrational element is at least as important as anything else. More, even, it is probably the only one for which there is no substitute.

In Clausewitz's favor it must be said that he realized this fact. Still, out of almost 900 pages in *Vom Kriege*, all he does is give it a few pages. He was probably worried that, had he written much more in an attempt to describe what it is really like, he might have degenerated into mere sentimentality, as has happened to so many others before and since. His followers, particularly those who pride themselves on being "neo-realists," have done much worse. With them, words like "honor," "sacrifice," and "heroism" are often accompanied by a sneer. Like those of my teachers who looked down on Plutarch as a "moralist," but with less reason, they close their eyes to the fact that there is more to life, and especially to death, than interest alone.

To the extent that war does not have a rational objective, it resembles a game of the kind described by Schiller, Huizinga, and Piaget, among others. Moreover, and here I return to Luttwak, it is the kind of game that is played not against fate—though there is an element of that, too—but against an opponent who is as strong and as intelligent as oneself. It is certainly true that each belligerent is constrained by circumstances. At the same time, however, each belligerent is to a large extent free to do as he sees fit. Being free, he does what he can to achieve his own objectives while trying to prevent the enemy from doing the same. Since the same is true of many different games from chess all the way to football, the same kind of logic governs all of them.

Whatever the kind of game in which you engage, to win you will have to study your opponent and understand the way he operates so as to devise countermeasures. Studying your opponent, without fail you will become like him. The longer the game or the conflict, the truer this is. By this process, if you start out much stronger than he is, unless you can defeat him quickly, you will end up weak. Unless the game you play is of the kind that is based on pure luck, the outcome is always the same. I personally know this from many years during which I used to play table tennis with Jonathan. Being a fair player myself, at first I beat him every time. He, however, displayed his usual persistence until I no longer stood the slightest chance.

Not only does fighting weakness with strength generate weakness, but doing so is a crime. In so far as he can desist from fighting, the strong one has a choice. In so far as the weak one cannot do this, for him necessity knows no bounds. Morality is a product of the balance of forces, not of the objectives that each side pursues or claims to pursue; as, speaking of the "underdog" and sympathizing with him, most of us readily recognize. For this reason, *the same* activities that are condemned when committed by the strong—for example, killing noncombatants—are tolerated, often even applauded, when committed by the weak.

In so far as the strong one, simply by being strong, commits crimes, he will be forced to try to conceal them as best he can, lying as only spokesmen and spokeswomen can. As time passes, the lies will corrupt his chain of command. In the case of the American Armed Forces in Vietnam, this was carried to the point where nobody believed a word they said. Tens of thousands went AWOL. An estimated thirty percent of the troops were on hard drugs, and sixty percent of all those evacuated from the country for medical reasons in 1972 were diagnosed as suffering from post-traumatic stress disorder (PTSD). Worst of all was that an unknown number of officers were "fragged," or blown to pieces, by their own men. As to the IDF, the Palestinian Intifada brought it to a point where it had never been before. Nowadays, when I tell students how walls in Jerusalem and elsewhere used to be covered with graffiti reading "hats off to Tzahal," they can scarcely believe their ears. Whether that is due to in spite of the fact that most of them have served in it is not clear.

In sum, *Transformation* does two things. First, it calls attention to the fact that we are in the midst of a transitional period. That, of course, is no great discovery. To say that the future will not be like the past has become part of the accepted wisdom. Anybody who does *not* agree risks being considered an idiot. The difference between *Transformation* and other works dealing with the same subject is that I was probably the first to suggest that military history, overshadowed by nuclear weapons, had ceased going forward as it has done for long. Instead, it seems to be taking us backward. Backward, that is, toward more primitive forms of war of the kind which are even now being waged in places as far apart as the Middle East and the Congo; backward, perhaps, toward more primitive political constructs as well. This view has now been adopted by some others as well.

Second, it argues that morality is not a function of the belligerents' objectives and the way they conduct themselves, as "just war" theory from Augustine through Thomas Aquinas to Michael Walzer would have it. Instead, what counts is the balance of forces. You cannot be both strong and just. The longer the conflict, the truer this becomes. However, no man is so foolish as to risk his life for a cause he considers patently unjust. As the ancient Chinese sage Lao Tzu put it more succinctly than I ever could, a sword, plunged into salt water, *will* rust. Looking back on the futile wars in Afghanistan and Iraq, let those with ears to listen, finally listen!

* * *

Whereas Kennedy owed some of his success to the timing of *The Rise and Fall of Great Powers*, *The Transformation of War* was not as lucky. It happened to come out on the very day that the 1991 ground campaign against Iraq began. A worse moment could scarcely be imagined. Here, after all, were the Coalition forces employing just the kind of conventional technological superiority I had denounced as more or less useless in order to turn their opponents into mincemeat. The war gave rise to a vast literature about something known as the Revolution in Military Affairs (RMA), which, people said, had already happened, or was happening, or was about to happen. I was the only one who argued that the future did not lie with more computers, data-links, and precision guided munitions. Instead, it would bring terrorists whose most sophisticated weapon might well be explosives made of a mixture of fertilizer and diesel oil. To counter them, armed forces would have to change by doing away with their principal major weapon systems and by adapting their methods until they themselves began to resemble terrorists.

Accordingly, the first reviews were, if not downright hostile, at least condescending. Even Walter Laqueur, whom I had asked for a blurb, expressed himself in rather cautious terms. Most people frankly thought I had gone off my rocker.

Sales were disappointingly slow at first, and it was several years before they started picking up. In a way, that was a good thing; it taught me there is such a thing as life after death. Slowly, the climate of opinion changed. We humans find it difficult to keep things in perspective, particularly those that happen to us. As a result, at the time a historical event takes place it always assumes momentous dimensions, overshadowing anything that happened before. Then, within a few months or years, it tends to fall into place as just another event. This is what happened to the 1991 Gulf War. I remember how, soon after it ended, a journalist asked me whether, as a military

historian, I could remember another victory as complete as the one
that had just taken place. Since then, that victory has been cut down
to size. It took place not over some great and mighty opponent, as
was claimed at the time, but over a third-world country with a GDP
about one percent that of the U.S. Saddam Hussein was left alive
and kicking, which, of course, is why the Bush Administration in its
wisdom felt impelled to launch another campaign against him twelve
years later.

To speed up sales, I thought of contacting Abu Nidal, who at the
time was considered the world's most dangerous terrorist. I would ask
him to blow up the Twin Towers; next, we would share the ensuing
book profits. In any event, that proved unnecessary, and 9-11 made
my work into the new orthodoxy as two new editions saw the light
of print. The time came when, just as I had advertised my work by
comparing it to Clausewitz, new books coming off the press were
being compared with mine. Their authors held forth on asymmetric
war, fourth-generation war, postmodern war, informal war, gray-area
war, hybrid war, and so many other kinds of war as to confuse even
the expert.

There was, however, a difference. Without exception, all the rest
claimed that an entirely new age in warfare was dawning and tried to
explain the principles that would govern it. My goal was exactly the
opposite: I wanted to put forward a theory of war which, unlike the
old Clausewitzian one, would fit both future wars *and* those of the
past. Whether I succeeded the future will tell, but in the meantime
I have had moments of great satisfaction. The most memorable one
took place late one hot night in the summer of 1994. I was just taking
a shower in preparation for bed when the telephone rang. A high-
pitched female voice told me that this was the White House on the
line. President Clinton wanted to know where he could obtain my
volume! Feeling like Moses in front of the burning bush, I answered
that he could buy it at such and such a bookstore. Had I possessed
any brains, I would have promised to autograph a copy and send it

to him. On second thought, perhaps it was the hope of getting a free copy that made him place the call to begin with. Given what we know of him, it seems quite likely.

Long before, watching the queues of tourists waiting to visit the White House, I had sworn to myself that I would only enter it by the front gate. Now, having blown my chance of being asked, I started getting invitations to numerous other places, albeit less august ones. I had made my debut as a guest speaker on the international circuit in 1982. I remember how, staying in a Washington, D.C. hotel, I was almost bowled over by the fact that my bathroom had a telephone. Still, it was only after *Transformation* was published that the pace really picked up. Most of those who invited me to their schools, academies, colleges, universities, institutes, centers, conferences, workshops, forums, or whatever had either read *Transformation* or one of its numerous spinoffs. Most wanted me to talk about the waning of "trinitarian" war and the advent of other forms of armed conflict. A few, however, were interested in other, to my mind even more important questions, such as the nature of war, its relationship to law, and the factors that make men either put their lives on the line or refuse to do so.

Many thought my vision of the future of war was incorrect, to put it mildly. At least one critic gave it to me straight between the eyes by calling me "a wet blanket." Others, misinterpreting what I had to say, called me "Doctor Doom." What they did know, though, was that my thesis was provocative and that it always made people argue, sometimes to the point where one or two of them seemed on the verge of apoplexy. I, of course, did my best to help them along—toward more argument, not a heart attack! I talked about "The Future of War" until I was blue in the face in places as far apart as Trondheim, Norway, and Dunedin, New Zealand, Newport, Rhode Island, and Johannesburg, South Africa.

The place I liked visiting best was the British Army Staff College at Camberley, England. I went there for the first time in late 1988, and the invitations kept coming for a decade after that, by which time the college had been closed and amalgamated with the Armed Forces' College, first at Bracknell and then in Swindon. Dating back to the mid-nineteenth century, the college was housed in an Italianate building that had once belonged to Queen Victoria's cousin, the Duke of Cambridge. For thirty-nine years (1856–1895) he served as commander in chief, British Army. Perhaps that was one reason why the place was chock-full of army memorabilia such as paintings, sculptures, old uniforms, and weapons.

Among the most interesting items were the bathroom fixtures. They looked as if they had come straight out of Oscar Wilde and probably did. If memory serves me right, there was no shower, only two separate taps that poured hot and cold water into the iron tub with its ornate legs In the mornings there was a kindly old lady who would come to wake you up, asking whether you cared for "a cup'a tea" and reminding you what a class-conscious society Britain is. Later, I learned that only unimportant guests were put up at the college whereas important ones were lodged at Camberley House. There, Mr. and Mrs. Commanding General reigned in a sort of neo-feudal splendor with valets, gardeners, and drivers. Indeed, I was told that, should the lady decline to act as hostess, her husband would not get the job. My visits must have been a success, for within two or three years after the first one, I graduated from the college to the house. Dvora, too, stayed there with me a few times, and like me, she has nothing but good memories both of the place and its occupants.

The memorabilia apart, what made Camberley unique was the civilized air it exuded. While certainly no loafer, I have long believed that too strenuous an atmosphere is bad for study, particularly if it is mock-strenuous, as at NDU. At Camberley there was no danger of that. The dining room was paneled with dark wood with an oil-portrait of Her Royal Highness Princess Ann hanging on the wall. For starters there were all the British newspapers, including the *Sun* with Page 3 carrying a fresh naked girl every day. The food was excellent. I was told that, in the good old days, it had been even better. It was served by waitresses in white aprons. The leather armchairs in the conference rooms were deep and comfortable, and you were expected to answer questions while sitting on one of them without any kind of partition between yourself and your audience.

Most of the officers, colonels with the occasional junior or retired general thrown in, did some sports, be it horse riding, rowing, or jogging. But they did not overdo it. As a result, they looked slim and elegant instead of big and heavy like weightlifters. Lunch came with no fewer than four different wine glasses, and come evening, everyone spent considerable time drinking at the bar. At Camberley, I used to drink more in a day than I usually do in a month. Returning home with every pore reeking of alcohol, I used to cure myself by a few days' total abstinence.

It may have been the generous quantities of alcohol which account for the fact that, though few of the officers held higher degrees as American ones do, the discussions were uniformly excellent. I learned a lot. In particular, we used to talk about events in Northern Ireland, where many officers had served not once but several times. One of the most vivid memories I have is of General Patrick ("Paddy") Waters. At the time we met, he was Commanding Officer at Camberley but had already been designated to take over the British Army in Northern Ireland. One evening, having lost my way in a typical English fog, I accidentally reached his door and knocked on it. He opened it, dressed in white socks. He invited me in, poured me a glass of sherry, showed me the eight books he was reading at the same time, and told me something of the way he saw his coming job. Compared to what some others have been doing and are doing in similar situations, I think the British performance in Ireland was magnificent. In a way, it was not surprising. As I was once told, one reason why Britain succeeded in building the largest empire in history was that its troops were good at "the smacking business."

Totally unlike Camberley is the Bundeswehr's Command and Staff College, AKA Führungsakademie, in Hamburg. It is located in the Clausewitz Caserne, a group of nondescript, nineteen sixties-style buildings located in the well-to-do suburb of Blankenese. While the fixtures are among the most modern I have encountered anywhere, the atmosphere is completely sterile. In part, this is due to the Spartan nature of the facilities provided. The first time I visited my room did not even have soap, and my request to have a bar was received with mild astonishment. The mattress was stone hard; I was told that Prussian officers have always been expected to make their own beds. Later, the bed remained as it was, but they did make some concession to modernity by providing a large TV set.

In part, the atmosphere is due to the very great difficulties the Germans have with their past. The Clausewitz Caserne had some statues of nude athletes clearly dating to the 1930s, but I seemed to be the only one aware of that fact. In other Bundeswehr installations one will hardly see any memorabilia dating to any period after 1918. Those that are older must be handled with caution lest they give rise to accusations of "militarism" or worse. In fact, almost the only more or less safe subject is the 1813–15 "Wars of Liberation," and even here one must take care lest Prussian symbols be displayed too prominently. This and many other things prove that the Germans, especially but not exclusively the government, are doing what they can to cope with their history. Had they not done so, I would not be prepared to live in their country or address them. However, it also serves as a reminder of how hard it is to set up a military without tradition. See my book, *The Culture of War* (2008).

Then there was the World Economic Forum at Davos. The meetings are huge, comprising about a thousand guests selected and self-selected from among the very powerful, the filthy rich, and the famous. In addition there are thousands of relatives—the gatherings serve as a market where the sons and daughters of those just mentioned can meet potential partners—as well as hangers-on of every sort. Finally, there are hordes of very pretty girls brought in to act as waitresses at the sponsored dinners. What they made of it all is a mystery to me. The presence of so many aristocats meant that security was quite tight. Guards, submachine guns at the ready, stood at the entrance to the Congress Hall where the meetings were held. Anybody who had forgotten his or her ID in his or her hotel room was sent back to pick it up, not a very pleasant thing to do on the freezing streets.

I was invited as part of the program, which is designed to create the impression that there was more to the meetings than a bunch of businessmen running after one another in order to cut deals and politicians following them, cap in hand, in order to beg for investments. Of course the most important people only came to listen to one another, if they listened to anybody at all. The common herd went to listen to the most important people—for Dvora and me, one of them was Palestinian leader Yasser Arafat. In case the ski slopes happened to be closed for the day they might also attend a seminar or two given by the likes of me. Partly because nobody took the seminars seriously, partly because the gatherings were much too large, as far as I know, neither a great stirring message nor real scholarship ever came out of Davos. In their favor I must say I enjoyed reading the magazine they published, *World Link*. That is, until they stopped sending it to me.

As to the forum itself, what irritated me was the stinginess of it all. Here were gathered people who, as founder Professor Klaus Schwab proudly pointed out in the 1996 opening session, had no less than eight trillion dollars to back them up—the world's third largest GDP after the U.S. and the European Union. Yet, for the likes of me, transport from Zurich took the form of a crammed minivan shared by several people and their luggage. At Davos—*da wo es teuer ist*, "there where things are expensive," as the Germans say—itself the hotel was good, considering that every last room was crowded to capacity. However, if you so much as wanted to take your wife to a meeting at which you were supposed to hold forth, she had to pay for her own meal. Speakers did not receive an honorarium, and the *per-diem* barely sufficed for a decent lunch.

Obviously, most of those present were not bothered by such considerations. They were the kind for whom all lunches are free by definition; besides, when *they* ate lunch, the paintings of a famous artist such as Kirchner served as decoration. As to those who were bothered, obviously, the organizers thought that merely rubbing shoulders with the great was reward enough. As Paul Kennedy, who served us as a kind of guide, told us, there was such a thing as a Davos groupie. The experience taught me how the very rich get their wealth: namely, by never overpaying for anything.

For me, the most memorable event at Davos was a seminar I gave on drugs. It is true I knew nothing about them. However, it was typical of the organizers that they never asked me about that. Made to sing for my dinner, I prepared as best I could. Whether because I am Dutch or because I consider myself a liberal if not a libertarian, the line I took was that the one thing wrong with drugs is the fact that they are illegal. At first the people around the table were unsympathetic. Later, after I had explained how desperate need and astronomical profits create a problem that simply cannot be controlled and whose "cure" is probably worse than the disease, most of them seemed to come over to my point of view. Not that they cared much one way or another.

To the general indifference, there were two exceptions. One, who sat there glowering at me, was a big, powerfully built, dark-haired man from the U.S. The other, who kept silent throughout, also had dark hair—it was carefully smeared with brilliantine—but was small and swarthy. It turned out that the former was the head of the American Drug Enforcement Agency. The latter was the foreign minister of Colombia. Each for his own reasons hated every word I said. Their tacit alliance was the best possible proof I (and my stepson Jonathan, who did his dissertation on that topic) was right.

That is also evident from the fact that, even as I am writing this in 2015, more and more countries have begun to decriminalize marijuana.

Flying from one conference to the next always reminds me of medieval knights going on tournament or of grand-prix drivers who compete now on one circuit, now on another. The main difference is that conferencing is not as risky to life and limb. Most of the time the only danger is to one's waistline as lavish breakfasts are joined by more or less formal dinners and, of course, countless coffee breaks. Another difference is that academics rarely find bevies of half-naked girls eagerly waiting for them after they have done, though, that too has been known to happen. After a time, not only do you become familiar with the different places you visit but you also keep meeting the same people and crossing swords with them. It can be boring, but it can also be fun. Some of us got to know one another quite well and liked to crack jokes about one another. When I started in this business, I was one of the youngest. Now, some thirty-five years later, I am among the oldest. Such is the way of all flesh.

I once read that most people see having to speak in public as the most stressful thing in life short of getting a divorce. I, however, have never been shy and never experienced any difficulty in doing so. Of course, experience helps. Over the years I have developed my own methods, which I am sure will not suit anybody else in their entirety but which may nevertheless be worth recording. The first rule is always to come prepared but, as far as you are able to, pretend you are inventing everything on the spot. My own method is to prepare well in advance and to refresh my memory at the last moment. The second is to limit your notes—if you need them—to a single page of paper. Whatever does not fit into that is better left at home. The purpose of this rule is to guarantee you will not be tempted to read your text, which is the way German professors like to do it by way of making absolutely sure nobody listens to them. Another reason for having only one sheet is that you do not want to be in a situation, which is almost certain to arise, where the audience tries to count those that still remain.

Unless you are very famous, dress up. But do not do it in such a way as to make everybody else feel uncomfortable. Since I am just a professor, and an Israeli one at that, there is not much danger of that happening. Reach the agreed-upon place in plenty of time so as not to feel flushed when you start. This is my advice; some people, apparently in the belief that a lecture is a form of combat, declare it is better to arrive somewhat tense. Make sure you know exactly what you want to say and how much time you have to do so. In my experience you can fit any subject into any time frame, provided, that is, you know in advance just how much time you have and what your subject is. To help you, you may want to divide your notes into numbered paragraphs. Never go on beyond the agreed-upon time since doing so will make everybody present, the chairperson included, hate you. If you can make do with a little less time than was allotted you, so much the better.

Check the room or hall where you are going to speak ahead of time. The shape of a table can make a big difference; you want to make sure you can see everybody and that everybody can see you. If it is up to you, select the place you are going to sit or stand in advance. Ask how many people are going to be present. Once, at the Air Force Academy in Colorado Springs, I thought I was going to address a small number of faculty members only to find the commandant, a three-star general, and 800 people waiting for me. That is not a situation you want to be in. I personally prefer to speak standing up even in quite small gatherings. The reason is that, owing to an operation I underwent, my voice does not carry very far. However, if the room is small enough, I will speak sitting behind a table or, if the occasion is suitable informal, while sitting on it.

Talking of tables, here is a story from my time at Webster University, Geneva, in 2012, Coming in for the first class, a seminar, I found that the tables and chairs were arranged as they sometimes are at school, i.e. in rows one behind the other. Since this put some of the twenty or so students at a disadvantage, I immediately asked them to help me re-arrange the furniture as so as to form a flat U with me in the center so all could see and hear me equally well. Each class after we were finished, we put them back again. When the time for evaluation came, I got 19 out of a possible 20 points. One student, however, using the rubric "various notes," complained about the difficulty of having to rearrange the room each time!

Remember that it is the show you give, as much as what you say, that will decide whether they like you and whether they ask you back. Therefore, however much you may hate the occasion, start by telling a white lie and saying how much you love it. Next, tell a joke. If you cannot think of a suitable one, say so and tell one that is not suitable. Or else make a joke of the fact that you are unable to think of one. From this point on you are very much on your own, and there is precious little I can do for you.

Make sure everybody can hear you and that you speak neither too slowly nor too fast. Don't rant, but do put some passion into your words. If you don't care about your subject, nobody else will either. Don't yell, but do modulate your voice to emphasize the points you consider important. Don't turn your arms into windmills, but do move your body sufficiently to keep them watching you. Don't look down and don't move your head from side to side like an oscillator. But do look people in the face and make sure they can look you in the face. Make them feel your confidence, but not your arrogance. Illustrate your ideas with concrete examples and an anecdote or two, but do not pile up too many lest they miss the point. If you feel you are losing them, get their attention by asking a question. To show them how clever you are, you will want to make fairly sure that it is one to which they do not know the answer. My own favorite, which always comes in handy during discussions of future war, is which international organization has more member states than the United Nations does.

By announcing that you are about to present your conclusions, you can cause those in the audience who have taken a nap to wake up in the hope you will finish soon. This is another good moment to tell a joke; having done so, you should put on as serious a mien as you are capable of. During the talk you are allowed to ramble a bit, especially in order to present examples. But the conclusions themselves should be presented in as clear and incisive a manner as possible. Limit their number to three or, at most, four. If you don't, then by the time you reach the last one, they will have forgotten the first. Display your confidence and generosity by inviting people to ask questions, but make sure it is the chairperson and not you who decides on the order they do so. If a question is too long, *encouragez les autres* by asking whether that was question or a lecture. Never trade insults with anybody, but always answer even the most obnoxious questions calmly and respectfully. The best way to deal with somebody who bears ill will toward you is to compliment him or her, thus drawing his or her teeth. Better still, ask for a favor. With some luck, he or she will learn a lesson.

Nowadays, everybody talks about audio-visual aids. To me they are one more manifestation of the feeling of inferiority that the humanities and social sciences have developed *vis a vis* modern technology; whatever it is, it cannot be any good unless it comes accompanied by a whole array of kaleidoscopic colors and stereo-phonic sounds. To be sure, a well-placed slide containing a figure or caricature may be extremely useful and/or provide comic relief, provided, of course, that you are able to display the right slide at the right moment and that it does not appear on the screen upside down. In that case, of course, you yourself risk turning into comic relief. Even if no such disaster takes place, and even when they are well selected to illustrate your theme, the aids you use are likely to draw attention away from you. Instead of listening to what you have to say, people will be reading the bullets you so conveniently provided them with or, which is much worse still, trying to make sense of the organization charts. That, of course, is the last thing you want. On balance, I think that a presentation with insufficient aids is better than one that has too many of them.

Perhaps the most successful talk I ever gave was to 3,000 Australian Air Force personnel in the summer of 1996. Having arrived on the previous day by way of New York and Los Angeles, I was suffering from a bad case of jetlag. Still, instead of going to bed, I did what one does in Australia, i.e. go out to look at kangaroos. Later that evening there was a bagpipe concert, and I did not want to miss that either. Whatever the reason, when it was my turn to speak, the Spirit descended on me. The idea behind the conference was to honor the seventy-fifth birthday of the Royal Australian Air Force. (It had been founded in 1921 and is the second oldest in the world.) My theme was that, since warfare was changing from something that states waged against one another into terrorism and counter-terrorism, twenty-five years hence there would be no air forces left. As manned combat aircraft such as fighter-bombers and bombers disappeared, most of those present would be unemployed. I ended by telling them that, in case my forecast was wrong, I would be very happy to attend their centenary meeting as well. In spite, or perhaps, because of its dire message, so successful was the talk that I had them standing up, cheering repeatedly as if I were a Spice Girl or something.

Since then, most air forces around the world have cut down their orders of battle by over one third. Wherever one looks, for every new fighter-bomber entering the service, there are numerous unmanned ones doing the same. More important in the short run was the fact that, among those present in the auditorium were the ex-commander of the Australian Air Force, Air Marshal Ray Funnel, who was then in charge of the National Defense College, and his Canadian colleague. Consequently, I received three more invitations, two to Canberra and one to Winnipeg. Of both cities it has been said that, though they are twice as large as Manhattan Cemetery, they are only half as lively. That, however, was hardly the fault of those who asked Dvora and me to come. In both cases the hospitality was first class, and we enjoyed our stay very much.

The highlight came at Winnipeg. After I had finished explaining why, in my opinion, air forces did not have a future, the Commander, Space Command, USAF, a four-star general as tall as a tree, strode onto the stage. First, he dramatically threw away his pre-prepared speech. Next, he proceeded to answer "that bastard." In his favor I must say that, when we spoke briefly afterward, it turned out that our differences were not as great as might be thought. We agreed that manned combat aircraft, which have long formed the core of existing air forces, have had their day and that space operations were there to stay. I, however, thought that much of the latter might safely be privatized. Three years later, visiting the U.S. Air Force Academy in Colorado Springs, I had as my escort a young captain. He told me that his wife, an Air Force lawyer, had just flown to Washington, D.C. to help deal with the legal aspects of the process.

Though people say I am a good academic speaker, I never developed into a public one, and the few occasions when I addressed a non-academic audience were only a qualified success. I may be too much of a highbrow for most people's tastes. I take it for granted that they know things they do not and thus make them feel bad about themselves. Or perhaps I am too much in love with the give and take of argument. Though I can come through forcefully enough, I never deliberately try to impose myself on a crowd, which, as some experts see it, has a female nature and loves to be imposed on. Had I made the effort, I probably would not have succeeded. Finally, I may not have what it takes to read their minds and to adapt myself. Since I rate freedom of expression above almost anything else, I am not even certain I want to try.

As the invitations I got multiplied, so did my encounters with the media. There used to be a time when, particularly at places like Oxford and Cambridge, for a professor to talk to the media was considered degrading. Doing so might, indeed, lead to his dismissal. Things have changed since then, though whether this indicates that the media have gone up or academia down I am not sure. Normally, the authorities at the university to which you are affiliated will beg you to speak out. They will even use their public relations department to send the media to you; of course their reason for doing so is their hope that you will mention them so as to give them some free publicity at your expense.

Though I have never done anything to attract the media, they keep coming to me on their own accord. The reason is probably that I tend to be provocative, even, as sometimes happens, when I have no intention of being so. By now I must have given newspaper, radio, and television interviews to hundreds upon hundreds of journalists. Like most things, good and bad, they tend to come in waves. As a result, periods when emails arrive and the telephone never rings alternate with others when they never stop doing so. Given my field of specialization, one could almost measure the state of the world by the frequency of their calls. As the Chinese curse goes, may you live in interesting times.

I think I learned the art of giving an interview as I went along. Never talk about methodology, and never hee and haw. Make your answers snappy, particularly on radio and TV. Even more important is making them "pregnant;" in other words, formulating them in such a way as to invite the next question even as the first one is being dealt with. To do so, you'd do well to talk to the interviewer ahead of time so as to understand his requirements and what it is all about. If he is wise, he'll do so on his own initiative. Television in particular is not a good medium for passing abstract messages. Hence you will do well to prepare some concrete examples and use them as you go along.

Always take the experts' advice concerning location, lightning, posture, dress, and so on. Do not forget to look at the interviewer or, as the occasion may demand, straight into the camera. Whatever the medium on which you appear, do not laugh at your own jokes. When you write for the papers, make sure you meet the editor's requirements. If the editor asks you for 400, or 800, or 1,200 words, don't argue but give him exactly what he needs. Keep your sentences short and your language simple. Use the active mode. Avoid long strings of polysyllabic words, though putting in an occasional one—no more than one per article—may have its uses. Most important of all, submit your contributions on time. Unlike many academics, editors know only too well that time is money. If you miss a deadline, they will think twice before asking you again.

Never forget that the journalist interviewing you is merely doing his or her job. Whatever else, you will get free publicity. Some will also pay you for talking to them. Most journalists are intelligent and try to be nice as well. After all, they are coming to you, cap in hand, and asking for a favor. Partly because they make me think aloud, partly because many of them have seen as much or more of the world than I have, I usually enjoy talking to them. Some have become good friends. A few don't know what they are talking about, like the one who once asked a colleague of mine for the address of the monks at Mount Sinai so he could ask them for the recipe for manna. Worse still are those who want you to confirm what they already know or think they know.

Worst of all are those who, not getting what they want, try to dictate to you. Those I shake off as fast as I can. I particularly remember one journalist who, many years ago, refused to believe me when I said that the IDF's decision to retain its force of paratroopers—they used to have one entire air-mobile division and several scenarios for using it—might not be due simply to brain damage. He told me that this did not interest him and put down the receiver. Of course one should not let the fact that one is often asked to address the media go to one's head. On the other hand, I was gratified when a colleague told me how, passing through Immigration at Vancouver, the responsible officer heard that he worked at the same university as I do. He said he read everything I wrote and gave him his visa on the spot. Who wouldn't be?

Whereas, abroad, I have often discussed things with some of the most high-ranking officers alive, my relations with the IDF remained problematic. I have it on good authority that this was due to the critical views I have often expressed. In 1994 Ehud Barak, then near the end of his term as Chief of Staff, asked me to address the Assembled General Staff (Forum Matkal) on the future of war. I did so, and what I got for my pains was a reception I can only call disgraceful. Both before and since, I have spoken about that subject hundreds of times all over the world and would certainly not say that everybody agreed with my vision. Nowhere, however, did I meet an audience, let alone an audience consisting of officers, whose members insisted on the *right* to be late, the reason being that they had to finish their sandwiches first.

The meeting took place in a room that looked as if it had not been refurnished in the last quarter century. Even the arms of the U-formed table did not run parallel to each other. Having been ushered into it by Barak's secretary, a female colonel, the generals, mostly in their late forties, would not sit still and listen to an invited speaker. Instead, they played with paperwork or with calculators. Others talked among themselves, interrupted me with sarcastic remarks, and briefly behaved like a troop of disturbed children. In part, they were trying to hide their ignorance. They were probably good practitioners, but never in all my appearances did I meet a group of people less familiar with the theory and history of their own profession.

Having said a word about Clausewitz, I immediately regretted it because, with the exception of Barak himself, none of them seemed to have read him. Hence his name being mentioned only increased their resentment still further. Repeatedly, they had to be calmed down by Barak. Seated to my right, he acted like a kindergarten mistress, telling them to shut up. Nor did the fact that he obliged each one to ask a question or give a comment endear him to them. After the meeting had ended, I asked him whether it was always so bad. He answered it was usually worse. At the time I thought it was a brilliant answer. Since then, I have often wondered whether it did not reflect the truth.

I am deeply aware that, without the IDF, my country would not exist for a single day and that their—our—sacrifices have been exceptionally heavy. I am also well aware they can manage without me, as they have now been doing for almost seventy years. Still, I would like to cooperate with them, offering whatever I may have to the best of my ability. I am not, however, prepared to surrender my right to criticize them or change my views to fit their, in my view deeply mistaken, policies.

What I would really like is to engage them in the kind of serious dialogue I often have with students, colleagues, and journalists all over the world, raising questions and exchanging views. We should do so as free, equal human beings whose loyalties are on the same side. If I recognize that many of them do what they do out of a deep sense of commitment, instead of ostracizing me, they should recognize that the same is true of me. To paraphrase Simone de Beauvoir, those who most harshly criticize the society of which they are members are by no means necessarily those who love it least. As it is, except for the occasional officers who take a course with me or who come to my home in order to talk to me, we must do without each other. My work gets published all over the world except in the Israeli equivalent of *Military Review*, *Ma'arachot*.

Meanwhile, as the years go by, attending conferences is becoming less of a challenge and more of a chore. As one gets older, traveling does not become easier, and all airports look alike. I have the good fortune that I can sleep almost anywhere. As long as I have a good book to read, I am content even when jammed into an aircraft seat with somebody else's inquisitive baby next to me. Once, a British Airways crew presented me with a bottle of champagne for cheerfully putting up with exactly that. The real problem is having to listen to things many of which you already know. Some conferences are better, others worse. I spend the worst ones doodling, or else I play word-games with myself.

Very often, the most important part is not the sessions but the breaks when you meet interesting people, talk to them, and exchange business cards (normally I forget to take mine along). Still, though the temptation is often strong, I am not of the kind who flies in, says his piece, and disappears. If you want people to pay attention to you, you should do the same to them. Nor is playing hooky up an acceptable way of treating those who invited you and who did what they could to make your stay a pleasant one.

In the end, both media appearances and conferences are trivial matters. At their best they may provide my life with some extra spice. But they do not fill it up. In 1899 Sigmund Freud, then 43 years old, published *The Interpretation of Dreams*, probably the most important work on human psychology ever to see the light of print. Some years later, looking back, he said, "Such discoveries one only makes once in a lifetime." In a way, he was right. Having founded psychoanalysis, he still had many important contributions to make, including *Civilization and its Discontents*, *Moses and Monotheism*, and others. However, he never challenged the foundations he had built, such as the belief that people keep reliving the experiences they had during their childhood and that dreams represent wish fulfillment. Nor did he conclude that analysis might not, after all, be the right method for looking into people's souls. Truth to say, there was little else he could do. To write another book as important as *Dreams*, he would have had to rid himself precisely of those of his ideas in which he had invested his greatest efforts and of which, with good reason, he was proudest.

When I published *Transformation*, I was two years older than Freud had been. Though I doubt whether it is as important a book as *Dreams*, I too came to feel that such discoveries one only makes once in a lifetime. For good or ill, I could not, would not, move away from the light I had seen. To speak in Biblical terms, doing so almost amounts to renouncing God and turning toward idol-worship instead. Wittingly or unwittingly, before I wrote *Transformation*, I had merely elaborated on the ideas of others, primarily Clausewitz. In *Transformation* I struck out against the master's ideas, overturned them, and replaced them with my own. Having done so, from now on to do original work in the same field would mean renouncing those ideas. That is a much harder enterprise for which I may be both too strong and too weak.

I, however, could not fill my life the way Freud did. I never had patients to treat and cure. I did not hold Wednesday evening seminars, sit on committees, organize congresses, lead a movement, or appoint and dismiss would-be successors. Except for Jonathan, who always helps me with my computer, I never even had a part-time secretary working for me. My teaching duties apart, in essence all I had were my books, my word processor, and my spare time. What I could do with them remained to be seen.

Chapter 5

As I Please

As the reader will no doubt have realized, I have been leading the scholar's life, the *vita contemplativa*, as it was known during the Middle Ages. Compared to some others, I have devoted less time and effort administration. Compared to some others, I spent more of it giving lectures and writing books.

It is possible to exaggerate the importance of what we scholars do. One reason for this is that even those of us who are interested in administration, such as heading departments, distributing grants, or hiring and firing people, only wield very modest power compared to some others in government and business. Another is that not too many people ever read our work. Neither Clausewitz nor many of the other authors mentioned on these pages received wide recognition in their lifetimes. Machiavelli's best known book, *The Prince*, was considered an abortion while he lived and only saw the light of print after he had died. Even Freud's *Interpretation of Dreams* only sold 350 copies during the first six years after publication. As the history of the Military Reform Movement demonstrates, the situation of those of us who work for the great and the mighty is only marginally better. It may even be worse, given that some of our products are not even published, but disappear into a drawer where no one sees them at all.

To be sure, I have not done too badly. A famous journalist once described how, living with guerrillas in a Burmese jungle, he was given some old books to use as a pillow. Waking up next morning, he discovered *Transformation* among the assorted dictionaries, handbooks, and so on. The way he told the story, it was a revelation. My work made him realize that the armed conflict he was covering was not just a godforsaken war in a godforsaken hole but a real harbinger of things to come. That realization is becoming truer and truer every day. Other people from all over the world have written to me, arguing points, providing or requesting information, or simply thanking me for my efforts. Some of my colleagues have done better than I and succeeded at getting their works onto best-seller lists. In so far as this reflects real quality and not some passing fad, I congratulate them. Still, in the age of television not even the most successful scholar can compete with soccer players and supermodels. As a rule of thumb, a pair of naked breasts gets as much attention as a thousand books.

Yet one should not underestimate the power of scholarship either. On several occasions I engaged on a debate as to who, Clausewitz or Napoleon, has played a more important role in military history. Of course I know that, at the time Napoleon was commanding hundreds of thousands of men and busy conquering a continent, Clausewitz was a little-known staff officer. I also know that Napoleon won the Battle of Austerlitz, and lost the battles of Leipzig and Waterloo, whereas all Clausewitz ever did was write a book which, at first, had so little popular appeal that it had to be sold by subscription.

On the other hand, the emperor himself once said that the pen was mightier than the sword. This is particularly true in the long run; especially because the pen does not destroy the hearts of men but enters them. To see how right he was, all you have to do is open a recent issue of one of the scholarly periodicals that specialize in strategic studies. Chances are you will find numerous articles on Clausewitz but not one on Napoleon. Chances are the *only* personalities who lived more than a hundred years ago you will meet are Clausewitz and, perhaps, Sun Tzu.

Judging by this criterion, the best I can think of, Napoleon might never have existed. Thus have the humble risen and the mighty sunk. Moreover, so pervasive is Clausewitz's influence that, thinking of Napoleon, we invariably wear Prussian glasses. It is Clausewitz who tells us who and what Napoleon was. To convince yourself of the truth of this, try to write a history of Napoleonic warfare that does *not* revolve around decisive battles and does *not* rest on the assumption that war is the continuation of politics by other means. If you can do that, you can do anything.

Another way to look at the matter is as follows. I once attended a conference on World War II. One of the speakers, a young Dutch scholar, presented a paper on the way decision-makers in Washington, D.C. had treated the social scientists whom they commissioned to do studies. He ended by comparing the former to dogs and the latter to lampposts. At that point the fun began. Most of the "decision-makers" who commissioned the studies worked for the War Department. Military or civilian, in their own time they may have been quite influential, but by now all of them have long been forgotten. The same was not necessarily true of the social scientists, one of whom just happened to be called Ruth Benedict. An anthropologist, a friend of Margaret Mead, and an exceptionally beautiful woman to boot, during the war she got a contract for doing a study on the Japanese national character. Later, it was published as *The Chrysanthemum and the Sword*. Not only did it influence an entire generation, but she was also paid for doing what she might have done anyhow. This makes one wonder who watered whom. To top it off, Ms. Benedict did not know Japanese. At the time she did the study, she had never visited Japan either. I am not sure what the moral of this is.

In July 1991, four months after *Transformation* was published, Dvora, Adi, and Jonathan, plus two dogs and one cat, went to Quantico, Virginia, to spend a year at the Marine Corps University. The person who had arranged it was my old friend and fellow military reformer, Colonel Mike Wyly. At that time he was the university's vice president. However, a few weeks before we arrived, he learned that he would soon have to retire after thirty years in the Corps. Initially, he was very downcast, but he quickly recovered and went on to grow vines and to run a ballet company in Maine. When we visited him there, he had started wondering why he had stayed in as long as he had.

The house we were assigned was located on "Colonels' Hill," not far from where the O Club used to be. Though the club served iced tea instead of alcohol, the rest of the food was as good as at Camberley. Like so many things at Quantico, the club itself was pleasant but slightly seedy. True to the name, most of our neighbors were colonels about the same age as me or slightly older, many of them ex-fighter pilots and some of them serving out their last years prior to retirement by filling all kinds of odd posts. The lieutenant colonels

Dvora and I at the Quantico Marine Corps Ball, 1992. The ball dress Dvora is wearing belonged to her grandmother in the 1920s. I have never worn a tux either before or after.

lived further down. The generals had a separate hill of their own and, probably because they wished to retain a certain aura, did not show themselves too often. The junior officers had their neat rows of cottages located in a remote part of the base where nobody would see them, and the enlisted men lived in their barrack-like apartments. *Ordnung muss sein*, order is necessary, as the Germans say. Though the Marines are not Germans by any means, the percentage of officers whose surnames indicate their family ties to that country is conspicuous. So is that of southerners and Catholics.

A few days after we had arrived, General Boomer, who had commanded the Marines in Desert Storm, took over the base. On the strength of his performance he had hoped for a promotion, if not to Commandant then at least to Deputy Commandant. Instead, he found himself in charge of a rather small training base. No wonder he was in a foul mood. To prove it, he made the entire base come out on parade to welcome him. In the lead, sword in hand and looking as sour as sour can be, marched the University Commander. I am told Boomer was a bona fide hero of the Vietnam War, but on the few occasions we met he and I did not get along. Once, having been seated together, he told me the following story. Early during Desert Shield, he and his staff were at work when two official military historians presented themselves at his headquarters and asked him for his instructions. He told them to do whatever historians do and sent them away. I took the hint. Since then, I have met many generals who were more senior than him. Some of them, I am happy to report, were more interested in military history or were, at any rate, more polite toward historians than he had been.

We were the first civilian family ever to live on base, and the experience was fascinating. Unlike NDU, Quantico was a real community, "The Crossroads of the Marine Corps," as it called itself. At the center of the crossroads, it was claimed, stood the local McDonald's. Almost as important was The Globe and the Laurel, a restaurant near the base gate whose restroom walls were entirely covered with visiting cards of Marines past and present. With most distances so small that one could cover them on foot, we soon led a social life busier than any I have known before or since. We were guests, and honored ones at that. Still, we obeyed the standing orders that governed everything from the date you had to rake the autumn leaves to the washing of cars. Once again, *Ordnung muss sein*. The only rule we ignored was the one that obliged the dogs to be kept on a leash at all times. They loved their freedom, and we were happy to let them have it.

At Quantico, too, everybody played sports. As you entered the base, there was a huge golf court which we, coming from poor, little Israel, thought was very strange. To our mind an officer was a rough, tough guy carrying an assault rifle. It did not include funny creatures dressed in shorts and walking about trying to hit a little ball. Some even drove about in golf carts. Every day around noon life would come to a halt. Students and faculty—not I, since I much preferred to do my runs in the late afternoon—went exercising, working out even harder than at NDU. In part they did that because they, or at any rate the students, were younger by about six or seven years. In part, they did that because they were, after all, United States Marines and very proud of the fact.

Whatever the reason, not a day passed without some of them sustaining an injury. Now somebody broke a finger playing softball or volleyball. Now somebody else had sprained an ankle and was hobbling about on crutches, and now a third officer had so overstrained himself trying to be Iron Man that he could scarcely walk for a week. Many suffered knee trouble, the result of years of exercises during which they jumped out of helicopters with full gear. If what I saw represents the benefits one gets from sports, then I want no share of them.

Wonder of wonders, the few women around—the Marines have proportionally half as many women as the other services—were as bad as the men. Once, in the middle of winter, I spoke to one of them who told me that she had spent an hour that morning rowing. I expressed my admiration and my envy, saying it must have been wonderful to go out into the crisp cold and enjoy the view of the Potomac which, depending on the weather, can be breathtaking. Not at all, she countered. What she meant was that she had been "rowing" in a gym. I myself hate gyms and have only entered them once or twice in my life. The hardware is a cross between torture engines and gynecological chairs. Besides, running in place, or swimming from one end of the pool to the other, bores me to tears even without having to monitor the speed at which I go, or my heartbeat, or whatever.

Compared with NDU, the difference consisted in that most of the people lived on base or not far away, so they did not have to get up as early in order to get to work. As a result, they remained tolerably fit until 2130 hours, when most of them went to bed. No wonder Quantico had a very low crime rate that made it among the safest places in the U.S. Our place was even safer, given that the provost-marshal lived right across the street. We had a direct line to him, and he, in turn, made sure our car was not subjected to a drug search when, as occasionally happened, we returned to the base in the middle of the night.

My students were about 200 majors in their mid-thirties, some 12 of them non-Americans from countries as far apart as Norway and Colombia. Meeting in the U.S. caused several of them, the Europeans in particular, to discover how much they had in common and how different America was. Every Monday morning we would meet at Breckenridge Hall, popularly known as the Master Bedroom, where I explained the evolution of war since the Middle Ages. The technicalities of lecturing in the military are different from those that attend civilian life. There is no such thing as an uninterrupted 90-minute class, the reason being that Marine bladders cannot stand it. Instead, they have a five-minute "stretch break." Of course it stretches out to ten and even fifteen minutes, proving that Einstein was right and that time is relative. On the positive side, sometimes there are announcements to be made. On such occasions the class will rise as a file of uniformed people marches stiffly toward the podium in strict order of rank. They will say whatever they have to say and then beat a retreat. It reminded me of an old limerick: "The Duke of York he had/ten thousand men/he marched them up the hill/he marched them down again." I always thought it was fun to watch.

They, in turn, saw me as a figure of fun, applauding when my name was mentioned and replying with a good-natured chorus of "Good morning, Professor van Creveld" each time I greeted them. Once, they even prepared a sketch about me. It was supposed to be performed at one of those late-night parties where the need to toast countless dignitaries serves as an excuse for heavy drinking. However, not knowing what was coming, I disappointed them by going home early. Later, they put on another performance especially for my benefit. It ran as follows:

Here's my story. It's sad but true.
The art of war is starting anew.
War as we knew it has gone away.
Nontrinitarian war is here to stay.

Well I should'a known it from the very start.
This guy he'd leave you with a broken heart.
Ah, listen, people, what I'm telling you.
Jomini wouldn't get you through school.

Harry[3] tried to put me down;
But I'm here to stay around.,
Clausewitz is out of touch.
Read my books. I know so much.

The moral of the story is a simple state.
Nuclear war is not our fate!
It's OK to wanna disagree.
But don't you ever disagree with me!

Ah, rosy cheeks and a grinning bright,
Preaching 'cause he knows he's right!
So if you don't want to cram like I do,
You'll listen to van Creveld, too!

By that time we had come to know one another better. If it is true that there is a large gap from theoretical knowledge to professional military competence , then there is an even larger one from ignorance to competence. As one of my Marines wrote, my course had grown on them. I too came to like them, especially those who seemed interested in what I had to say. Of course there are exceptions, and one of them later penned an article in which he dismissed what I had taught as an "elegant irrelevancy." Still, doing so is his good right, and I do not think he crossed the line between bona fide criticism and personal attack. In sum, based on my experience with them, I would say that the claim that "military" and "intelligence" represent an oxymoron is much exaggerated.

At Quantico, as at NDU, the real problem at the school was that neither I nor any other faculty member had any influence on an officer's career. The decision to send them to Staff College had been made by Manpower on the basis of so and so many decimal points in the evaluation forms. Once it had been made, everybody graduated. Gathering my courage, at one point I asked how that was possible. The answer I got was that Manpower's predictions as to who would do well in the course were so good that they never had to make any changes.

To be sure, at the end of the year there were exams. I personally read and corrected every one of them. The colonel in charge of the staff college, thought, mistakenly, that I had failed about one quarter of the class. Consequently, he became quite agitated. When it turned out that there had been a misunderstanding and that I had only failed a handful, the sigh of relief could be heard as far away as the Pentagon. It was agreed that those who had failed would correct their papers. This was duly done, making everybody happy. The only exception was the Israeli student, to whom, all unknowing, I had given a grade that prevented him from ranking first in his class. All's well that ends well. Still, recalling the commandant's remarks during the farewell party, I suspect that nobody had expected me to correct the papers as thoroughly as I did.

Though things were not as bad as at NDU—perhaps because the students were younger—the fact that results did not matter gave the course an air of unreality, not to say ticket-punching. This was not the pre-1945 German Kriesgakademie. The latter had been among the most prestigious institutes in the entire country, much more so than most civilian universities. Here, by contrast, the college was lucky if it received accreditation from a bunch of civilian institutes of higher learning. There, the course lasted three years; here, one only.

There, though there were no formal examinations, an officer's entire career might be decided by the written assignments he submitted and his performance in class as well as the impression his instructors, who were experienced general staff officers, formed of him during staff rides and the like. Here, as at NDU, the very fact that an officer was on the faculty usually meant that his career was about to end or had already ended. The students in the course for future instructors, known as McWar, sadly called themselves Children of a Lesser God. How, working under such a handicap, they were ever to develop into role models is a mystery. Yet when a teacher cannot act as a role model, he cannot be effective either.

Things were very different at the other class I occasionally taught, i.e. the School of Advanced Warfighting (SAW). SAW, like its counterparts in the staff colleges of the other services, is a second-year course for a few outstanding officers. There, I met some of the most able students I had ever had. Besides, so aggressive were they that they seemed about to devour their instructor alive. I particularly remember a few classes when we played out the debate held between Hitler and the German High Command in the summer of 1941 as to whether the next objective should be Moscow or the Ukraine. As the Chief of the General Staff, General Franz Halder, noted at the time, the decision was going to be "decisive for the outcome of the war." Both courses of action had a lot to be said for them, including not only military considerations but economic ones as well. The trick consisted of having the students, and myself, present first one side of the question and then the other. At one point I, playing the Führer, "threatened" to decide the issue by putting the Gestapo on my opponent's tail. However, it was all done in good fun. I learned a lot, and so, I think, did they.

Though nothing was ever said about the matter, unofficially, I was also on permanent standby for anyone on base who needed a lecture on any subject he did not feel competent to speak about or was simply too lazy to prepare. All in all I was kept fairly busy. I did not mind, considering myself a kind of friendly neighborhood guru. At other times I thought of myself as a battleship majestically sailing along, with all guns firing broadsides. What the targets were I can no longer remember, but they must have been any number of sacred cows. My reward came when they asked me to stay another year, but, unfortunately, it did not work out. Our daughter Adi was about to be drafted, and we wanted to be as near her as possible. Though she would have made it without us, I am not sure we would have made it without her. When I left, they gave me a framed picture of the staff college, signed by the entire faculty. I still treasure it.

Just before arriving, I had finished writing *Nuclear Proliferation and the Future of Conflict*, a small volume that sought to apply the lessons of *Transformation* to the situations in Southeast Asia and the Middle East. It was the last study I did for Mr. Marshall. I did it because he asked me to, not because I was excited about it or because I thought it would interest many people. Still, as an attempt at predicting the future of war in those two regions, the book seems to have hit the nail right on the head. Some of the countries I dealt with are Jewish, some Moslem, some Hindi, and some Confucian. Each developed its own way of thinking about nuclear weapons, which was the product partly of culture and partly of politics and strategic requirements.

The differences notwithstanding, broadly speaking, the introduction of those weapons seems to have had the same effect on these countries' strategy as it had on the freedom-loving U.S. of A. and the communist, atheist Soviet Union. In all cases it caused large-scale interstate warfare to wane in favor of non-trinitarian war or, to use the current term, hybrid war. In 2003, the year I wrote the original draft of the book in question, Iran looked as if it would soon join the nuclear club. In 2015, the year when I revised it for publication, it *still* looked as if it would soon do so. Either it will, or it won't. If it does, then almost certainly the outcome will be the same as everywhere else.

At the time I had already started thinking about *The Rise and Decline of the State*. As usual, the idea came partly from various discussions I had with friends, partly from my previous work, and partly—these are the mysteries of inspiration—out of thin air. The way I saw it, the blade of the knife, namely war, was about to undergo some very radical changes. If that were true, then inevitably the hilt, namely politics, would also have to change. I worked on the *State* from about the middle of 1993 to the middle of 1996. As I was doing so I was finally compelled to give up my old Apple II, which at the time I bought it in 1985 had been the wonder of the Faculty of Humanities. Much against my will, I had to switch to an IBM compatible I inherited from Jonathan; he, of course, used the opportunity to get a better computer for himself.

Deciding what the outline of the *State* should look like was very hard. Two years passed before I concluded that the main difference between the "modern" state and all its predecessors was the impersonal nature of the former; in other words, the state was a corporation. That point having been settled, the rest was a little easier. However, I still felt awed by the need to gather vast quantities of material on subjects I had never studied before. The list started with the way tribal societies were governed, or not governed, which for the first time caused me to delve into anthropological literature. Next, I had to study every important Western political scientist from Plato to Lenin and Carl Schmidt. Other topics included the nature of Athenian democracy, the origins and nature of feudalism, the struggle between Church and secular rulers, the evolution of central banking and of taxation, the political history of Russia, Latin America, and the British colonies, and the rise and fall of Western imperialism in Asia and Africa.

At the time the list seemed endless, and now that I think of it, it seems more endless still. Compared to this, even *Technology* was small fry. I had to develop entirely new methods not just to classify my material but also to read it. More than once I found myself consulting works on how to organize files only to discover that they did not contain any solutions I could apply. More than once I found myself cursing the moment I had embarked on this monstrous project, only to feel I simply could not withdraw. Partly this was due to the fact that I was afraid of wasting the work I had already put into it, partly due to the fact that I could not think of anything else to do. Mainly, though, I considered the subject absolutely fascinating and was determined to do it the way I thought it should be done.

In the end *The Rise and Decline of the State* was published by Cambridge University Press. Translated into several other languages, it did quite well, attracting favorable reviews and bringing me the usual reward in the form of invitations to speak. A particularly interesting invitation came from the Mises Institute for Austrian Economics at Auburn, Alabama. I confess I had never heard of it, but once I went there, I found it fascinating. Auburn is miles from anywhere. The only ones who visit it are students' parents, whom nobody expects to stay for more than a night or two. As a result, the food at the university inn was deliberately lousy. I was told that, by the time visitors feel they can no longer stand it, they are gone.

The institute itself is less like a university as I understand it than like an Islamic *madrassa* or religious school. From morning to night, they keep intoning that there is no God but Free Enterprise and that Ludwig von Mises, assisted by Murray Rothbard, is His prophet. However much I agree with some of the economics they teach, the idea of privatizing political power seems naive to me. After all, it has been tried and found wanting. Few would like to return to the days when, in ancient Rome, people left their wealth to the emperor in the hope that, as long as they lived, he would leave them alone. Still, I liked the fact that they refuse to accept any money from any government and contributed a small sum to the cause. Much later, I did the same with Wikipedia; another organization whose mission, as I understand it, is to enabled free thought to spread and flourish.

Other invitations to speak about subjects relating to what I like to call The Fate of the State came from Europe, particularly Austria. On such occasions I was often asked whether, in my view, the predictions I make in the book had come true or were coming true. I responded by briefly listing the main factors I thought I could see at work. The first was the end of major interstate war that was brought about by nuclear weapons. The second was the retreat of the welfare state that made people less dependent on their governments and forced them to look after themselves. The third was the bundle of processes collectively known as globalization, which submerge national economies and enable people everywhere to communicate with each other behind their governments' backs. The fourth was the decline of internal security owing to the rise of terrorism; the fifth, the loss of public faith that is partly the outcome of these factors and partly their cause. Next, I asked whether, in my interlocutor's opinion, one or more of these are at work in his country, too.

There are exceptions, mainly in the Far East, where states such as Japan and South Korea do not appear as if they are about to relax their iron grip on their citizens. In Singapore, I am told, the government even meddles in matchmaking. It seeks to hitch the brightest women to the brightest men in an attempt to make sure that their genes will not be lost to the state. (Once, discussing these things with some officials, I mentioned that people may not like to breed in captivity;

one could literally see them jumping through the roof.) However, we usually ended up by agreeing that three or four of the processes do in fact have an impact. Some are more prominent here, others there. Which is as one would expect it to be.

* * *

In 1996 I started working on my history of the Israel Defense Force, and once again Luttwak had something to do with it. Years before, he had suggested that I write a sequel to his and Horowitz's *The Israeli Army* (1975). I told him I might, but that in that case I would take the opportunity to rewrite the first volume as well. I said so partly to get my own back at him and partly because I do believe in doing *ganze Arbeit*, a complete job, as the Germans say. Though nothing came of it, the idea stuck in my mind.

Now, it seemed that the time had come. In *Transformation* I had examined the metamorphoses of war. In *The Rise and Decline of the State* I looked at the way the changing nature of war affected, and will affect, the nature of the political entities that wage it. In *The Sword and the Olive* I also reexamined *Transformation*, but the angle from which I did so was completely different. I took what many see, or saw, as one of the twentieth century's greatest fighting machines. First, I traced its history from the time when it consisted of seven members in what was half private security firm, half semi-legal band of extortionists, called Hashomer, to the time when it had been developed into one of the most formidable armed forces on Earth. Next, I used that history to see what happens when such a force confronts another, i.e. the Palestinians, which is so much weaker than itself that it is really no contest.

The results are there for all to see. In 1991, coming under Iraqi missile attack, Israel had the dubious honor of being the first country in history to go through a war in which more people died of panic, either putting on their gas masks the wrong way or suffering heart attacks, than by enemy action. In 2006, during the so-called Second Lebanon War, its ground forces barely functioned. Entire columns were held up by a few Hezbollah warriors with anti-tank weapons and machine guns. Some of my military friends tell me that their performance during the various skirmishes with Hamas in Gaza was not much to boast of either.

I shall not discuss all the books I have done since then. The interested reader can find a list of them in the appendix. Suffice it to say that, the older I got and the fewer the hairs left on my head, the more I found my interests broadening. Having started by writing an acerbic, highly specialized, academic monograph, I gradually focused on military history which, for some twenty years, formed the center of my work. Starting around 1995, though, I found myself researching a much wider range of fields: including political history, women's history, American history, Israeli history, the history of conscience, and the history of equality. At one point I also considered writing a biography of Adolph Hitler but ended up by rejecting the idea because there was nothing new to say. Until, upon thinking the matter over, I realized that if one approached the subject as an *autobiography*, there was actually a lot to say. This book, now completed, will be published soon by Castalia House.

Nor was it a simply a question of writing. Though I had always tried to avoid becoming what the Germans call a *Fachidiot*, or professional gnome, I had long focused my "serious" reading mainly around military history. Now, at long last, the difference between "serious" and "non-serious" reading largely disappeared. I have branched out into philosophy, politics, and political theory as well as the history of law, administration economics, and statistics. To this I added Freudian psychology, Jungian psychology, anthropology, sociology, socio-biology, evolutionary theory, and quite a lot of fiction from Edit Caldwell and J. M. Coetzee to Jose Saramago and, believe it or not, J. K. Rowling. At one point my then eight-year-old grandson Orr brought me, as a present, a book on the ways mathematics is or is not related to the physical world. He had seen it and thought I might find it interesting. He turned out to be right. Last, but not least, there is an illustrated edition of the *Kama Sutra* I own and like very much. Most people, including many who have never read it, see it as a list of sexual positions and techniques whose purpose is to excite and titillate. They are wrong: it is a treatise on how to "consecrate" one's life by making love, both mentally and physically, in such a way as to receive the blessing of the gods. In the whole of world literature nothing more tender, yet realistic, has ever been written. *Honi soit qui mal y pense!* The reason I mention it is that, some years ago, my friend Professor Benjamin Zeev Kedar wrote a new preface to a Hebrew edition of Bloch's work. From it, I learned that Bloch had treasured erotic literature. The difference is that times have changed. I never saw any reason why I should keep the few "pornographic" works I own secret either from my children or from anyone else.

Gradually, Dvora's interests and mine broadened to include anything from an exhibition of ancient Egyptian perfume bottles through the architectural sketches of Karl Schinkel to the paintings of Philip Pearlstein. As this happened, I have often thanked my stars for the privilege of working at a university rather than for some research institute or think-tank. Here, I thought, I could roam where I wanted. There, I would have been tied to some specific field and unable to leave it. At some stage in my career I might even have to take orders as to what to study. Whatever others may feel, to me that is perhaps the worst thing I can imagine happening to me. As Bismarck is supposed to have said, either I play my own violin or none at all.

In the event, proceeding by trial and error, I climbed hills and entered dark crevices I had never known existed. Quite often, I lost my way and had to start afresh, as happened, for example, when I tried to write books on the history of nudity. More often, though, I was delighted by what I found. Delighted or not, *nihil humanum mihi alienum puto* (nothing human I consider alien to me). Once it was Marx's favorite motto; now it is mine. As far as I can see, the only disadvantage of freedom is that the books I own occupy much more space than they used to and that keeping track of them has become much harder than before.

I incorporated my reading into my teaching, or perhaps things worked the other way around. Since the demand for military history was limited, I had never at any time taught courses on that subject alone. Now I deliberately started teaching the history of utopia, the Industrial Revolution, political thought, Nazi Germany, the state, the U.S., and as many other subjects I thought I could master sufficiently well to introduce undergraduate (though not graduate) students to them. Some proved so interesting that I taught them for years on end. Others only lasted a year or two before, having squeezed them dry to my own satisfaction, I let them go.

My goal in selecting the subjects was to have one completely new course every year. The more I did so, the more I found that not just teaching but writing about several subjects at once became much easier. Here and there, students ask me how I do it while pointing to the three meters of my books (comprising as many different editions and translations as I have been able to put my hands on) that grace my shelves and wondering if and how they are ever going to catch up. I always tell them that, when I was their age, I used to ask Talmon the same question. The students take the hint.

My social life, too, has changed. To be sure, I remain something of a loner. The Nobel Prize-winning Egyptian writer Naguib Mahfouz, once wrote that amusements are meant for couples who are bored with each other. It may also be that, to allow one's thought to roam far and wide, one has to follow the calm and orderly life of a bourgeois. Try to do more, and it may be too much for your sanity; certainly, I feel that it may be too much for mine. Be this as it may, Dvora and I seldom go out and attend very few parties. Even when we do, what I like best is to stand in a quiet corner and talk to two or three people I find interesting.

By way of compensation, we get quite some visits from family, friends, journalists, officers, and students. Some we invite to dinner, proving Herman Melville's dictum that anyone who does so can feel like an emperor. Almost always, the conversation is excellent and is only eclipsed by Dvora's cooking. Afterward, I like to think about what I heard while washing the dishes. That lasted until Dvora insisted that, to prevent my thoughts from interfering with hygiene, we buy a dishwasher. I cannot say how much my life and work have been enriched by these meetings. What I do know is that, without them, neither would have been the same.

Above all, I no longer felt Clausewitz or anybody else held the key to wisdom. To be sure, my admiration for him remains as strong as it has ever been, and I never regretted the short article I penned on him entitled "The Eternal Clausewitz." I did, however, feel I could talk to him, and other great thinkers, as an equal, if only in my own mind. My favorite, incidentally, is Friedrich Engels. I first became well acquainted with him when I taught a course on nineteenth-century military theory. In his own day he was considered a first-rate pundit on military affairs, and that point of view was later carried into the Soviet Union. There and in other communist countries, I was told, you had to open every article and book with a quote from him. Homage having been rendered in this way, you could do more or less as you wanted.

Later, my knowledge of Engels deepened as I gave a seminar on Marx and Marxism. Marx, whom Ronald Reagan, when he was still an actor, once described as "sick in body and mind," was a man of towering intellect. His inclination to be a bookworm and admiration for Antigone I share. Nevertheless, personally, I found him too opinionated, too self-centered, and not always sufficiently considerate of the feelings of others. Not, of course, that he was the only one. You could listen to him and learn from him. But it was impossible to argue with him. If you disagreed with him, he would call you nasty names. Especially, but not exclusively, behind your back.

Engels too had an excellent mind. As a journalist, he was at least as good as Marx, many of whose articles he wrote for him. But he was also the kind of man I would like to have as my friend. He was stable, loyal, courageous, exceedingly generous, and capable both of loving and forgiving. If, as in *Herr Eugen Dühring's Revolution in Science*, he attacked rivals in print, he always did so in a spirit of magnanimity. The older he became, the truer all this was. To my mind, no greater praise is conceivable.

Another major influence on my life has been Friedrich Nietzsche. Most of my other books keep going from the basement, where there its lot of room, to my study, which is rather small, and back. But his are always right in front of my eyes. Like Engels, Nietzsche had a lot of facial hair. But here the similarity stops. He was self-contradictory, peevish, inclined to sponging on others, and, from time to time, full of his own importance. Still, I would argue that, in this case, that feeling may have been more justified than in almost anyone else before or since. As he wrote, he was not a man; he was dynamite. As my colleague Professor Steve Aschheim, a Nietzsche expert, says, the German philosopher's writings are so diffuse that they can be interpreted almost any way one wants. That is true, but it is also true that one can follow Nietzsche's own teaching by subjecting him to one's will and making him serve one's own purposes. As he says, he teaches how to philosophize with a hammer.

To me, the most important thing Nietzsche is about is casting off constraints, both those that have been imposed on you during your childhood and those you imposed on yourself later in life. If you are lucky, he can help you close the gap between what you are and what you want to be; in short, become yourself and rid yourself of the most poisonous of all human qualities, *ressentiment*. The final outcome is, or should be, freedom. The highest thing there is, and one of the very few really worth having.

As my self-imposed professional restraints melted away, I thought I was finally free to do as I please. Little did I know I would soon run into others of a different kind. It came about as follows. While working on *Transformation*, I had for the first time taken a serious interest in the psychological factors that make men risk their lives in war—this being the obverse of my realization that war is not primarily a rational instrument serving rational ends. Looking to Clausewitz for answers, I noted that he did not seem to have any; as he says, that was a question he left to the philosophers.

More remarkable still, in his *magnum opus* women are not mentioned even once. This was true even though a woman, the famous Queen Luise, was co-responsible for starting the disastrous war of 1806 in which he had been captured, and even though he himself was happily married to Marie von Brühl. After his death, it was this highly intelligent and well-read woman who edited his book and arranged its publication. She also added a moving preface in which she explained how strong their love for each other had been. I thought there was something very wrong with a volume which, claiming to be the best ever written on war, ignored one half of the human race, and not the least important half at that. I still think so now.

At that time and now, the burning question was whether women could or could not, and should or should not, participate in combat. My own first contact with this debate came in the late nineteen eighties, when I suggested to Mr. Marshall that I do a study of it. However, he rejected the idea. I think the reason was almost certainly that he considered it a hot potato uniquely capable of getting those who touch it into trouble; at that time I had no idea this was so. Next, in 1992, I was asked to testify in front of the President's Commission

on Women in Combat as it held its meetings in Washington, D.C. It
was my first experience of the kind, and I was very impressed by the
dignified and deliberate way the commission went about its work.
The commissioners called on cartloads of expert witnesses: some
military, some civilian, some active, some retired. It questioned them
on everything from physical strength to the effect that setting up
mixed units might have on morale; the fact that incoming President
Clinton, kowtowing to the feminist lobby, ignored their recommen-
dations is hardly their fault. I said my piece, explaining that the myth
of the Israeli fighting woman was just that, a myth. Later, I was glad
to see that my testimony had been reprinted in the official journal of
the Army War College, *Parameters*.

I am, however, a historian and not a physiologist, psychologist,
soldier, defense official, or policy maker. Whether or not the U.S.
Armed Forces would or would not be damaged by the inclusion of
women in combat did not concern me much. What I did find interesting was another question altogether: why, with few exceptions,
had women hardly ever served in the military in the past? Obviously,
there were the physical differences between the sexes to consider. In
overall strength the difference is as 10 to 7, in upper body strength
alone as 10 to 5.5. In terms of aerobic capacity, a man of fifty is equal
to a woman of twenty. Intensive training will cause the gap to grow.
If the sisters Williams look strong on TV, then the only reason is that
they don't play Boris Becker. Still, I did not think these differences
constituted the entire story. After all, we all know that some men
are quite weak and some women very strong. Had war really been
a rational instrument for a rational end, then society ought to have
examined all men and all women and drafted, or selected, those who
meet the requisite criteria without regard to sex.

I shall not guide the reader through every mental step I took.
Suffice it to say that the most important reason why women have
never, or almost never, taken an active part in war is not necessarily
because they cannot. Rather it is that men do not want them to. By

and large, men are stronger than women. Therefore, following my own logic as explained above, a man who fights against—or side by side with—a woman and loses, loses; a man who fights against, or side by side with, a woman and wins also loses. To use the terms of game theory, a branch of strategy that between one incomprehensible equation and another is sometimes capable of explaining things clearly and succinctly, doing so puts those who do it into a lose-lose situation. The situation in sports is exactly the same. Which is why, in practically all its branches, there are separate competitions for men and women.

So why were women allowed to penetrate the modern military as they did? Remember that, at this time, I had already concluded that there was about "modern" war a strong element of make-believe. It could take place, if it took place, only when and where the most powerful weapons of all were either absent or virtually certain to go unused. In other words, war was turning into a game. At no time since Vietnam did any Western armed force suffer more than a handful of casualties. Particularly after the Cold War ended, the West felt secure as never before. Its armed forces were melting away like snow under the sun. Following the Gulf War, the American ones alone lost a quarter of their strength. In Germany, the once proud Bundeswehr was cut by no less than two thirds. Many seemed to have no real function left. Therefore, why not fill them with women?

To put it differently, the real reason why women were entering the military was not that feminism was making progress. Rather, it was due to the fact that those militaries were in full decline. As usual, in social life, where cause and effect are notoriously difficult to disentangle, things probably also worked the other way around. The more women entered militaries, by definition, the fewer men those militaries had left. The fewer men they had left, the faster the militaries declined.

One need not be a social scientist to see that, other things equal, the more women there are in any field, profession, or organization, the lower its prestige. The lower its prestige, the smaller also the economic rewards it can command. For good or ill, that is the way the world works and, if I am not completely wrong, will always work. Of course, different conditions meant that women's movement into the military did not proceed in exactly the same way, and at the same speed, in different countries. Still, trying to take a global point of view, I thought my theory provided the best explanation of the facts. At any rate, it was better than the feminist one, which always sees "discrimination" and "oppression" everywhere. And which, doing so, ignores everything else.

When *Men, Women and War* was fin-ished, it proved too politically incorrect for most. My German and French publish-ers were ready to bring it out at any mo-ment. However, English-language ones turned down the book so many times that I began to fear it might figure in the *Guin-ness Book of Records*. That position, inci-dentally, is occupied by another work on a somewhat similar subject. Steve Gold-berg's *Why Men Rule* (1973) was rejected dozens and dozens of times before it finally saw the light of print. In the end my vol-ume went to an English firm, Cassell.

The German cover of Men, Women and War.

Even so, there was a difference. The German and French editions have on their covers a picture originating in Atelier Menasse. The firm's owners were a wife and husband team of Yugoslav origin. They worked in Vienna during the 1920s, specializing in symbolic paintings that showed women with titles such as *Revenge* and *As You Want Her* and gaining a near-legendary reputation. The picture I liked I discovered in a Berlin Museum. It was called *Return from the Field*. The lower part showed long columns of heavily laden troops on their way home. However, most of the painting was taken up by a young, blonde, completely naked, woman opening her arms to welcome them.

The painting reflected another idea I had expressed in the book. In my view women's role *as women*—encouraging men to fight, waiting for their return, welcoming them (and sleeping with them) after they do so, celebrating the victors, dressing the wounded, mourning the dead—cannot be overestimated. A single woman escorting her son, brother, boyfriend, or husband to the mobilization center is more important to the conduct of war than a thousand uniformed female secretaries, medical personnel, or even combatants. So it has always been, and so it always will be.

Confirming the saying "No sex, please, we're British," Cassell refused to have this picture but designed a new cover instead. The book's publication date was timed to coincide with the expected unveiling of a report by the Ministry of Defense, which was to rule on the thorny question of women in ground combat. However, the publication of the MoD report was delayed. Later, a British journalist whispered in my ear that this fact had something to do with my book. When it finally appeared, it recommended that existing policies be retained, i.e. that women should not be permitted to join the ground combat arms. In thirty years, this was the first serious setback to feminist-inspired attempts to expand women's role in the military.

Not that any of this affected me personally. Out of my five children and step-children, four—two male and two female—have served in the Israel Defense Force. So have both our "adopted" sons, Shmulik Alkelai and Amihai Borosh. However, none of them developed a particular liking for it. Only one, Uri, decided to stay in for longer than he had to and was commissioned as an air force officer. But even he did so only because they used a stick and a carrot on him. Thus, to me, the question was an academic one like any other I have ever studied.

Still, I have spent over four decades teaching at several Israeli universities. Often, I had to console my male students who, having been called up for reserve duty, came to apologize for being absent from class. Here and there, one of them has never come back. I particularly remember one who was killed in the 1973 war and another who, along with twenty of his comrades, lost his life in 1980 when the plane in which they were flying crashed. Others have spent time in prison rather than carry out orders they, after due consideration, saw as illegitimate or inhuman. For all the fashionable talk about equality, in all those years not a single female student has ever missed a single hour for this reason.

If women were, in fact, called up as men are, it might reduce the burden on the latter. That would be a development I, as a member of that much-maligned species, can only welcome. To put it in a more brutal way, ever since humanity first evolved—say, for the last fifty thousand years—countless men have died in the hope that, by sacrificing themselves, their women (and children, of course) might live. Perhaps it is high time for the situation to be reversed. However, for good or ill it is not going to happen. In this respect, like so many others, women are the privileged sex.

When *Men, Women and War* came out in September 2001, it attracted considerable critical fire. One female reviewer, claiming I had taken the debate to "new lows," took offense at my mentioning the fact that many women develop large, pendulous breasts, which impede movement and require special protection. A second called me "an incorrigible chauvinist and biologist." A third thought I was a "patriarchal dinosaur." On the other hand, both in Europe and the U.S. there were also some male reviewers who thought that, far from being sexist, I had not hit feminists as hard as I should have and as they deserved. In their view, the only good women are either dead or in bed. I wish to have nothing to do with these people.

The most interesting discussion came from Julie Wheelwright, author of *Amazons and Military Maids; Women Who Dressed as Men in the Pursuit of Life, Liberty and Happiness.* Like most other female reviewers, she did not like my work. Unlike most other female reviewers, she was sufficiently fair minded to postpone judgment on whether I was right in saying that women's progress in the military was largely an illusion until more was known about the War in Afghanistan. Now, in 2015, more is known, and the results are very clear. First, recall that war is always a two-sided business. Suicide bombers apart, there are few if any women among the Taliban, Al Qaeda, and Daesh fighters (though I would not be surprised if there were some in support). That means I won half my argument before I even started.

Now look at the Americans as the most important Western forces of all. On each of the four aircraft carriers that participated in the opening moves of the war in Afghanistan there were about 500 women, making up some ten percent of the crew. Of those a few worked above deck. But most did "traditional" female work in administration, communication, medical services, food preparation, etc. Of the roughly 1,200 pilots aboard all the carriers combined, only one was female. In Afghanistan itself there were a few American female administrative personnel and nurses on the ground. However, when the troops there went hunting for Taliban and Al Qaeda, they stayed behind at Camp Rhino, and with very good reason. Only a few went along, and then not as fighters, but as translators and mediators responsible for looking after Afghan women and children. What the war in Afghanistan proved is that where the bullets fly, there are few women, and where there are more than a few women, the bullets do not fly. The same was true in Iraq, where only 2.5 percent of all American casualties have been female. I rest my case.

* * *

It was the first time I had taken an academic interest in women. When I told our librarian, the late Ms. Haggit Arbel, she smiled and said it was time I did. From the start, I found the subject absolutely fascinating. Coming to grips with the history of women and feminism was like pulling a thread from a knitted sweater. At first, you proceed gingerly; then, as you go along, you gradually watch the entire garment come apart.

On the whole I think my new field of study has made me more conservative. Or perhaps I am simply getting older. It has been said that a young person who is not a revolutionary has no heart whereas an old one who is not a conservative has no head. Be this as it may, as a graduate student, I had the good fortune of studying Marx's writings under the guidance of one of the world's leading experts in the field, Professor Shlomo Avineri. I was particularly impressed by Marx's claim that human nature is determined by the underlying economic realities which form the "infrastructure" of history into which people are born and over which, as individuals, they have little or no influence. Later, I concluded that, *pace* Marx, economic reality is but one part of the "infrastructure." Even that may be going too far. In reality, "infrastructure" and "superstructure" are inseparable. Toward the end of his life, Engels, now freed from Marx's overbearing presence, seems to have moved in that direction. This, however, did not affect my belief that what we call human nature is to a large extent the product of circumstances in which we live. Therefore, as they change, so do we.

Marx in his writings paid only very limited attention to women. (Engels had more to say about them, but he is not at issue here.) I, however, was becoming interested in the factors that govern relations between people of both sexes and their position in society. The more socio-biology I read, the more I felt that certain things have never changed. Here, I shall only list a few obvious ones without trying to justify my beliefs in detail. Women have wombs and can give birth whereas men do not. That fact has some important consequences for the psychology of people of both sexes as well as their role in society. Humans are mammalians, with the result that, in all societies without exception, it is mainly women who raise young children. Since women spend so much of their energy bearing and raising children and are, in addition, physically weaker on the average, normally, they depend on men for a living. One might, indeed, see human society itself as a system whose principal purposes is to save women and children from having to compete with grown men. For children, this applies until they grow up; for women, as long as they live.

Most women depend on men for a living, and almost all do so for defense against other men. Hence, the higher one goes on the ladder of riches, power, and fame, the fewer women one meets. That explains why so many women are jealous of men. They try to emulate men in ways that range from wearing trousers to having a career. Perhaps feminism itself is simply the greatest manifestation of penis envy in history so far. I believe these facts, and many others like them, rest on a firm biological basis. Hence no amount of social engineering, let alone feminist ranting, can or will make them change. At most the changes are cosmetic. And even they only affect a minority of women. For every "liberated" career woman, there are usually several others who cook for her, clean for her, and look after her children for her. This is one reason why feminism has never been able to reach lower-class women. For them, the problem is not the right to work but how to escape from it.

To pursue my interests I took a Humboldt Fellowship, the second time that generous foundation has assisted me. It enabled Dvora and me to spend the academic year 1999–2000 in Potsdam near Berlin. The center of Potsdam had been obliterated by the Royal Air Force in April 1945. It was the last German city to receive that treatment. We had been there in 1993 and had noted how shabby it all looked. Like any other visitor who knows something about German history, we started by asking about the whereabouts of that most famous symbol of the Prussian spirit, the eighteenth-century Garnisonkirche. We were told that it had been blown up on Walter Ulbricht's orders in 1956. One day, driving by the half-ruined edifice, he had asked what it was, got the answer he got, and ordered the deed to be done. In this case, as in so many others, stupidity has been its own punishment.

We enjoyed the town which, like Sleeping Beauty, was waking up from forty-five years of Communist vandalism and neglect. Potsdam is probably the most beautiful city where I have ever lived. It was crowded with flowers and trees and parks and palaces and was sufficiently close to Berlin for us to enjoy the cultural life there, too. Whatever the sins of the past, nowadays, the atmosphere is anything but militarist. When the mayor, seeking to attract tourists, tried to revive the eighteenth-century battalion of *Lange Kerle* (tall fellows), people pelted them with eggs. We took countless walks, looking over the magnificent buildings as well as the subdued, slightly sad, character of the landscape. Best of all, we went swimming in the surrounding lakes whenever the weather permitted. This, we decided, was every day the outside temperature was at least 14 degrees centigrade. What the temperature of the water may have been, I have no idea.

Starting from the fact that women have never been *obliged* to serve in war, I spent most of the year working on another book, *The Privileged Sex*. Like any other Western person from the 1960s on, I have spent my adult life being subjected to an interminable barrage about men "oppressing" women. Looking back, I think I was the first to try to see whether the accusations are true. I soon concluded that, for every disadvantage under which women labor, there exists a privilege they alone enjoy. Had I wanted to list all the privileges I found, I would have written not five hundred pages but ten thousand.

Our immediate circle of German friends apart, very few people knew what I was doing. Nevertheless, back in Israel things started happening. In January 2000 I filed the list of my courses for the next academic year, including one called "Feminism and Its Discontents." As I said, I enjoy teaching new courses. Having encountered feminism when working on *Men, Women and War*, I thought I might learn more about it by teaching others. I did not give it another thought; it was only when I returned to Israel that I became aware there might be problems ahead. I started hearing rumors that some people in and out of the university were very unhappy with the title of my new course, but I had no idea why. After all, I had taken it straight from a female scholar, Mari Jo Buhle, who had written an excellent book on the relationship between feminism and psychoanalysis.

As to the course contents, there was no reason why I should share my ideas with anyone. I had never tried to tell my colleagues what to teach, and I did not expect them to do the same to me. Next, the telephone rang, and a female reporter from *Haaretz*, the Israeli daily that claimed to address "people who think," asked me for an interview. I had often dealt with them before, talking and writing about military history and strategy. This time, though, the subject of the interview was women and feminism.

By that time I knew something about the history of women, the psychology of women, the positions of women in various societies at various times and places, and so on. After all, the original version of *The Privileged Sex* had almost 2,000 footnotes. In both Germany and Brazil it has reached the covers of leading news magazines. In a long telephone conversation, I said that feminist claims about oppression and discrimination were greatly exaggerated. Women's allegedly inferior position in society is due mainly to biological differences between the sexes; indeed, one might argue that oppression and discrimination, to the extent that they exist, are not so much the cause of those differences as a symptom of them.

First, lower testosterone levels make women less aggressive and less assertive on average. Second, whereas women can usually find a man to earn a living for them, the reverse is not true. This may explain why most of them seem less determined to get ahead; they have a choice whereas men do not. Third, over a lifetime women spend far less time in the workforce than men do. Finally, I said that, on the basis of American SAT scores, there was some reason to believe that, at the very top of the intellectual ladder, men outnumber women by a considerable margin. In other words, there are more male geniuses than female ones. Since average intelligence is very similar, this also means there are more male underperformers than female ones.

None of these ideas is original. All can be found in the literature, much of it written by female researchers from Margaret Mead down. At the time I gave the interview, I was aware of the demands of political correctness and tried to conform. I was very careful. I used many qualifying phrases such as "research shows that," "I sometimes think that," and "perhaps." This, however, was the daily for people who think. They took out the qualifications, fabricating a text a hundred times more aggressive than anything I had said. When I protested in a letter to the editor, at first they refused to print it. Later, they edited it in such a way as to draw my sting. Now the fat was in the fire. The interview was published not only in Israel but also in English on the Net. There were God knows how many readers' letters, all of them denouncing me. Some also denounced Dvora, whom they called a little dependent woman, for living with me. I regret to say that some people whom I thought were our friends stopped her on the streets and told her things they did not dare tell me.

I was branded number-one male chauvinist pig in the country, a title I rather enjoyed. It did not prevent me from doing my share of the supposedly "inferior" housework, something I also rather enjoy. Yet I must have struck a chord, for I was told that some female faculty members used the interview as a text for teaching Hebrew. Others, seeing me in the corridor, pointed at me as if I had horns; others still harassed my students and tried to steer them away from me. Equally petty were the many letters and petitions that followed, calling on the university to punish and/or dismiss me.

When the course started, there was a demonstration attended by about a hundred people. Needless to say, none of the protesters knew anything about the course except its title. Even that they did not get

Mount Scopus Campus, where I taught for twenty-seven years

first hand. Instead of looking it up in the curriculum, they took it from the newspaper; as a result, the posters they carried had the wrong words written on them. When I invited two of them, women, I am sorry to say, into class so they could see for themselves what it was all about, they started yelling at the students and me. In the end, to get rid of them and the rest, I had to call security. Somewhere I still have a copy of the poster calling for the demonstration.

Later, it turned out there had been a conspiracy. A female colleague of mine to whom I had shown an early draft of *Men, Women and War* to read had become very upset about it. Somehow she convinced herself I was trying to put down women; in fact, what I was saying was that the problem lay with men who, for good or ill, find having to compete with women intolerable and, if forced to do so, prefer to withdraw. She had unleashed the reporter, and the rest followed. I taught the course, and the students were very happy with it. There were one or two complaints from my female students in my other courses. Apparently, they thought I should teach the history of the IDF, the only armed force in history that has conscripted women, without mentioning the fact that it has done so; but those complaints I was able to handle.

Meanwhile, I was becoming the object of petty guerrilla warfare. At Hebrew University, as at other universities, many professors hang various posters on their office doors. Mine kept being torn off or defaced (I had a supply of new ones, and I kept putting them back). There was an attempt to smuggle a microphone into one of my courses, and the offprints of articles I left in the library for my students to read were either stolen or had unprintable things written on them. The university, to which I reported several times, did nothing. Still, since the harassment was petty, I did not mind too much.

Next, things became nasty. Some female students went to the head of the student union, Mr. Guy Yarnitsky. They themselves did not have what it takes to approach the Rector but wanted Yarnitsky to do their dirty work for them. He went over some of the things I had allegedly said but could not find anything offensive in them. He told them so and added that, in his view, academic freedom came first; his curiosity having been aroused, he decided to take a course with me.

Another female student launched a sexual harassment claim, alleging that I had made a pass at her and, having been rebuffed, avenged myself by giving her low grades. She enlisted a female faculty member, whose name I do not know and do not want to know, and together they went to Admin. To my great good fortune, the person who received the complaint was fair minded. Instead of making me defend myself, which is all but impossible, he took off both our names. Then, he had somebody else read the papers I had graded, only to be told that the grades were fair and square. He only told me about it a year after it had happened. By that time I could not even remember what the woman looked like. On these two occasions, as the Hebrew saying has it, "The righteous ha[d] their work done for them by others."

In the autumn of 2000 I attended a conference in the United States, the topic being the future of the state. In the breaks between the sessions I spoke to several of my colleagues from the humanities and the social sciences. Most happened to be slightly older than I, and all complained about political correctness. The way they saw it, there was always some student waiting for them to make a slip. Some of the slips were real. Nobody is perfect. Others were imaginary. Once the slip had been made, there would be a complaint to the authorities at the college or university. If, by twisting a remark every way, it could possibly be interpreted as "sexist," then this proved one had always been a "sexist." And sexists, as everybody knows, do not even deserve to live. Having been turned into the least free of men, my interlocutors said, all they wanted was to retire as soon as they could so as to either do their work in peace or go fishing. I told them it was an American disease and that in Israel things were quite different. Since then, I have learned how wrong I was.

As I understand it, the essence of political correctness is that nobody should be taken to task for what he or she is rather than for what he or she thinks or says or does. Having been born with a cleft palate, when young, I used to be called "Crookie." Since the air escaped through my nose, talking without grimacing was almost impossible. I had to listen to many "funny" imitations of the way I spoke. I also have vivid and not very pleasant memories of being pursued by an entire troupe of kids, all of whom were jeering at the shape of my mouth. Finally, half-weeping and half-screaming with rage, I would take out my false palate and scare them off. And yet, perhaps because two of my own children have the same problem, looking back half a century later, I think it upsets me more now than it did then.

With this experience behind me, I am all in favor of political correctness. Conversely, I can think of more than one historical figure who, having been mocked and persecuted for having been born the way he was, turned into a monster. No sooner did he have the opportunity than he avenged himself by every available means. Had political correctness existed in their time, the world might have been spared a lot of pain and trouble.

Here, however, the objective is not to offend but to understand. By definition, the first step toward understanding is classification; one that will recognize both similarities and differences. The fact that there are similarities between men and women I take for granted. As to the differences, their existence is, or ought to be, obvious even to the most purblind observer. For example, we all know that some men are smaller than some women and that some women are taller than some men. However, this does not mean either that most men are not taller than most women or that the average man is not taller than the average woman, let alone that being tall, or small, is inherently "better" than its opposite. Not even the most powerful infusions of political correctness can change these and similar facts. Of course it is possible to ignore them or to prohibit people from mentioning them. However, doing so merely leads to a gross misunderstanding of social reality, one equally harmful to men and to women.

During much of history women were considered the weaker vessel. True or false, it seems to me that women who complain only confirm this belief. A female professor who, instead of confronting a male colleague who has said or written something she finds unacceptable, complains about him, violates the first rule of academia. In fact she behaves like a little worm. This is all the more so if, as in my case, that colleague has never heard of her and has no authority over her; the same, needless to say, applies if the sexes are reversed.

A female student who does the same is only slightly more excusable. That student, sitting in the professor's office and being made a pass at, should have the courage to tell him, politely but firmly, that she does not want him. She should also have the wisdom to do so without offending him. If offend him she must, then there are no doubt some circumstances under which doing so is both warranted and worth the risk.

To be sure, doing so is not easy. Standing up for oneself seldom is, and that is at least as true for men as it is for women. Still, I think the alternative is even worse. Years ago I became friendly with a young female student who, since she came from the U.S., had no relatives in Israel. One day she entered my office, sobbing, threw herself into my arms, and said she had been diagnosed as having breast cancer. Fortunately, later, the diagnosis turned out to be erroneous. Had she done the same today, I probably would have recoiled in horror. Who knows what she might have done next? Not only have we gotten to the point where few male professors will even see women in their offices unless the door is open, but I am told that, in the U.S., they will never leave their desks while they do so. They cannot get up and show a female student a book for fear that, if they touch her accidentally, all hell may break loose. As a result, many of them would like all female students to disappear to the devil cares where.

If things go on as they do, some people might get it into their heads that the Taliban are right and that segregation, chaperoning, the veil, and the *burka* are the only answers. Since I adore women—long ago, somebody wrote a newspaper article about me to that effect—I think that will be a great loss to me. Since what research exists on the subject shows, and my own experience with Dvora confirms, that female students are as at least as interested in their male professors as the other way around, I think it will be a great loss to them, too.

In any case, it is my view that the "yammering"—the term comes from Betty Friedan, *Life so Far*—about sexual harassment only serves to undermine the justified quest for equality. It may, indeed, be understood as a tacit admission that full equality, the kind under which it will no longer be necessary to "yammer," is not attainable and will never be attained. One may have either equality or special protection, but not both. A woman who cannot say no to a man, or who claims to have been traumatized by a look at her cleavage, can hardly complain if she is neither promoted to company CEO nor sent to combat terrorists in Afghanistan.

Personally, I find that the peculiar feminist combination of strident hatred for men with whining self-pity makes me sick. It is the main reason why, in spite of several false starts, I do not intend to pursue my studies into women's history. I leave that to my female colleagues in the various women's studies programs. They are welcome to stay in those programs, talking almost exclusively to one another, producing sob stories instead of scholarship, and blaming men for every possible evil under the sun. One female scholar has even produced an entire volume to show that "gender" does not refer exclusively to members of her own sex. This is something we all know but about which nobody cares.

In the end those who complain only hurt themselves—a point on which Ms. Friedan, whom it was my good fortune to interview in May 2002, seemed to agree with me. Hence I cannot really feel angry at them. Besides, doing to them as they do to me violates the principles of sound strategy. To paraphrase Nietzsche, he who fights a worm should beware not to become one himself. Much worse are those universities, including my own, which show signs of surrendering to their demands. They tolerate, even support, the attacks on freedom of thought. Doing so, they betray their main mission on earth; from what I read and hear, it seems that this phenomenon has now reached even the greatest and most important institutes of higher learning in the world. Not that I find it particularly surprising. Writing *Candide* about two hundred and fifty years ago, Voltaire said that "philosophers" are cowards. It was probably true then, and it is very often true now. If this represents the universities' way of proving their responsiveness to social needs, it is clearly the wrong way to go.

As for me, all I have ever sought in history is truth. Along with doing what I can to make Dvora and the other members of my family happy, it is the quest for truth that has given my life whatever meaning it has. Since there can be no truth without freedom, freedom is as necessary to me as the air I breathe. That is why, back in 2006–7 when a female student complained that I had "offended" her by daring to suggest that women are not necessarily oppressed, I decided not to answer the charges but to take early retirement instead. Being able to do so was a stroke of luck in two ways. First, as Steven Pinker in *Blank State* (2003) shows, many eminent colleagues who dared voice opinions similar to mine have suffered much worse punishment at the hands of their academic institutions. One of them was Edward Wilson who, after he had published his seminal book, *Sociobiology: The New Synthesis* (1975), narrowly escaped being thrown out of Harvard. Second and more importantly, for years people had been telling me that retirement was wonderful. I did not believe them then; now I know how right they were.

Unfortunately, the universities are not the only place where political correctness and sheer bigotry have caused freedom of expression to come under threat. At present I still hope and pray it will never depart from the country where I have spent my life and which I love with all my soul. Should it do so, however, then so shall I.

Chapter 6

Looking Forward

When I started working on this book, all I wanted to do was answer Jonathan's probing questions. I had no idea where it would take me, much less where I would be twelve years later. The many titles I gave it reflect this fact. At first, I wanted to call it *History and I*. But that seemed too pretentious, so I added a subtitle: *An Intellectual Odyssey*. That still seemed too pretentious, so I substituted *Journey* for *Odyssey*. However, I was worried that, in case my work made it into print, the word "intellectual" might scare off some readers.

At one point, Dvora suggested *Living with History*. Since it is she who sees me "glued" to my word-processor for hours and hours every day, I understood what she meant. However, in other ways I do not "live" with history at all. Unlike some of my colleagues, I neither surround myself with antiques nor, I hope, spend my days boring people by telling them about what happened 1,000 years ago. All I do is contemplate the past, try to find out what happened in the past, assess how what has happened in the past may affect the present and the future, and write down what I think I have learned for those who want to read my stuff. At one point I even considered *The Young Historian's Guide*. However, that was both pretentious and not exactly what I had in mind. Finally, realizing that one cannot satisfy everyone, I took to the suggestion of my publisher, Vox Day, to call it *Clio & Me: An Intellectual Autobiography*.

What, then, is this book all about? In the past, I have often missed the answer to this question until some reviewer thrust it into my face. This time I shall do what I can. First, it is about some of the people I was lucky to meet. The most important ones are the members of my family who have given me, and are giving me, more than I can tell. Next come my teachers, colleagues, co-workers, students, and many others. Some were very well known, but I shall not list the politicians and generals who have listened to my lectures or discussed things with me. Others were just "ordinary people." Some are now dead, but others are very much alive and, thank goodness, intend to remain so for a long time to come.

The latter include the great figures of the past whom I admire and who have taught me so much of what I know. In some ways they seem to be more alive than many of those I meet every day. For example, Engels did not have a PhD. Instead of limiting himself to articles, he was so foolish as to write books, at least three of which are still in print and are likely to remain so for some time. Nevertheless, I would gladly trade him for many of my colleagues at Hebrew University and elsewhere. The same is true of Machiavelli, Adam Smith, and Clausewitz.

Among military commanders, my sympathies go to the likes of Scipio Africanus, Julius Caesar, the Duke of Marlborough, Frederick the Great, and, closer to our own day, Field Marshal Archibald Wavell. All five were great commanders. No less important, all five were also civilized men. As the story about the first, who at one point freed a beautiful Spanish female captive who had been offered him, illustrates. Still, the one I'd like to meet the most is Helmuth von Moltke. Like the others, he was one of history's great commanders and one of the few who never lost a battle, let alone a war. Like them, he was a highly educated man who was both prepared and able to explain what he did and why he did it. Last, but not least, there is no record of him ever saying a harsh word to anybody. that is proof, if need be, that boorishness is not a necessary quality on the way to military excellence.

Some of the people I met have dropped out of sight, but others keep in touch. Some have changed their roles with respect to me, as when students became valued colleagues. Some have taught me a lot of what I know even if, like Geoffrey Warner and Elisabeth Erdmann, they did not necessarily realize it. With many I have had splendid arguments. If, as so often happens, neither of us changed our views while we were at it, then equally often our conversations caused us to have second thoughts after they were over. At any rate, that is what happened to me.

One of the best moments I recall is associated with my American friend, Bill Lind. Lind, who must be at least six feet six, is a Christian conservative and attends church every week. Years ago he asked me, a liberal agnostic Jew who has not entered a synagogue for years, to appear on a television program he was running. I readily agreed, but warned him that he and I did not see things eye to eye. Speaking very softly, he answered, "I know, and it does not matter." That, to my mind, is the hallmark of a great man. I am proud to have him as my friend.

Second, the book is about my joy in studying history. My definition of the latter has broadened over the years. It now includes whatever can help me understand the way people, past, present, and perhaps future as well, function in this world of ours; whatever the term that comes before "logy," I am prepared to look at it. Even greater is the joy I find in discussing history, teaching history, and writing history. Very often, far from having to make myself work, I have to force myself to stop. In a way, I am studying even when I am taking a break. Recently, I have begun carrying about little slips of paper to write down ideas much as some other people carry their pets.

The greatest joy of all, which thanks to my switching from one subject to the next, has not abandoned me even after *Transformation*, is that of making a discovery. I am thinking of those magic moments when, in the words of our Jewish prayer book, the sun, rising "with all its might" tears away the clouds of confusion and misunderstanding; I feel I have arrived at "the truth." Whether that truth is of earth-shaking importance or, as is more likely, a very small one that only exists in my own mind, is, in the end, immaterial. It is the feeling that counts.

For example, I remember how I experienced it in the spring of 1981 during a visit to a Berlin museum. I was looking at one of several paintings Rembrandt did of a man with a golden helmet. I had often seen other versions of the same painting, particularly the one at Kenwood House, which is located near my beloved Hampstead Heath. They had always mystified me, given that golden helmets are by no means common. Suddenly, I realized that the point Rembrandt was trying to make was the contrast between the polished perfection of the helmet and the creased, care-worn face of the wearer. Though he was its creator, it was going to outlast him; what this says about our vaunted "mastery of the physical world" I am not sure.

Since then I have never bothered to check whether others before me have come up with the same idea. All I know is that the joy I felt was as intense as if I had discovered relativity; with one exception, that joy is the greatest I have ever known or think I am capable of knowing. I have often thought that, had I been a painter, I too would like to try to capture the contrast on canvass. Though my chosen means of doing so would be not helmets but bathrooms. Which reminds me that Rembrandt also did etchings of his mistress, Hendrickje Stoffels, washing herself.... Did he have the same idea?

Thankfully, the joy does not last for very long. Had it done so, it would have been too much to bear. Besides, I fully recognize that, to us who are born of women, finding "the truth" is almost certainly impossible. In part, the reason is that the past is irretrievably lost, so we cannot put ourselves in our predecessors' shoes. Even if it were possible to experience things the way they did, no mere human work is remotely capable of capturing the full richness of the reality that surrounds us. By merely trying to grasp it, let alone explain the way we understand it to others, we probably make it more coherent and more rational than it is.

Even if all these obstacles could be overcome, we might discover that "the truth" simply does not exist. There are other objections, some of them weighty. But I do not think they should make us give up. Doing so is the council of despair. It may even be tantamount to giving up our humanity. Indeed, that humanity may well consist of not giving up in spite of knowing we are doomed to fail; here is tragedy, but here is greatness, too. Besides, from my point of view as a military historian, there are practical problems. When the bullets start flying, telling people that experience cannot help them find the true way to avoid being hit does not strike me as very useful. And what is history if not experience that has been collected, sifted, and systematically arranged?

Since they add cynicism to despair, the "postmodernist" and "deconstructionist" claim that all truths were born equal are, in some ways, even worse. I may regret the fact that truth does not exist as well as my own inability to get at it. However, I do not think this means we should open the door to every kind of nonsense simply because it is there and because somebody feels that his (or her) subjective experience gives him (or her) the right to spout it.

Here, as elsewhere, we should let the marketplace—not the marketplace of the moment, as it manifests itself in the form of some bestseller, but the *longue durée* marketplace—decide. We can only hope it will lead us, if not to *the* truth, as close to it as we are capable. Some people may use unkosher means, from lying through censorship to the execution squad, to corner some of the truth for some of the time. However, I do not think they can do so either entirely or for very long. What Stalin did not succeed in doing, presumably nobody else will. At any rate, that is what I hope.

To make sure, I take my news from as many different sources as

I can. Thank heavens Israel is not, nor has ever been, a totalitarian country with thought control. Still, the electronic media are government owned or at least censored. If only for that reason, I do not allow a day to pass without watching foreign TV. I also read parts of the international press either in printed form or, increasingly, as they are posted on the Net. Finally, I recognize that, though I personally cannot think of a better way to spend the gift of life than looking for truth, it is not the only way. In particular, creating beauty—as Dvora, who is an artist, successfully does—and helping others are pursuits at least as worthwhile as searching for truth is. The trouble, as far as I am concerned, is that I am not very good at them. At times, I wish I were.

As to the purpose of truth, I think it is an end in itself. *Causas rerum cognoscere*, as the Latin saying has it. Like anyone else, I would like to have money and fame. Like anyone else, I would like to see people reading my work, thinking about it, and enjoying it. I would also like it to nudge society in the direction I consider desirable. It would be nice if my books could help make people a little happier or, at any rate, a little less unhappy than they are. By and large, my thoughts concerning the social and political prerequisites for happiness follow the ideas of John Locke, Thomas Jefferson, and John Stuart Mill. By and large, my thoughts concerning the way I, as an individual, should live coincide with those of Nietzsche. Yet in the end none of these objectives is as important as truth itself. If, as can happen and sometimes has happened and may happen again, they clash with what I see as truth, then I can only hope I will find it within myself to put truth first and reject whatever threats or blandishments I may encounter.

Not that I have much choice in the matter. In the past, there have been some moments when, tempted by generous offers that came my way, I tried to write things I did not know enough about or did not really believe in. There have also been moments when, worried that saying what I saw as the truth might prove harmful to me, I made half-hearted attempts to lock it up and to prevent it from bubbling out. I always did so at the cost of strong nausea and always, in the end, to no avail. It simply kept coming. Sometimes it did so at inappropriate moments and in inappropriate ways; for that I apologize. I console myself by thinking that my experience is anything but unique. Just read Jeremiah 20:9: "Then I said, I will not make mention of Him, nor speak any more in His name. But His word was in mine heart as a burning fire shut up in my bones, and I was weary with forbearing, and I could not stay."

The third thing this book is about is freedom. "The truth will set you free," said St. John. On the other hand, no one can even try to get at the truth without being free first. Freedom to explore as I please, without *internal* constraints, driven only by my desire to know, understand, and share my thoughts. Freedom to explore as I please, without *external* constraints, driven only by my desire to know, understand, and share my thoughts. As I have explained, the second kind is now coming under attack, which only makes me even more determined to maintain it at all costs. The first kind I think I have earned by many years of hard work.

In retrospect, perhaps even more important were the repeated periods of frustration and despair. So intense were they that I am not sure I would wish them even on those who want, or think they want, to take the path I have taken. There may be among us some playful conquerors who can arrive at truth, or what they honestly take for truth, without having to undergo this torment first, almost without any conscious effort on their part. If so, then I think they are a small minority. By and large, the more I study the minds of the great men I admire, the more I think that most are not too different from my own. If this is *hubris* on my part, then I think it is the positive side of *hubris*. *Per ardua ad astra*, as the saying goes.

Needless to say, freedom for myself also means freedom for others. Of the great men I admire, none could have done their work if they had not been free to think, speak, and write as they chose. Had they lived under a totalitarian regime, many of them would have been silenced or worse; however much they differed in other respects, this was something the liberal Mill, the communist Marx, and the aristocratic radical Nietzsche had in common. To use an analogy I often use to explain my country's situation *vis a vis* the Palestinians, he who does not grant others what he demands for himself is like a policeman chained to a criminal. "Look at how free I am," he keeps shouting, "Whereas that guy is not!"

As to the future, just how I am going to use what freedom I have I do not know. I often feel like a little boy—some people, I know, think I *am* a little boy—skipping along the beach. I pick up a brilliant pebble and examine it until my curiosity is satisfied. Next, having recorded whatever I found most beautiful and most interesting about it, I put it aside and pick up another. As I do so, the great ocean of truth stretches in front of me. it is sparkling bright, practically untouched, and brimming with more than enough rich and strange secrets to fill the lives not of one person but of millions. Much will depend on the future of my country. As I write, it is under a cloud; the reason is that, as Nietzsche wrote, he who fights a monster should beware not to turn into a monster himself.

Like everybody else, I live inside a soap bubble. As in the case of anybody else, that bubble could burst at any moment, torn apart by a suicide bomber, or a road accident, or a disease, or, which is perhaps worst of all, bereavement. But my personal life is the concern of nobody except me and my family. Being very happy with it, I have no intention of changing it.

In my professional life, if that is the term for somebody who has enough to live on and no ambition to climb the greasy pole further than he has, I may be lucky enough to be presented with another idea for a book, just as the idea for this one came from Jonathan. Here is one possibility. For over a quarter century—ever since I studied the problem of sex and family in Plato's *Republic*—I have thought I might do a history that would go backward, from the present to the past. Such a work would run directly counter to the idea of causality that underlies modern historical thought and, perhaps, historical thought as such. At the moment I have not the slightest idea how to do it. Still, the results could be interesting.

I already spend one morning a week making mosaics, a relaxing activity that requires patience and a little skill. I have just completed one of a kimono-wearing Japanese lady. Feeling like Pygmalion, I called her Shonagon, after a famous 10th century A.D. courtesan who wrote an even more famous book. Perhaps, one day, I shall realize another old dream by learning to play the harpsichord. Be this as it may, there are some things I shall not do. Contrary to my previous plans, for the time being I shall neither do a history of feminism nor try to explain why, in my view, it has failed. Having mastered the field, the thought alone is almost enough to make me gag.

For me, the only thing at all like studying history is falling madly in love with a woman. At first, there is hesitation and embarrassment. Two strangers meet. They look at each other, and something mysterious passes between them. Is it mere chemistry, as so many scientists say, or is there more to it? They enter a complicated mating dance, now coming close, now withdrawing to take stock and consider their next move. It is anything but easy, and there are many anxious moments. To love, after all, means to trust and to surrender.

Then, suddenly, the walls between us start crumbling. A meeting of minds takes place, the most wonderful thing there is. Soon, she becomes me; I become her. Hers, mine, ours, mix and fuse until we no longer know which is which and who is who. As our joy in each other grows on us, eternity is in our lips and eyes. The world fades away; we lose control. We melt in a smile so radiant one could almost mistake it for a grimace of pain. Looking backward on my sixty-year-long love affair with history, I think it is far from over. Looking forward, I hope it may only have begun.

Some Works Consulted

Bloch, M., *The Historian's Craft*, Manchester University Press, 1967 [1942].

Dayan, M., *Story of My Life*, Weidenfeld & Nicolson, 1976.

Finley, M. I., *The Use and Abuse of History*, Viking, 1987 [1975].

Geyl, P., *Debates with Historians*, Wolters, 1955.

Heuser, B., *Reading Clausewitz*, Pimlico, 2002.

Howard, M., *The Lessons of History*, Yale University Press, 1991.

Hughes, H. Stuart, *History as Art and as Science*, Harper & Row, 1964.

Huizinga, J., "My Path to History," in *idem, Dutch Civilization in the Seventeenth Century and other Essays*, Collins, 1968, pp. 244–76.

Krepinevich, A. G., and Watt, B. D., *The Last Warrior: Andy Marshall and the Shaping of Modern American Defense Strategy*, Basic Books, 2015.

McCullagh, G. Behan, *The Truth of History*, Routledge, 1998.

Mosse, G. L., *Confronting History: A Memoir,* University of Wisconsin Press, 2000.

Nietzsche, F. *Beyond Good and Evil*, R. J. Hollingdale, trans., Penguin, 1987.

Nietzsche, F., *Ecce Homo; How One Becomes What One Is*, R. J. Hollingdale, trans., Penguin, 1988.

Nietzsche, F., *Thus Spoke Zarathustra*, R. J. Hollingdale, trans., Penguin, 1969.

Popper, K. R., *The Poverty of Historicism*, Routledge, 1972.

Singer, P., *Hegel: A Very Short Introduction*, Oxford University Press, 2001.

Taylor, A. J. P., *A Personal History*, Hamish Hamilton, 1983.

Wilson, E. O., *Letters to a Young Scientist*, Liveright, 2014.

List of Publications

More on War, Oxford University Press, 2017

Pussycats: Why the Rest Keeps Beating the West, and What Can Be Done About It, Createspace, 2016.

Equality: The Impossible Quest, Castalia House, 2015.

Conscience: A Biography, Reaktion, 2015.

The Privileged Sex, CreateSpace, 2013.

Wargames: From Gladiators to Gigabytes, CUP, 2013.

(ed., with John Olsen), *The Evolution of Operational Art*, Oxford University Press, 2011.

The Age of Airpower, Public Affairs, 2011.

The Land of Blood and Honey: The Rise of Modern Israel, Public Affairs, 2010.

The Culture of War, Random House, 2008.

The American Riddle (Russian), Irisen, 2008.

The Changing Face of War: Lessons of Combat from the Marne to Iraq, Random House, 2007.

(ed., with K. von Knop and H. Neisser), *Countering Modern Terrorism*, Bielefeld, Bertelsmann, 2005.

Defending Israel, St. Martin's Press, 2004.

Moshe Dayan, Cassell, 2004.

Men, Women and War, Cassell, 2001.

The Art of War: War and Military Thought, Cassell, 2000. Also published as *A History of Strategy: From Sun Tzu to Bill Lind*, Castalia House, 2015.

The Rise and Decline of the State, Cambridge University Press, 1999.

(ed.), *The Encyclopaedia of Revolutions and Revolutionaries from A to Z*, Facts on File, 1996.

Airpower and Maneuver Warfare, Air University Press, 1994.

Nuclear Proliferation and the Future of Conflict, Free Press, 1993.

The Transformation of War, Free Press, 1991.

The Training of Officers: From Professionalism to Irrelevance, Free Press, 1989.

Technology and War: 2000 B.C. to the Present, Free Press, 1988.

Command in War, Harvard University Press, 1985.

Fighting Power: German and US Army Performance, 1939–1945, Greenwood, 1982.

Supplying War: Logistics from Wallenstein to Patton, Cambridge University Press, 1977.

Hitler's Strategy 1940–1941; The Balkan Clue, Cambridge University Press, 1973.

Notes

1. Etzel was a pre-1948 underground organization that fought the British.

2. W. Kross, *Military Reform*, Washington, D.C., National Defense University, 1985.

3. The late Colonel (ret.) Harry Summers, Author of *On Strategy* (1992), with whom I once had an unpleasant exchange.